NAW'LINS

by

Ben Cherot

ISBN 0615543812

Chapter One

     A road-weary blue delivery van pulled to the curb on the north side of Saint Charles Avenue in the Garden District, an upscale locality of New Orleans.

     The lanky man with wire-rimmed glasses in the passenger seat peered past the driver and through that man's opened window to scan BELMONDE'S, a trendy restaurant across a wide thoroughfare divided by trolley tracks. He glanced periodically at four glum-faced men huddled on the floor behind him. All wore dark clothing and dark woolen skullcaps, and all but the driver cradled shotguns on their laps.

     The chubby one sweated, with no windows back there for ventilation, and mid-March sultry already enveloping southern Louisiana. He slid on his bottom to behind the driver to gasp fresh air and craned his neck to stare at the restaurant. A passing trolley momentarily blocked their view, poking along as languidly as most things in the *Big Easy*. It finally clanged past, allowing them to again scan Belmonde's.

1

Sporadic vehicles rolled along both sides of the trolley-track-median with the casual tempo of the few people strolling on the sidewalks of the wide avenue. In that torpid climate folks didn't necessarily consider time a measuring device.

"When the hell they coming?" Chubby whined.

Lanky-guy grimaced annoyance and turned away from the pesky questioner, passing his eyes over his side of the street. However, he paid little heed to the Victorian-styled mansions of a by-gone era, set back and isolated from the sidewalk by wrought iron gates, now rusted and deteriorating. Inhaling tolerance, he returned his gaze to the restaurant.

His mouth twitched when a limousine pulled up to the front of it. Forcing himself to breathe, he watched the limo chauffeur open the door on the sidewalk side for three men in suits and ties to exit. Some of the tension-lines in his long face receded as he identified two as African-Americans. The third had a light complexion and straight black hair, rendering him racially indistinguishable.

"We hunting titsoons?" Chubby asked in his whiney voice as he shifted impatiently.

Lanky-guy didn't reply. He gritted his teeth while fondling the shotgun on his lap, the only double-barreled among them. Then his expression eased when a Mercedes coupe parked behind the limousine and two white men got out, also in suits and ties. They surrendered their car to the valet while exchanging salutations with the three from the limo. After a few moments of chatting, all five ambled into the restaurant.

"Whatta' we waiting for?" Chubby asked.

Lanky-guy pursed his lips, but didn't respond. He inhaled patience while glancing periodically at his watch. After ten minutes he growled: "Let's do it."

The driver poked the dirt-streaked blue van into traffic then darted to the left lane of Saint Charles Avenue, from which he took a hard left to bump the van across the trolley tracks. Cruising down the oft-repaired road alongside the restaurant, he ignored the sign that restricted that stretch as a loading zone, and eased to a stop near the door close to the rear of the building.

Lanky-guy and the others clambered out, holding their shotguns against their sides to conceal them as much as possible while hurrying across the sidewalk. Reaching the building, they pulled the bands of their knitted caps down to form ski masks while barging into the kitchen.

Workers garbed in white froze in place and gaped as each in turn became aware of the masked men with awesome weapons. One screamed.

"Quiet!" commanded Lanky-guy, threatening them with his double-barreled shotgun. All fifteen capitulated to being herded against a sidewall, their frightened eyes mesmerized by the large-bore muzzles.

Lanky-guy and Chubby hurried to the small frosted window in the wall that separated the kitchen from the bar area to aim their weapons at the shadowy figures on the other side of the frosted glass.

"Which one is Brent Kenman?" Chubby asked, loud enough for everyone to hear. When he received an approving nod from Lanky-guy he added as loudly as before: "They all look the same."

Lanky-guy leveled his double-barreled weapon, then nodded to Chubby. Both fired in tandem.

The small window exploded. Screams of terror rent the air —most from the dining room but some from those held at bay and now cowering in the kitchen. Lanky-guy took down the man from the limousine that had been difficult to distinguish racially. Chubby fired

3

over the head of the bartender and one of the white guys from the Mercedes coupe.

Then Lanky-guy fired the second barrel, flinging one of the black men backwards. Breaking down his shotgun, he ejected the spent shells to clatter on the floor. After fumbling to reload, his grip restricted by latex surgical gloves, he snapped the breech closed. Searching around he spotted the other black man kneeling and tending to one of his fallen companions—barely visible at the end of the bar. And he took him out.

"Whatta' ya' doing?" Chubby squealed.

"Shut the fuck up!" Lanky-guy swung about and hurried for the door, unconcerned for the high-pitched pandemonium engulfing him. Many of those held hostage in the kitchen screamed hysterically.

"Why'd you shoot alla' them mullenyams?" Chubby asked, his face contorted by confusion as he trundled behind.

Lanky-guy didn't reply as he hurried through the door and into the van. Chubby followed while the other three backed out in quick-step, keeping the help covered until they turned to scramble into the vehicle. The delivery van sped up the street as its doors slammed shut, lurched around the first corner and disappeared.

#   #

Chapter Two

     Mike Molino paused at the entrance to the executive office to inhale resolve. Yes, he knew he'd be reprimanded, having brought this grief on himself. So he needed to show character and convince his boss he deserved a chance to redeem himself.

     Nodding to that, he ventured into the chamber where half a dozen men and women vied for attention for respective objectives. Attorney General of Louisiana, Jason Morreau, glanced up at him from behind the impressive desk. But his bushy mustache denied Mike determining his disposition, consequently get a hint of what to expect.

     "Mornin', Director Molino," came from a woman with an armful of documents bustling away from the flurry of activity.

     Mike nodded to her drawling greeting while resigning himself to biding his time until the departmental frenzy subsided, after which he'd learn how much trouble he had to contend with. So he ambled to the double windows on the wall across the room to avail himself of that view from the twenty-fourth floor of the thirty-four-story State Capitol Building, the tallest of any state in the union.

     Below him, in the center of a sward of lawn surrounded by neatly trimmed shrubbery and majestic trees, stood the twelve-foot-tall bronze statue of Huey Long, back-dropped by the modernistic office buildings of downtown Baton Rouge. The passing years since that man's burial in nineteen thirty-five hadn't diminished the veneration of the ex-Governor fondly remembered as *Ole' Kingfish*.

     A couple of older gals departing the office tittered to each other how fifty-two-year-old Mike Molino been widowed near two years now, consequently fair game for the older single ladies. One babbled how he'd inherited his dark virility from his Mexican daddy and his Cajun and Choctaw mama.

Like most who lived in southern Louisiana, they knew that the descendants of the Acadians who migrated from Canada three hundred years ago, generally referred to as Cajuns, are as commonplace in their part of the state as Creoles, the progeny of the original French colonists. With the exception of seasonal migrant workers, Mexicans are more numerous on the western border with Texas, while Choctaws reigned as the dominant Indians in Louisiana, as well as in Alabama, Mississippi and Arkansas.

Attorney General Morreau rose from his desk and shooed everyone except Mike out of his office. He plodded over to join Mike in front of the windows that glinted the rays of the mid-March sun. "Thanks to one of your dumbest damn decisions you've saddled this office with a big-time scandal."

Mike shuffled in place while holding his boss's probing glare. Knowing Jace, he'd likely get raked over the coals, so prepared to show character.

"Did you consider, even for a tiny minute, what the hell you were doing when you created that fiasco in Shreveport?" the AG asked.

"You need to fire me, Jace, to placate folks, just go ahead. No hard feelings. I'll understand." God a'mighty, he hoped Jace didn't take that literally.

"To what end? The damage is done, and can't be erased. Exiling you into oblivion won't come close to cleansing the stain off this administration. So let's deal with the scandal by convincing the general public that you're a moral man who plain goofed, and can redeem yourself."

Mike blinked, struck by that he indication of reprieve. God a'mighty, he needed to survive this ordeal, didn't want to be axed from a position that filled him with pride . . . a lofty station he'd earned by years of application.

"The Governor's in a damn tizzy," the attorney general grumbled as he paced the length of the window wall with his hands clasped behind him. "Demands we get his worried ass off the hook."

Mike stifled commenting that Governor Birch Murdock is oblivious of wallowing around in a pool of his stagnant administration. Instead he said: "I'll hold a press conference and take the heat for stupid judgment, so it doesn't splash on y'all."

"Jeezus H, the fall-out from that screw-up isn't one of those things you can put some kind of damn spin on. Nobody but nobody is going to accept any kind of lame-ass excuse."

Mike swallowed the urge to ask what in hell his boss wanted from him.

Jace swung about to glare at his subordinate. "Political rhetoric just isn't going to cut it, and please don't even think about claiming you didn't realize what you did wouldn't end up being construed as suborning justice."

"Said I'll go public and take the heat, then resign if that's what it takes to salvage your reelection." He sucked in breath, again hoping not to be taken literally.

"Mine's secure," Jace grumbled as he resumed pacing.

Mike nodded to that, aware that the AG had a rock-solid record for the nigh-on eight years he'd been in office. Not likely the public will turn him out, especially since term limits dictates this next four will be his last. But he doubted anything will get Birch Murdock reelected after four years of fumbling and bumbling.

7

Mike breathed deeply and asked: "What in hell would you like me to do?"

"Redeem your damn self by justifying to Lu'ziana folks why my first official act in this office was to appoint you Director of the Investigation Division."

"How exactly you suggest I accomplish that miracle?"

"Haul your rusty-dusty down to Naw'lins and clear that high-profile assassination of three African Americans, two of which qualified as the most prominent in the state. Make such a damn splash as a super-cop that it'll shuffle that Shreveport mess off the front pages and raise your image back to what it was."

"You 'spect folks are that gullible?"

"Lord, yes. They'll forgive their heroes most any kinds of transgressions if given reason enough."

"However, the NOPD will resent my interference."

Jace snorted. "Two damn days later the NOPD admits they don't have clue one concerning five damn ghosts blowing away three prominent black men in one of the finest damn restaurants in Naw'lins."

"Not the first time supremacists pulled off stunts like that."

"Don't even think about palming this off as engineered by racial repugnance rather than motivated by political ambitions. We do and the black community will damn sure condemn us for pandering. Darby Williams is too prominent, or was, especially down in Naw'lins, to sell it as simply a hate crime."

Mike hunched acceptance that it sure has the earmarks of a professional hit, rather than that of a wildass raid by some redneck yahoos. Yep, it's being complex is why the NOPD is having a hard time clearing it. Like as not, they're working overtime to clean that brazen killing off their slate. And two, three days isn't a lot of time for a crime

8

that was apparently carefully planned and executed..

"You damn well need to get your rusty-dusty down there," Jace said. "Sticking your damn nose in that fiasco and rooting out the damn facts is the only damn hope you have of getting favorable publicity . . . needed to retain your status as top-cop in this state."

Mike nodded to his boss' rationale, having decided against reminding that they generally extend the courtesy to local law enforcement to invite them into an investigation, as opposed to bulling their way in. And they damn sure hadn't received any calls for assistance from that bunch.

"Birch Murdock wants us to poke our damn noses in there," Jace growled, "or anywhere else to clear up this damn mess. I've sworn as the damn attorney general to uphold the damn law and assure justice throughout the whole damn state. Nobody down there best not to oppose my damn authority."

"Granted, Jace, but having had more than enough truck with those ole' boys, I'd as soon defer to them for a week or so. At least if they haven't made any progress by—"

"No! No! No! It's too damned political. Like the governor said: we can't afford not to have our finger on the pulse of that heinous incident, especially since winning the black vote this fall just might hinge on the way we react, or fail to. No way he or I can sit up here and allow those hooples down there bungle the investigation."

Jace resumed pacing. "To avoid condemnation requires we convince the public, white, black and ever' other color, that we're making ever' damn effort to get to the bottom of things and bring those responsible to justice."

Mike nodded but refrained from reminding his boss that it wasn't the first time ambitious scoundrels sought to grab a political office by blowing away their competitor—especially in that smoldering caldron of iniquity. He did, however, say: "The minute they learn we're sticking our noses in there they'll close ranks against us, like it was a challenge of honor."

"Which is reason one, two, three and four why I want you down there."

"In spite of those cops having a giant-sized hard-on for me?"

"They created the damn corruption you exposed last year. That sits on them, not on you. More importantly, you damn well need to redeem yourself to prove to the citizenry that you deserve to retain your position in this department."

When Mike didn't respond, Jace spun around to him. "Well?"

"You know damned well I value this job, Jace. It's been a hell of a run, these past seven plus years. And I wish worse than you that I hadn't fouled-up."

"My fault as much as yours." Jace strode over and placed a hand on Mike's shoulder. "I saw that you needed help when your sweet wife got killed in that pile-up. Hell, I picked out a shrink for you before the wreckers towed those three tangled vehicles apart. Why'd you refuse that help?"

"A mistake, considering it from hindsight, especially since I lost Miriam six months after losing Arlene."

Jace hung his head and nodded repeatedly as he resumed pacing. "Losing your sweet daughter on top of losing your wife is exactly why you'd have been wise to let a shrink screw your damn head back on."

"The dumb decision I made in Shreveport had nothing to do with those tragedies."

Jace swiveled around to gape at him. "A bunch of folks likely will characterize that denial as delusional. You damn well need to go on down to Naw'lins and put a shine back on your damn image."

"Doubt I'll get a whole lot of cooperation from that bunch."

"You don't need their damn cops, what with having our own investigative staff there. And a damned good one, if I say so myself. Hell, I handpicked Armand Dupuy to head it."

Mike nodded to that, having nothing but the highest regard for Armand. However, he knew damn well if you want to solve a crime in any city you need to work in concert with the locals. So he ventured to say: "You sure as hell will get better results with someone other than me ramroding that staff there."

"You're the one needs redemption, Mike. So you damn well need to apprehend those yahoos shot down Darby Williams and those other fellers in cold blood. And you need to accomplish it before folks all across this damn state start demanding your damned hide gets nailed to the damn barn."

"Okay, Jace—you're asking me to go, I'll go."

"I'm not asking you to do a damn thing, Mike. I'm telling you that you go to Naw'lins you got you a chance to redeem your damn status as top cop. You don't clear that damn case, you can tender your damn resignation."

#   #

11

Chapter Three

"Special Agent in Charge Dupuy be right with you, Director."

Mike nodded to the receptionist, then paced the small reception area of the New Orleans office complex located in the modern tower of One Canal Place, barely more than a block from the Mississippi River. That section of the skyscraper, designated as Three Sixty-Five Canal Place, competed with other impressive edifices in the southwest corner of The French Quarter, at the apex of a rehabilitated area that had become one of the most trafficked sections of the city—day and night.

From the twenty-seventh-floor window Mike scanned an architectural conglomeration that exemplified the diverse influences of the *Big Easy*. Harrah's Casino with its Byzantine domes contrasted with the modern structures of the Double Tree Hotel to the right of it and the Hilton to its left. Behind Harrah's, the traditionally designed Lykes Building rising imperiously toward the wispy stratus clouds served as home-office of the shipping magnate.

Close to the river the World Trade Center towered above the sprawling Convention Center, as well as above the mile-long Riverwalk Mall. Ships from all over the world occupied the docks, piers, and moorings along the *Big Muddy*, interspersed by steel cranes swinging cargo onto and off those vessels.

"Hey, Mike," greeted roly-poly Armand Dupuy with his bush of gray hair as he emerged from the inner office. Black horn-rimmed glasses teetered on his nose as he hurried over to vigorously shake Mike's hand. "Good to see you, guy." They pounded each other's shoulders.

Then Armand hooked an arm in Mike's and ushered him along a hallway to a conference room, where four people sat around an oblong table. Armand gestured to Mike, who towered a full head above him. "For any of y'all unfamiliar with the Director of Investigations, this is the man, Mike Molino."

Those at the table murmured and nodded greetings. Mike nodded back as he placed a hand on Armand's shoulder to project solidarity. He recognized three of the investigators, having worked cases with them.

Three were mature, demonstrating the kind of experience Mike liked to have in an investigative staff. The fourth, bright-eyed and eager, looked like he had a few years before turning thirty. But that probie would learn from the vets and personify the process that perpetuated a dependable law enforcement team.

Mike thought he read resentment on the face of Nelda Washington, a tall and big-boned black woman. He'd worked a number of cases with her during her seven plus exemplary years with the AG's office, all in New Orleans. Before that, he knew, she put in nine years with the NOPD, from whence Armand Dupuy recruited her, as his first act after Jace anointed him to ramrod the city's investigative staff.

Mike always complimented Armand for assembling the ideal team for a complex city. Steamy and torpid most of the year, New Orleans served as the cauldron of descendants of immigrants from France, Spain, Africa, and French Canada—spiced with Irish, Italians, Asians, Caribbean blacks, and Canary Islanders—plus the influx of legions of migratory Americans. That agglomeration commingled with Cajuns, Creoles and Native Americans, plus African-American descendants of slaves, created uniqueness unmatched in any other metropolis in the United States.

13

Gustave Jawarlska, seated across from Nelda Washington, postured professorially with his close-cropped blonde hair and square face adorned by a neatly trimmed beard and mustache. Mike stifled chuckling, remembering the man objecting to being addressed as Gus, demeaning it as an appellation befitting butchers and plumbers.

Gustave Jawarlska was the only investigative holdover from the previous administration, which had been headed by the opposition party. That retention spoke volumes for him in a state ridden with rabid politics.

Julius Provenzano sat on Gustave's right. His thinning brown hair laced with specks of gray softened an otherwise pugnacious appearance. Short, stocky, and slightly round-shouldered, his squinted eyes sparked with intensity. He'd spent the past three years with the AG's office after serving eleven with the state police, where he earned a reputation as an astute detective and a specialist in organized crime.

"Say hello to Chi Chi O'Brien on his first day here," Armand said to Mike, gesturing to the newest staffer, seated alongside Nelda Washington. Glossy black hair and a pencil mustache underscored the man's swarthy complexion and Hispanic appearance.

A bemused snort burst out of Mike. "O'Brien?"

"I'm Puerto Rican," the serious-faced young man said.

The ensuing chuckling eased the tension of confronting the agency's director of investigations. "You from these parts?" Mike asked.

"No, sir. I'm from the Bronx." Receiving no immediate response, he added: "That's the number one barrio in New York . . . a city in the northeast."

"Is that Bronx a separate municipality?" Gustave Jawarlska asked, chuckling with the others.

"Don't they hire Puerto Rican cops in that rotten-ass city?" Nelda asked.

"Hell yeah! They only hire gringos when they run out of Puerto Ricans."

"So why you hustled yo' skinny ass way down here to get you a damn job?" Nelda asked, her acerbic tone laced with humor.

"Bad marriage. Me and that gringita were both in the job. No way I wanted to see her mean ass every time I reported to the station house."

"You work in investigations there?" Mike asked.

"Most of the last year in plainclothes, sir, in Organized Crime."

"Why'd you pick Louisiana?" Mike asked.

"Served near here in the Marines, sir. Liked the place, so decided to head this way when I split with that bitch. My cop experience in The Apple, and fluency in Spanish, gave me a leg up in getting hired here."

"Okay," Mike said, "so much for the bio of a misplaced Puerto Rican. Let's talk about the reason I'm here. Both the governor and the attorney general demand we clear the murder of Darby Williams, Jerome Sessy, and Antwan Croix."

"Amen!" issued from Nelda. "About time the wanton murder of black folks rated administrative attention."

"We're obliged," Gustave said, sniffing haughtily, "to find and punish the assassins of all our citizens, regardless of ethnicity."

"However," Armand Dupuy said, "three days after the commission of that crime the NOPD doesn't have clue one as to the identity of the perps."

"Nor do they have a defined motive for that rash act," Gustave added.

15

"They haven't even found that stolen delivery van," Julie Provenzano said.

"Do they at least appear to have a direction to pursue?" Mike asked.

"Everybody in that kitchen," Armand Dupuy said as he pushed his heavy-rimmed glasses back up his nose, "heard them state loud and clear that they went there to light up Brent Kenman."

"Apparently they were color-blind," Nelda said, and sucked her teeth in criticism.

"Let's concentrate on method and motive." Mike said.

"Sure looks like a mob hit," Julie Provenzano said, intensity in his eyes.

"If it was home boys," Chi Chi said, "they'd more likely wield automatic weapons, relying on a stream of bullets rather than marksmanship, with little regard for who-all they take down in the process."

"Rednecks," Nelda said, "tote high-powered rifles or large-caliber pistols to intimidate folks."

"Mob buttons," Julie Provenzano said, "will do multiple hits with shotguns, and are precise, killing only their marks unless they need to eliminate witnesses."

"Besides," Nelda said, "homies kill to protect turf, especially where they peddle dope, or to avenge one of their own who somebody put a hurting on. Yeah, and when they resent some outsider hitting on their ladies. They don't have care one about politics . . . which is what this appears to be about."

"Interesting," Gustave said, "that those pols competing for the candidacy converged at that window at that particular moment."

Mike pointed a finger of commendation at Gustave for that

16

contribution.

"Those assassins appear to have expected them to be there," Julie Provenzano said.

Mike pointed a finger at Julie.

"But why'd they take out those three brothers?" Nelda asked. "Like as not they were the only black folks in that fancy-ass restaurant?"

"In spite of claiming to target Brent Kenman—a white guy," Julie Provenzano added. "Maybe we need to lean on that guy for a heads-up."

"Not a good idea," Armand Dupuy warned.

Mike compressed his lips as he conceded Armand Dupuy his wariness since Brent Kenman had become the city's most prominent up-and-coming politicos. He'd clawed his way up the ranks of campaign managers to mastermind the election of Big Willie Hoke, the only nominee left to contend for the governorship against Birch Murdock. Success would make him a damn king-maker.

"What bothers me," Nelda said, "is that good ole' boy being the only one standing, in spite of supposedly being the damn target . . . and sure couldn't pass for a brother."

"His sidekick, Nicky Boheemer, also walked away unscathed," Julie reminded.

"We talking about doing three prominent brothers," Nelda said, "and you better believe this sister has some hard eyes on the local fuzz, to make sure they don't sweep this one under the damn porch."

"We've been scrutinizing their reports," Armand said, "making certain they aren't pulling any shim-sham."

"Hereon," Mike announced, "this office will administer its own investigation." He glanced around, his demeanor defying resistance or opposition.

17

"They may object," Armand said. "to our infringing on their jurisdiction."

"Every damn thing," Mike said, "in the state of Louisiana is our damn jurisdiction. That makes it our damn responsibility to make certain this case is investigated thoroughly."

"Sounds like the way to go, boss man," Chi Chi said, "with everything pointing to hit-men as opposed to politically motivated extremists or KKK loonies."

"Racists," Gustave said in his affected way, "may well have camouflaged their action by making it appear political."

Julie Provenzano shook his head. "It's plain as pesto on penne that we're dealing with professional buttons, not a bunch of backwoods rednecks. They planned and efficiently executed that triple rub-out, taking out exactly who they targeted."

"The question," Gustave said, "is who engineered it and why?"

"Exactly," Mike said. "We need to learn why pros who expertly covered their tracks ended up supposedly shooting the wrong guy."

"And why after offing the opposition candidate," Armand added, "did they blow away the black banker and an assistant campaign manager?"

"Suggests motives other than political rivalry," Gustave said.

"Perhaps intent to obscure," Armand said.

"Requiring that we delve into this thing ourselves," Mike said, "and not depend on pretexts fed us to cover up an inept investigation."

"Lead the way, boss man," Nelda said. "I'm ready, willing and eager to follow."

Mike gestured to Armand. "You and I are going to visit the cop house in the Sixth District, to personally inform them of our intention to institute our own investigation."

18

"Been preparing for that contentious meeting," Armand said, "since informed you were coming. Sure hope we don't set no whole lot of fur to flying."

"How they react is their problem," Mike said. "When we return the lot of us are going to Belmonde's to sweep that three-day-old crime scene . . . compile our own reports."

# #

Chapter Four

     Armand Dupuy drove the black SUV up busy Canal Street, a wide thoroughfare divided by a median that paved over the trolley tracks. An occasional dare-devil pedestrians darted across the street choked with trucks, cars, taxis and buses.

     Droves of people swirled along the sidewalks, scurrying in and out of mid- and high-rise office building lobbies as well entrances of ground-level-stores with display windows topped by colorful signs. The maze of windows glinted shafts of sunshine, intermittent blocked out by gathering clouds. Wispy stratums of smog skirted the tops of towering buildings. Every sound and noise imaginable reverberated in the midday heat.

     "Is it my imagination that Nelda Washington appeared unhappy about my arrival?" Mike asked.

     "Like as not she's worried," Armand said, chuckling. "Thinks they've kicked you down here permanently, affecting her aspirations to succeed me in heading up this office when I retire in three, four months."

     "Tell her those worries are unfounded. I damn sure intend to redeem myself by clearing this mess up in jig time. I don't, I'll likely get the gate—as opposed to demotion."

     "Not necessarily, good buddy. Jace has the political savvy to know that if he exiles you to this turbulent metropolis, the rest of the state will consider it punishment—which'll likely pacify the critics."

     Mike made a wry face as he hoped Armand didn't rap that spike dead on. Damndest thing was, when Jace Morreau insisted he go to New Orleans to ramrod this case, he worried it had every possibility of ending up as his demotion. But he determined to damn sure clear this case and earn reinstatement as the agency top-dog in the state capital.

"Gustave Jawarlska also considers himself a candidate to head up the New Orleans office," Armand said, "resulting in he and Nelda butting heads." He turned left into Magazine Street, a one-way headed west, flanked by low- to mid-rise office buildings, many with storefronts on their first floors.

"Whichever of them gets the nod, " Mike said, "will inherit a good crew." He nodded to approval of Armand having put together an efficient bunch. Yep, he couldn't imagine a more valuable asset than Julie Provenzano, an authority on mob activities in a city with Italian, Irish, and Russian mobsters. Nor could they ignore the criminal antics of Jamaicans, Colombians, Chinese, Mexicans and Vietnamese.

"How's that Shreveport business going?" Armand asked as he turned right on Common Street, a one-way headed north, lined with hotels as well as office buildings.

"Glad you broached that matter, so's we can clean the air between us."

"Don't sweat it, Mike. That Jace didn't fire you is vindication I can accept."

"You're a good ole' buddy, Armand. Everybody isn't near as trusting as you. Fact is, all too many condemn me as having abused my authority."

"I know you better than most, having worked a bunch of cases with you through the years. You're clean in my book, with a record to support that faith."

"Truly appreciate that, good buddy. But failure to clear this case is my swan song."

"Then let's do it, making it your return to glory and my parting

21

gesture into retirement."

"Easier said than done, considering this assassination is headed for storage in a cold-case file cabinet. Incidentally, what's prompting you to take the farm all of a sudden?"

"Nothing sudden about it, Mike. Hell, I've put in nigh on eight years with the AG's office after thirty-two with the state police. Besides, I figure that Jace wants younger minds to ramrod things here— those in tune with this technology age. My old brain struggles to absorb all that modern hokum-pokum."

"But the agency always needs your kind of experience."

"Hell, I'll be sixty-four in October, Mike . . . time to smell me some damn roses."

Reaching the Howard Avenue interchange, where Loyola merged with South Rampart, they passed under the elevated highway of Interstate Ninety, resounding with the tire-singing of heavy traffic.

"You're one hell of a cop, Armand, and I hate to see you go. Find it hard to believe you don't have reservations about hanging it up."

"Oh, I got me a few. Mostly, it's spending twenty-four-seven with Ysette. No denying we have us a good marriage and get along better than most. But I only see her a few hours a day except on weekends, and not every one of those. Now I'm likely going to see more of her than I ever wanted to, even when I was a rutting youngster."

"You're lucky, from my point of view."

"Sorry, Mike. Didn't mean to remind you of that."

"Nothing you can do to prevent it haunting me."

"Ever consider marrying again?"

"Doubt I can love a woman that much again."

"Never know, good buddy. You just might meet someone turns your head."

Preferring not to expound on the subject, Mike focused on their surroundings, a neighborhood with conditions depreciating with every block they traveled west. Those small and narrow dwellings, virtual shacks the locals referred to as shotgun houses because a hallway ran from the front to the rear door with all rooms accessed from it. Battered by age and neglect, they had board or shingled exteriors ravaged by age and weather.

Streets as well as buildings revealed deterioration aggravated by a lack of maintenance. Scrubby bushes and weed-infested hardscrabble bordered the broken sidewalks. Trash flitted about. Invariably, the few people that emerged from the decrepit residences were African-American.

At the corner of South Rampart Street and Martin Luther King Junior Boulevard they pulled up to the Sixth District Police Station, a modern two-story brown brick building with a plate glass entranceway, an imposing example of public funds invested in a sea of dereliction. It and the fire department station stood out, incongruous in that neighborhood; both examples of political ineptitude motivated by patronizing that did nothing to improve the lifestyles of the indigent residents.

After parking, they climbed the short concrete stoop with blue-painted pipe railings. One of the glass doors swung open just as they reached it and a tall, thin guy with straw-colored hair exited. All three arched brows in recognition.

"You know Edmund Knuth," Armand said to Mike.

"Only too well," Mike said, scoffing at memory of the guy being introduced to him a couple of years ago as the award-winning investigative reporter. Sneering, he remarked: "You worked that Shreveport affair like a dog shaking the life out of a rat in a henhouse."

23

"Didn't have all that many choices with the black community clamoring about racial abuse," Knuth said, twirling his hands while shuffling in place, "leaving the media little choice but continually publicize the event. But you have to admit I refrained from embellishing the thing with lascivious assumptions like those tabloids."

"The reason I don't hold it against you," Mike grumbled.

"You needed to speak out in your defense," Knuth said, "to prevent those trashy scandalmongers spreading false perceptions so widely they became accepted as gospel."

"Probably didn't expect folks to believe that nonsense," Armand said.

"It's what was out there," Knuth said. "What else you want folks to believe? But, okay, if what I published is in any way incorrect or untrue, it's on you to set the story straight. Believe that if you give me facts I can verify, I'll publicize your side."

"Wish I could," Mike said. "That gal stymies every chance I have of bailing myself out by persisting she succumbed to me under duress."

"Hard to convince folks of something different," Knuth said, "after seeing her sexy photos in those scandal rags. They're not about to believe you didn't jump on those bones—you being widowed and all, and in a position to take advantage of her."

"Folks likely will keep arriving at that conclusion," Armand said, "so long as she persists in that claim."

"And she will," Knuth said, "long as those tabloids continue buttering her bread."

Mike spread his hands in a helpless gesture.

"You disprove her claim," Knuth said, "and I'll publicize it."

Mike grimaced criticism at himself for having sluffed off the accusations rather than establish his innocence and preclude the perception advanced by the rumor mongers.

"Always admired you as a good cop," Knuth said, "and was surprised when the story erupted. I'd be more than happy to help absolve you."

"I'll keep that in mind," Mike said.

"Dropped in here," Knuth said, "in hopes of getting a heads-up on the Belmonde assassinations. Running into you two suggests there's something in the wind I haven't been informed about. Y'all willing to share something I can use?"

"Learn anything from them?" Armand asked.

"Nothing everybody hasn't already printed. You fellows have anything for me?"

"We get anything," Armand said, "we'll keep you informed." All three nodded to each other as Armand and Mike pushed through the door to enter the police station.

#   #

Chapter Five

Armand flashed his credentials to the desk sergeant. "We have an appointment with the District Commander."

While the sergeant checked his schedule, Mike gazed around at the desultory activity of uniformed men and women intermingling with those in civilian dress; some with ID cards and/or badges dangling from around their necks.

The desk sergeant disinterestedly performed another repetitive task by calling the District Commander's office to verify the appointment then inform of the arrival of his guests. While clicking off he glanced at the second visitor and gawked. "Lookee here! We got us a visit from the renowned Director Molino of the AG's office."

A hush enveloped those collected in small groups in the wide concourse. Uniformed officers plus those in civilian dress displaying badges glowered at the two visitors. The civilians without official connection gazed around, mystified by the hostile murmur that thickened the air. Two scowling plainclothes cops advanced toward the subjects, but hesitated when others didn't back their play.

"Let's take this som'bitch out!" one of them called to stimulate the others.

"Time to get us some payback," the other one hollered to feed the drone of belligerence.

But all attention turned to a door opening from an inner office. A burly detective with a pink face strode out. In shirtsleeves with tie and collar loosened, he threaded through his fellows to the targets of antagonism. "How the hell are you, laddie?" he said as he proffered a beefy handshake to Armand.

"Hey!" one of the angry bunch growled at the burly detective. "Don't you know who they are?"

"Aye," the pink-faced detective responded, "and as well aware of that as I am, I consider Armand Dupuy one of the good fellows from that office. So let's impress these visitors by acting like professionals."

"Say hello to Sergeant O'Shea of homicide," Armand said to Mike. "He heads up the Belmonde's investigation. Patty, this is Mike Molino."

O'Shea thrust out his beefy hand. "Now I'm not going to embarrass my mama by forgetting my manners, while, in fact, I'm not all that happy to make your acquaintance, considering your reputation for axing cops."

A murmur of dissention riffled the air as the scowls deepened and a few menaced by inching closer.

"I only ax corrupt cops," Mike said while shaking hands. "You don't tarnish the badge or the shield you have nothing to fear from me."

"Then I've not a worry in the world," O'Shea said, "being as I respect my shield too much to bring shame to it." A less assertive wave of grumbling assailed them.

O'Shea grinned brashly while ushering Mike and Armand through the hostile environment, the flexed muscles bulging his shirt challenging interference. After a short walk down a hallway he waved the visitors into the expansive office of Captain Sebastian Shayde, Commander of the Sixth Police District.

A tall and handsome African-American, with an obvious Caucasian admixture, postured imperiously in his braid- and medal-decorated uniform. He rose from the leather throne behind his impressive desk to greet Armand vocally while according Mike Molino a grumble and a desultory nod.

"This is Lieutenant Jesse Montrose, the District Chief of Detectives," the captain said as he gestured to the black man with serious mien in civilian dress near his desk.

Lieutenant Montrose rose to shake hands with both visitors, after which everyone took seats. Captain Shayde however remained standing behind his desk. "Just so everyone knows: I fully intend to protect this department from any attempt to tarnish it."

"Not our objective," Mike said.

"Why else have you come to Naw'lins?" Captain Shayde challenged.

"To clear up that Belmonde's affair," Mike replied.

"We have enough pressure," Lieutenant Montrose said, "struggling to make headway with the case without additional interference."

"You burned us badly a year ago," Captain Shayde said.

"There's no correlation," Armand Dupuy said, "between that corruption investigation and this assassination case."

"So y'all claim," Captain Shayde retorted.

"All things considered," Lieutenant Montrose said, "we'd prefer to keep this in-house, excluding bureaucratic analysis and interference."

"You know that's not going to happen," Mike said, "considering this thing has state-wide political implications."

"Exactly the reason," Captain Shayde said, "we intend to protect this department from unwarranted criticism by antagonistic outsiders."

"There's the rub," Sergeant O'Shea said. "We're asked to suffer the interference and criticism of every ambitious office-seeker as well by the motor-mouths of the media, the lot of which inhibit our progress."

"We'll clear this case," Lieutenant Montrose said, his voice vibrant with assurance.

Captain Shayde nodded. "Knowing we'd better damn well serve up indictments if we want to retain viability, and keep our jobs."

"Believe that we will, sir," Montrose said. "But we'll be more efficient if free from being hampered by oversight and interminable evaluation."

"We'll try not to hinder your procedures," Mike said. "But we prefer to conduct our own investigation rather than depend on what's spoon-fed to us."

"Hardly desirable," Lieutenant Montrose said. "We have enough to deal with without stumbling over each other."

"That doesn't have to happen," Armand Dupuy said, "if we coordinate procedures."

"Sounds to me like another of your witch hunts," Shayde said, sneering at Mike.

"I don't do witch hunts, District Commander."

"How else can you characterize ruining the careers of nineteen of our police officers?" Shayde shot back.

"They ruined their own damn careers," Mike said. "I remind you that all charges of corruption were proved. Fact is, that cleanup should have been inter-departmental, but y'all made the mistake of trying to insulate yourselves from outside review rather than weed out your unscrupulous. Hopefully, captain, you won't repeat that mistake. Cull your bad cops before it's done for you."

"You insinuate anything uncomplimentary about our people in this mess," Shayde said, "and I'll go after you. You're vulnerable—scandal-ridden."

"Baseless allegations. Nothing's been proven against me."

"Baseless my ass!" Shayde shot back. "You're dirty. Read any

29

damn newspaper or listen to the radio and TV commentators criticize your reprehensible performance with that gal in Shreveport."

"With every innuendo unsubstantiated," Armand said.

"Smoke needs fire," O'Shea said, "and there's more than a little of that about."

"If I'd been found dirty," Mike said, "I'd have been axed, not dispatched here to ramrod an investigation your people have failed to make reasonable progress at."

"Now there's a pile of shit," O'Shea growled. "We've been working our asses—"

"Your protector, Jace Morreau," Shayde interrupted, "let you off the hook. But I won't sit quietly and allow any goddam politician, no matter how big and powerful, grant you dispensation . . . not when the charges include racial improprieties."

"I repeat," Mike retorted, "that they haven't been proven—"

"Hell they haven't," Shayde retorted. "That little gal in Shreveport repeatedly accuses you of shaking her down for her booty. Depend on those charges being pursued until your boss cashiers you."

"Do your damndest," Mike said, "but that won't obstruct our investigating this matter until we've provided answers that will satisfy the people of New Orleans—as well as those throughout Louisiana."

"You mean whitewash your sins in Shreveport," Shayde said.

"Our intent," Mike said, "plainly and simply is to clear this triple murder . . . with or without your cooperation."

"Hope you're not insinuating," Shayde said, "that New Orleans police personnel are involved in an assassination of one of the finest men who ever graced this city."

Lieutenant Montrose nodded emphatically, adding: "Darby Williams was a man among men."

"As was Jerome Sessy," Shayde said, puffing out his chest. "How many other black men in this country rose to top management in a major international bank?"

"In charge of billions of dollars in foreign exchange," Montrose added.

"Don't twist it," Mike said. "This is about uncovering assassins, not splashing around racial mud or singing the praises of successful African Americans."

"And what was that debacle about in Shreveport?" Shayde demanded. "You denying that was racial?"

"Yes, I am," Mike said, "in spite of whatever way the scandal sheets spin it."

"Then you had damn well better be able to support that contention," Shayde said, "since I intend to see that the media publicizes the reason your office is interfering in this case is to smokescreen that scandal."

"Remember," Mike said, "to remind the media that the guy you accuse of racial prejudice is part Mexican and part Indian."

Shayde waved contemptuously at that. "Why aren't y'all concentrating upstate, where the Klan is strongest?"

"Because," Lieutenant Montrose said, "there's no political hay in that direction."

"Ridiculous," Mike said. "Our office respects the rights of all its citizens, regardless of race, religion, or anything else."

"Tell it to someone gullible enough to believe that rhetoric," Shayde said. "You folks will make all kinds of claims in an election year. But upstate is still the white half of Louisiana."

"You're being overly cynical, Sebastian," Armand Dupuy said.

"Cynicism," Shayde shot back, "is acquired by wallowing in the grime of the criminal element and the despondency of poverty. You fancy cops rarely dirty your shoes, so lack our experiences of dealing with sub-human elements."

"We were both state cops," Mike retorted, gesturing to Armand, "and trundled through slums and trashy alleys the same as city cops."

Shayde sneered. "Only when you climb down from your holier-than-thou-perch to persecute local cops."

"To expose their corrupt practices," Mike shot back.

"Simply accept," Armand said, "that a cop is a cop, whether city, state, or federal. We all live in the same universe and play by the same rules."

"There's only three kinds in a cop's world," O'Shea said. "There's those of us in the job that impose the law. Then there's the civilians who benefit from our efforts and sacrifices, in terms of the times we put our lives in peril to preserve theirs, along with whatever little wealth the good citizens accumulate. Last but far from least are the scumbags who make it necessary to have cops."

"We're wasting time here," Mike said, "with a lot of meaningless psychobabble."

"Meaningless to you," Shayde snarled. "Jesse, why don't you take these meddlers to your office and brief them so they can see we have no need of their interference."

#   #

Chapter Six

Mike sighed audibly , relieved to exit that office and distance himself from contention with Sebastian Shayde. Damn, and he thought he'd braced himself to deal with the egomaniac.

Lieutenant Montrose led them to a smaller office, where files burdened the desk and tops of file cabinets. Three straight-back chairs crowded the rest of the space. O'Shea closed the door to muffle the clamor of activity typical in municipal cop houses.

"This immediate neighborhood is rundown," the black lieutenant said, waving them to take chairs while he sat behind his desk. "However, a goodly part of the sixth is comprised of some of the most desirable and expensive real estate in the city, consequently over all it's not your high crime area."

"However," O'Shea remarked, "what you observed outside our doors more than makes up for the tranquility in the quieter sections."

"Let's not digress into sociological deprecation," Lieutenant Montrose grumbled. "We're here to find a middle ground with the AG's office—keeping in mind that we're unreceptive to interference."

Mike leaned forward but the opening of the door forestalled his intended proposal. He and Armand arched their brows as an attractive female in a conservative navy blue skirt-suit entered and exchanged salutations with Montrose and O'Shea. The shield suspended around her neck identified her as a member of that official body.

"Sergeant Kaylee Boyle," Lieutenant Montrose introduced. Addressing her, he said: "Say hello to Director Molino and Special Agent Dupuy of the AG's office."

33

Both rose to shake hands with her and murmur greetings. O'Shea gave her his chair, then propped his haunch on the far corner of his superior's desk, far enough over so his bulk didn't block out the lieutenant.

"The municipal police department," Lieutenant Montrose said, "accepts its obligation to its residents to vigorously pursue the investigation and assure the citizenry that the perpetrators of those vicious murders do not go unpunished."

"I hear you," Armand said, adjusting his glasses.

"We sure as hell share that attitude," Mike added.

"Some of us have taken a personal interest," the lieutenant continued, "since the three victims were African-Americans . . . prominent ones, I might add."

"While all identifications of the perpetrators," O'Shea added, "imply Caucasians."

"To assure the AG's office we've no objection to opening our files for oversight," Lieutenant Montrose said, "we've had copies run off for you gentlemen to take with you." He gestured to a number of accordion envelopes stuffed to capacity leaning against the wall.

"Naturally," O'Shea said, "we'll appreciate reciprocation."

"Works for me," Mike said. While bobbing his head in agreement to the amicable arrangement he assessed the female sergeant as mature with a handsome face framed by brown hair.

"Both our agencies," Lieutenant Montrose said, "will be served by eliminating costly duplication. To achieve that we'd like Sergeant Boyle to liaise with both of our offices to keep us advised of each other's procedures and progress."

Mike tried to but couldn't suppress an amused snort. He and Armand exchanged glances, transmitting awareness that the locals were trying to burden them with an albatross. He ignored Armand's conspiratorial wink. Okay, he found her attractive, and estimated her age as in the late thirties or early forties. But he closed the door on personalizing a relationship with a gal intended as a mole to report on their activities.

True, he'd mourned beyond the generally prescribed period, but still felt queasy about pursuing women, as if it tarnished the memory of Arlene. Besides, he shuddered at the prospect of going through the preliminary overture phases. Hell, he hadn't done it since he surrendered bachelorhood, some twenty-odd years ago.

But Arlene was gone and he'd begun to rebuke himself for not seeking a normal life . . . especially to consider partnering. Still, he admonished himself to be careful. Didn't he have enough grief coming out of Shreveport? He damn sure didn't need any new innuendos to further complicate his life.

"Any other business to discuss?" Lieutenant Montrose asked.

"If you've no objection," Sergeant O'Shea said, "I'll offer a bit of commentary."

Mike inhaled to prepare himself to suffer a long-winded discourse, very probably regarding truth and trust between the two agencies—maybe even a few veiled threats.

"Everything we know about the assassins," the Irishman said, "came from interviewing the kitchen help, being as those folks in the dining area were too busy ducking and hiding to witness anything when that tiny window between the two areas exploded."

"Nor did the kitchen help serve up any useful intel," Lieutenant Montrose added, "having been traumatized by the experience."

"Their only descriptions," O'Shea said, "were that the thugs were scary-looking white guys wearing ski masks, and holding big-assed shotguns."

"However," Montrose said, "they were more explicit with the two shooters. The tall one wielded a double-barreled shotgun, while all the others toted single-barreled."

"Story I got," Armand said, "is that in spite of announcing they targeted Brent Kenman, the dumpy one on the left missed Kenman when his twelve-gage shotgun bucked, sending the shot high."

"With a load choked to spread laterally rather than vertically," O'Shea said, chuckling cynically.

"Fired too high," Lieutenant Montrose grated, "to harm a hair on that supposed target's head.

O'Shea nodded while adding: "All witnesses agreed that the tall guy shot Darby Williams and Jerome Sessy, then reloaded and shot Assistant Campaign Manager Antwan Croix."

"I'm convinced," Lieutenant Montrose said, "they anticipated those folks being there and went there to kill those black men."

"The reason," Mike said, "we need to learn a whole lot more about why those politicians met there and set themselves up as ducks in a row."

Lieutenant Montrose nodded animatedly while asking: "And how did those brazen killers expect them to be standing there?"

All heads bobbed to that, prompting O'Shea to say: "Those mobsters raced away in a blue delivery van reported stolen by Bubba's Delivery Service—which hasn't been located despite an APB out on it."

"We'll find it," Lieutenant Montrose assured. "The thing's too big to hide for long."

"You mentioned," Mike said, "that one of them reloaded his shotgun. I'm going to assume you collected the spent shells for ballistics examination."

"Had a CSU team there for two days," Lieutenant Montrose said, "without obtaining a lick of evidence."

"In keeping with our luck in this case," O'Shea said, "those shells contained no fingerprints. That mook obviously had the smarts to wear latex gloves while loading as well as handling the damn shells beforehand."

"Television shows are educating them," Armand said.

"Without the weapons to test," Montrose reminded, "there's no way we can connect those shells by hammer marks to any particular shotgun."

"By now," Armand said, "those ole' boys like as not disposed of those suckers by tossing them into Lake Pontchartrain or one of the many bayous."

Mike nodded, aware there was no end of deep water in the vicinity, what with all the damn canals, swamps and bayous around the city . . . not to mention the *Big Muddy*.

"Nobody with half a brain," O'Shea said, "is likely to trudge about in those 'gator dens in search of a damned shotgun."

"Plus," Armand said, "it's not likely you'll get identification from buckshot."

Mike nodded to that as he assumed those mooks were paid a bundle for that triple shooting, so could afford to ditch everything incriminating.

"We interviewed all those who remained until the police arrived," O'Shea said, "as well as many of those identified from the reservations list. Not one had more to say than they'd panicked and dove for cover."

"Did Kenman sustain any injuries?" Mike asked.

"He and his side-kick, Boheemer, had a few cuts and bruises

from flying glass," O'Shea said.

"Confusing aspect," Montrose said, "is that Kenman and Boheemer head up the campaign for Willis Hoke, the front-runner with a comfortable margin. Every poll projects Willis Hoke whooping Darby Williams in the primary, questioning political motives for that killing."

"That's the long and the short of it," O'Shea agreed. "Big Willie never had any other party opposition that threatened his primary bid, and there's not a bit of doubt that Little Orphan Annie beats Murdock in a general election."

"Had the senator been the victim," Montrose said, "we'd have reason to look at Darby Williams and his people. But since Darby didn't figure to close that gap against Big Willie, upstate anyway, there's no basis for suspicion of that sort, leaving us floundering for direction."

"Hard to believe," Armand said, "that those mooks expect folks to accept that professional shooters out to kill one particular person totally missed that target while taking out three others."

"Shooting blacks," Montrose rasped, "when Kenman, their supposed victim, is white. It's going to take doing to convince me they weren't racists."

"Lu'ziana has no shortage of the type to get spooked by the prospect of ending up with a black governor," O'Shea said.

"In spite of the country having elected a black president," Montrose added.

"No way of telling until we catch up to the perps," Armand said, "assuming they'll spill their guts if and when we do."

Mike turned to the woman. "You've been singularly silent, Sergeant. What's your take on all this?"

"Not a thing, sir, having had nothing to do with the investigation. You see, I've just been transferred out of PID for this assignment."

Mike nodded, aware that what most cities called the Internal Affairs Bureau, New Orleans Police Department referred to as the Public Investigation Division. Those cops investigated other cops, ostensibly to prevent or uncover corruption and wrongdoing in the department. It raised the question in Mike's mind why they didn't assign someone from homicide as liaisons. And why an attractive woman?

"It serves both our organizations," Lieutenant Montrose said, "to have the sergeant keep us all up to speed, eliminating duplication of efforts."

Mike chuckled, though he conceded that the lieutenant sounded sincere, but suspiciously eager to sell the idea, which Mike presumed originated with Shayde. "So you're saying the sergeant is to serve as a glorified courier."

"I'm an investigator, the same as you, Director Molino, with years of experience."

Mike noted the rancor in her retort, implying toughness. He winced when Armand informed her: "We're planning to spend the afternoon interviewing people at Belmonde's."

Mike hadn't intended to take the honey trap along. But shorn of that option, he shrugged and turned to O'Shea, who quipped: "Don't plan on taking lunch or dinner there, being its prices exceed those an honest peace officer can afford."

All chuckled as Mike and Armand rose, as did the lieutenant and O'Shea to shake hands. Sergeant Boyle stood also, though she appeared uncertain what to do.

"You coming with us?" Mike asked her.

"Not at this minute, sir. Folks taking over in PID need to be briefed. Mind if I meet you in an hour or so?"

"We'll welcome any info you can bird-dog," O'Shea said, as he escorted them back through the concourse, and past the glaring resentment of cops there. "No denying we're desperate for a heads-up."

#   #

Chapter Seven

    "We need to interview every waiter, busboy, cook, chef, and pot washer," Mike instructed the staff gathered in the reception area of the AG's office. "Grill them until you extract relevant information that can open an avenue of investigation."

    "What of patrons who were present?" Gustave asked.

    Armand shook his head. "It'd take too many man-hours to locate and interview every one of them."

    "And most," Nelda reminded, "weren't back in the bar area, so unaware of what really happened."

    "Even those back there more'n likely panicked," Julie Provenzano said. "Doubtful they can even identify any of the hoods that scared their asses off."

    "Those interviews supposedly have been done by the locals anyway," Mike said. "If they elicited any info it'll be in that pile of reports they gave us."

    Armand scoffed. "Expect the most of it to be useless prattle . . . intended to confuse as well as monopolize our attention and direct us away from probing that riddle."

    "Making it more productive," Mike said, "to concentrate on interviewing employees and arriving at our own conclusions."

    "Most won't be aware of the value of their experiences," Gustave commented.

    "Why we need to delve into their cerebral cortexes with pick and shovel," Mike said, "to mine nuggets they may not be aware of. Partner up. Armand is with me."

41

"Want to hang with me, New York boy?" Nelda asked Chi Chi, "and teach me how all y'all big-city folks do police work?"

Chi Chi glanced to the other two men, his barely perceptible grimace suggesting disappointment for not partnering with one of them. But he shrugged as he rose and loped toward Nelda.

"Why you dragging yo' Puerto Rican ass?" she harassed him. "You don't like partnering with a female? Or is it black females you have an aversion to?"

"Yo, lady, get off that shit with me. Puerto Ricans have their own baggage."

"Then why you drag-assing?"

"Hey, woman, you pull your weight and I got no complaints. That goes for a guy just as well."

"Hold on," Mike said. "Chi Chi, I'd rather you and Julie partner, since you two are familiar with mob and organized gang activities and can feed off each other, maybe pick up on something that those not as attuned might overlook."

"You saying I don't know my way around the damn streets?" Nelda demanded.

"I'm saying I think Julie and Chi Chi make a good team," Mike replied. Oh boy, he hadn't intended to antagonize Nelda . . . didn't need that cantankerous gal pissed at him.

Chi Chi struggled not to expose elation while catching up to Julie, who headed out the door, hunched forward with determination, his eyes squinted with intensity.

"Appears to be you and me, Nelda," Gustave said, stroking his beard.

She scowled but accompanied him to the second floor garage. Mike instructed each group to take a car so they'd be available if

42

someone was needed at a different location.

"I'll drive," Gustave announced.

"Why? 'Cause you a man? Or 'cause you white?"

"Let's not indulge in racial or gender absurdities. We're assigned to work together as two professional investigators. Let us prove that we are."

"Long as you know your place."

"What exactly does that infer?"

"When Armand takes the farm, I'm the one going to succeed his ass as case agent. You best accustom yo' conceited ass to subordination to this black woman."

"Your racial references are boringly repetitious. Aside from that, perhaps you're overlooking the possibility of our erstwhile division leader actually being permanently demoted, therefore the new agent in charge here."

"Not if we clear this case and get that sucker reinstated in Baton Rouge. Believe that this ole' gal is ready to work her ass off to achieve that."

"Still," Gustave said, "what bolsters your confidence that you, rather than I, will succeed Armand?"

"My damned credentials are a whole bunch better than yours."

Gustave chuckled as he tooled their car out the Iberville Street exit, then along that narrow and oft-repaired roadway before swinging into traffic onto Decatur Street. "Time will tell, sweetheart."

"I don't play that sweetheart shit. If Nelda is too hard for you to say, try Agent Washington."

"May I suggest, agent, that we make every effort to work in concert, keeping the best interests of this case in mind."

#   #

Chapter Eight

Armand drove, leading the three black SUV parade up Canal Street with its crush of auto, truck and bus traffic. They turned left onto Royal, which soon became Saint Charles Avenue, the juncture at which the metropolitan clamor converted to the dawdling pace of old New Orleans.

A clanging trolley lumbered along in the median that separated the east and west traffic lanes, as if it had all the time in the world to complete its run. Vehicular traffic poked along on both sides while pedestrians moseyed along the sidewalks, some mopping their brows. The breeze whispered too softly to allay the heat radiated by the afternoon sun.

The three cars traversed an area renowned for imposing churches of every denomination, plus some of Louisiana's most distinguished universities, including Tulane, Loyola, and Xavier— besides the Notre Dame Seminary and Sophie Newcomb College.

Armand turned left at Plato Street, leading the convoy across the trolley tracks to pull into the parking lot behind BELMONDE'S. Emil Gasse, the owner, greeted Mike and Armand at the back door, having been advised by Mike via cellphone of their intended visit. The rest of the AG staff gathered to be introduced to the entrepreneur of an establishment with prices that discouraged the patronage of civil service employees.

Mike assigned Julie and Chi Chi to interview the people in the kitchen, since they'd been closest to the shooters, while Gustave and Nelda conferred with the dining room staff. Armand supervised both

44

teams, freeing up Mike to tag along with Emil to the bar where the heinous crime occurred.

En route, Mike noted that there were few patrons at that hour, and those appeared to leisurely enjoy the company of their table companions. The staff busily reset empty tables with white table clothes and settings in two dining rooms in preparation for the supper crowd.

Mike and Emil dropped onto one of the banquettes that abutted the back wall of the dining area at a ninety-degree angle to the bar. When Emil suggested a drink, Mike opted for a coke, eschewing anything alcoholic.

Emil shrugged acceptance of what he considered official idiosyncrasy and told the bartender to make him a café brulot. Mike salivated, remembering that coffee flavored with cinnamon, cloves, orange and lemon peels, then dramatized with flaming cognac. But he forced himself to abstain, needing to be an example to his minions.

The two men, familiar through the years, traded small talk until served. After Emil sipped his café brulot and sighed satisfaction, Mike asked: "What can you offer to shed light on those killings?"

"I apologize for the inability of myself and my people to assist your investigation. Most of us were too frightened to take particular note of anything. Many still haven't gotten over that trauma. God, it was awful."

"I hear you, Emil, and sympathize with y'all for suffering that experience. Still, we have us a need to pry something out of someone's memory."

"The kitchen help may be your best hope, being as they were terrifyingly close to the shooters. However, because of what they experienced it's doubtful they're capable of offering little in the way of descriptions."

45

"Even those within a few feet of the shooters?"

"Those barbarians wore ski masks and similar clothing, making it difficult to distinguish them individually." He gestured to the small square window behind the bar with the letter B etched into its frosted glass. "Replaced only this morning. The assassins stood on the kitchen side of it, with a hazy view of the people at the bar, while it's doubtful those patrons became aware of shotguns aimed at them from behind that frosted glass until all hell exploded."

"Were you in the area?"

"Was at the entrance lectern trying to shuffle things around to arrange a table for five, a daunting task because the place had been overbooked."

Mike's eyes narrowed as Emil shrugged his helplessness as he explained: "Surprised me when Darby Williams and his people entered in the company of Kenman and Boheemer. If they had only—"

"Hold on. You telling me they met here without anybody making a reservation?"

"What was I to do? We're busy at lunch hour, as we will be in a few hours for dinner. There were no available tables, with more diners with reservations expected. What was I to do?"

"Which of them was supposed to make arrangements?" Mike asked.

"Kenman insisted that his office had called and done it."

"You believed him?"

"Didn't consider it politic to contradict someone of Kenman's standing. Besides, he's familiar with the restaurant, so aware of the necessity of reservations."

"Could someone here be responsible for that oversight?"

"Believe me, Mike, we're meticulous with that, considering that

46

our luncheon patrons are the elite of New Orleans business and government. Yes, there are tourists also, but generally only the well-off, with reservations arranged by their hotel concierge."

"So it's doubtful there was an oversight on your part."

"I certainly hope there wasn't, though Kenman and Boheemer argued volubly that one of their employees had phoned in a request for a table for five."

"To save face with Darby Williams and Jerome Sessy," Mike said.

"If they were lying," Emil said, "their performances deserved academy awards."

Mike tumbled that information around in the convoluted layers of gray matter in his cerebrum. It challenged reason that Kenman and Boheemer hadn't adequately prepared for a meeting with someone of the importance of Darby Williams and Jerome Sessy. But why in hell did the two political manipulators in charge of selling Big Willie Hoke to the voters host luncheon for the primary opposition?

According to the pollsters, Willis Hoke, a long-time state senator from Shreveport, held a comfortable margin to win that contest. Darby Williams, though heavily backed in the New Orleans area, had at best an outside chance of becoming their party's choice to become the first black governor of Louisiana.

Sure, he'd win the statewide black vote. But generally only about forty percent of African-Americans bothered to register and avail themselves of the eligibility to express political preferences. Less cast their ballots in a primary. Yes, more would with a black man in the race. Still, a greater percentage of white conservatives voted, especially when a candidate of color threatened their hold on political power.

An unexplainable exception was the election to the governorship of Bobby Jindal, son of immigrants from India. But that was then. Consequently, the probable outcome figured to pit Big Willie against the incumbent governor, meaning a sure win for Hoke, considering his popularity and Birch Murdock's pathetic record.

Responding to Armand Dupuy's signal, Mike patted Emil's back as he excused himself and joined Armand out of earshot of restaurant people. "Interviewed all of the employees," Armand said, "and failed to turn up anything."

Nelda Washington ambled over grumbling: "Sure didn't happen on anything to explain why those hooligans gunned down Darby Williams or Jerome Sessy."

"My take on it," Julie Provenzano said, as he, Gustave and Chi Chi joined them when leaving the restaurant, "is that the chubby guy with the single-barrel shotgun who missed Kenman was Italian-American."

"What makes you think that?" Armand asked.

"One of the guys I interviewed," Julie replied, "heard the chubby one ask the tall guy why he'd shot all of the mullenyams. That ethnic slur indicates that at least the chubby one was Italian."

"Suggests that the tall guy was also," Mike said, "since the chubby guy used that term when addressing him. We might conclude that all were Italian-Americans."

"Don't remember Montrose or O'Shea mentioning that," Armand said. "Didn't they pick up on it—or are they holding back?"

# #

48

Chapter Nine

Mike pulled open the car door on the passenger side to climb in when a Chevrolet Cavalier with a few hard years on it pulled alongside. The window rolled down to expose Sergeant Kaylee Boyle. "Leaving already . . . just when I arrive?"

When Mike shrugged, she asked: "Come across anything interesting I can report to my bosses?"

Mike's second shrug provoked: "Hope to hell y'all are not blowing smoke, director. I'm not the forgiving type. You run a game at me and you won't be happy to have this female around."

"I'm not all that happy about the arrangement under any circumstances," Mike retorted, rankled by her aggressiveness, which he'd interpret as insubordination if she worked for his agency.

"Play nice, kids," Armand playfully scolded.

"We'll check with you if we learn anything," Mike said to her as he climbed in.

"Let's visit Brent Kenman and get firsthand explanations," he instructed Armand. He flicked open his cellphone and punched four-eleven to get that man's office number, then called to advise them to expect their visit.

"Mind if I tag along?" Kaylee called to them.

Mike glanced up and realized she'd eavesdropped. He shrugged. "You have your car, so meet us there. I assume you know where."

"All too well."

Mike ran the implication of that reply through his mind as Armand got the car underway. Then he shared the information gleaned from Emil Gasse regarding the deficiency of reservations.

"Leaves a lot of room for conjecture," Armand said, "with regard to why they lined up at the bar—in front of that damn window."

Mike nodded. "Positioned by prearrangement for the assassins to take out those three marks."

"But who set it up?" Armand asked.

"And why?" Mike added.

"And how do we prove it?" Armand asked.

#

Mike and Armand shared lascivious interest in the receptionist who greeted them in sugary southern syllables. Her mauve knit dress accented her curvaceous figure. Kaylee ahemmed to reproach them for their lecherous behavior while the receptionist buzzed her boss on the intercom to inform of arrival of the visitors from the AG's office.

They continued to ogle the gal and exchange glances while being ushered into Brent Kenman's office. When she retreated, Mike took in the office appointments. Nodding to himself he approved the rosewood furniture upholstered in chocolate brown leather and complimented by brass polished to a sparkle. The multi-colored shag carpeting enhanced the executive aura.

Brent Kenman rounded his desk while introducing himself and shaking his visitors' hands. Mike noted his light brown hair and blue eyes. His average height and slender form added to his lack of outstanding features . . . his *everyman* appearance . . . the unseen guy in the crowd.

His custom tailored shirt and expensive foulard necktie, however, denoted affluence and taste. He greeted Kaylee familiarly, before gesturing them to sit in the comfortable club chairs set in a semi-circle facing his desk. "To what do I owe this visit?"

50

"Surprises us," Armand said, "that you need to ask."

"Considering," Kaylee added, "that you nearly became a victim at Belmonde's."

Mike stifled a smile, pleased by her bluntness . . . directed at someone beside himself. This ole' gal wasn't reticent. "You certainly anticipated being interviewed," he said to Kenman, "having been informed by the locals that the AG's office has joined the investigation."

Kenman frowned, but neither confirmed nor denied the supposition. Since the guy hadn't responded to that flyer it left Mike uncertain whether the locals had informed him.

"We're hoping for your cooperation," Armand said as he pushed his glasses up, "in bringing those cold-blooded killers to the bar of justice."

Kenman nodded, though he appeared to restrain his lip from curling. Leaning back in his chair, he scanned his two male visitors, then the female, where his eyes lingered. Returning his attention to the men, he said: "I'm surprised the local police haven't satisfied your need for information with regard to that distressing incident."

"We deemed it necessary," Mike said, "to hear it from the prime target—according to witnesses."

"And to view the miracle of your avoiding injury," Armand added.

Kenman displayed Band-Aids on his hands and arms. "Hardly avoided. Got hit by flying glass."

"But no wounds because of flying bullets," Mike said, "which is surprising considering they were expert hit men."

"Firing duckbill chokes—according to the NOPD report," Armand added, "to increase the strike potential by spreading their shotgun loads laterally."

51

"Exhibiting expertise," Mike said, "by executing three of their targets."

"Doesn't sound like amateurs," Kaylee added.

"Assuming killing those gentlemen weren't mistakes," Kenman said.

"That your take on it?" Mike asked.

"Having had no control over all that occurred there, I obviously can't explain it."

"Someone needs to," Kaylee said, "if for no other reason than to determine whether you really were the target."

Kenman turned hard eyes on her while struggling to suppress a scowl. "Thank the good Lord, even assassins are not perfect."

"Surely," Armand said, "you have some idea why they allegedly went gunning for you in particular."

"Sorry, folks, I don't have reason one why gangsters want to murder me."

"Maybe you need to look real hard," Kaylee said, "and might think of any number of reasons."

Kenman again glared at her. "Perhaps somewhere along the way I inadvertently created enemies that resort to violence of that sort—though I can't think of any."

"Let's separate fact from fiction," Mike said.

"Fact," Kenman retorted, "is that I never in my life realized anyone hated me enough to send hired killers after me."

"What makes you think they were hired?" Mike asked.

"According to the police, and based on your recent remarks," Kenman said.

"You saying," Kaylee asked, "you never rubbed anyone wrong?"

Kenman sneered at her. Turning to Mike, he said: "True, I'm

competitive, but not so much so that folks want me dead . . . leastways, I hope not . . . most especially in this case, where I serve solely as campaign manager, not as candidate."

"Maybe that's were we need to look," Mike said.

Kenman smirked again. "Killing me serves no political purpose."

"You're brainstorming the election of Big Willie Hoke," Mike said, "with prospects of becoming the foremost political manipulator in the state if Big Willie wins the governorship."

"But facing a loss of stature," Armand said, "if he's not."

Kenman scowled but didn't respond.

"Since Big Willie doesn't have any competition now that Darby Williams is dead," Mike said, "it suggests that poor old Darby was the target rather than you."

"While a good man, and deserving of high office," Kenman said, "Darby Williams never threatened to beat out Senator Hoke."

"Which gives me pause," Mike said, "that anyone bothered to kill him."

Kenman's face rippled with annoyance. "Every damn witness testified that the shooters mentioned me by name as their prime target."

"Reason we're mystified," Kaylee said.

"The fact that I'm not dead doesn't dispute that they went there to kill me."

"You telling us those yahoos weren't able to differentiate between white and black men?" Mike asked.

"Darby Williams was near white as I am," Kenman said. "Considering that the window they fired through is lightly frosted, they'd easily make that mistake."

"Or mentioning you by name," Armand said, "could have been a

53

ruse."

"Draw your own damn conclusions, gentlemen. However, I sincerely doubt you'll find any reason to consider me complicit in that unfortunate occurrence. Is there anything else I can help y'all with?"

Mike rose and started to turn away, then hesitated. "Who set up the luncheon at Belmonde's, you or Darby Williams and his people?"

"I did, actually, motivated by my hope of alleviating the bitterness of competition and garnering support for Senator Hoke in the coming election since he rather obviously was going to win the primary."

"Doesn't that generally occur," Armand asked, "as a matter of course once the candidacy is decided?"

"Consummate politicians," Kenman said, "don't take anything for granted . . . especially with the black vote impacting significantly in a statewide election. Concerned that we might lose a significant portion of it because of animosity born of defeating Darby, we made every effort to smooth over any bad feelings, especially after concluding that we need twenty percent of it to defeat Murdock. Hence our out-reach to Darby Williams to campaign for us."

"Why," Mike asked, "did you extend the invitation to Antwan Croix and Jerome Sessy, as well?"

"Croix is—rather was—an assistant of Josh Bigelow, Darby's campaign manager. It didn't surprise me that Darby brought a staffer along. I haven't the slightest why he had Sessy with him."

"Being a banker," Armand said, "and dealing with a cross-section of voters it's doubtful that Sessy would publicly express a preference that might alienate clients."

"Both are black and successful—or were," Kenman said, "therefore perfectly understandable that he supported Darby Williams."

54

"Perhaps there were other reasons," Kaylee said.

Kenman tried to suppress his sneer as he disregarded her by turning to address Mike. "If you folks have nothing more, you need to excuse me. I do have a few pressing chores requiring attention."

"One last thing," Mike said. "Since you'd arranged to meet for lunch with a man of the stature of Darby Williams, why didn't you extend him the courtesy of having a reservation at a restaurant as busy as Belmonde's?"

"One of my office people apparently fouled that up—or folks at Belmonde's did. Anything else, gentlemen?"

"Thanks for your time," Mike said.

#   #

Chapter Ten

Mike held the door for Kaylee and Armand to exit the building. As they separated to head for their respective cars she paused, then swung around and called to Mike. "How'd you know they hadn't made a reservation?"

He swallowed, concerned that she'd realize he'd violated their agreement by not sharing information. "Supposition," he said. Then his eyebrows knit in perplexion that her bunch hadn't gleaned that important nugget . . . or had they?

"You telling me you have the gift of prescience?" issued from Kaylee.

"Simple deduction. Why else did the five of them stand at the bar while waiting for a table to be vacated and prepared?"

"I've had to numerous times," she said, "in spite of having a reservation."

"You're not Darby Williams, Jerome Sessy or Brent Kenman," Armand reminded. He gave her an all-knowing smile before adding: "It's plain as warts on a pond frog that those killers expected them to be lined up facing that window."

"Sure sounds right when you put it that way," Kaylee admitted. "But it defies reason for Kenman and Boheemer to risk their lives by standing there if they set it up."

"Baffles us also," Armand said. He shuffled in place at the SUV driver-side door.

"Depends on the level of desperation," Mike said, "that motivated the rub-out of those three men."

Kaylee grimaced puzzlement as she stared into the beyond. She grunted to her thoughts and almost smiled in a wistful way. "Kenman has always been devious. However, can't figure this out, considering they're the front-runners."

"Couldn't help noticing," Mike said, "that Kenman takes a shine to you."

Her lips curled with distaste. "I don't consider his ogling as flattering."

"We need to know if there's a relationship," Mike said.

"No way! Not with that lecher." Kaylee scowled as she strode to her car.

Mike hesitated at the passenger door of the SUV with his hand on the knob and called to her. "Hard to believe that the man never sought your company, considering he has the reputation of a chaser, and you're an attractive lady."

"Thank you, kind sir, for that compliment." Kaylee pulled open her car door but hesitated stepping in. "Didn't realize you noticed."

"Hard not to." Then he wondered what impelled that confession.

She cut her eyes at him, a cross between skepticism and appreciation. "Let me state here and now that I've never had the kind of involvement with that man such as y'all infer. Only contact was when I served as an aide to Captain Shayde."

"Interesting," Armand said while settling behind the wheel, "that the district commander hobnobs with a political mogul."

Kaylee snickered. "Sebastian Shayde doesn't hide his ambitions or conceal his sucking up to those wielding influence."

"That your take on the district commander?" Mike asked.

"Really successful guy," she replied, "deserving of what he's

57

achieved by clawing his way up the ladder, in spite of barriers."

"You sound like a fan," Armand said.

"What can I say besides admiring a successful black man in the Deep South?"

"Changed dramatically," Mike said, "over the past forty or so years."

"How true is the rumor that Shayde exiled you to PID?" Armand asked.

"However, I'm back. Thankfully, I might add. Never comfortable in the rat squad, spying on and jeopardizing the careers of cops, then being shunned by other cops."

"Any of them harass you?" Mike asked as he settled in the passenger seat.

"Only once. I kicked the guy's butt in the squad room. No one else cared to be embarrassed by being taken down by a female, so they kept their remarks to themselves thereafter—or, at least, didn't utter them for me to hear."

Mike grinned. "And I had you pegged as the sedate type."

"Except when I'm riled. Then I lose my lady-like demeanor. So if you're not anxious to deal with my mean side, don't lie to me or blow smoke up my parts."

#   #

Chapter Eleven

Mike leaned back and closed his eyes after Armand pulled away from the curb and headed down Poydras Street, with its grassy median serving as a landing field for foraging pigeons. Increased cloudiness presaged inclement weather as they tooled between modern office buildings and luxury hotels.

"Sergeant Boyle is a woman catches your eye," Armand remarked, glancing at Mike. When Mike shrugged, Armand snickered. "Tell me you didn't notice."

"I'm not embalmed yet."

"Glad to hear it. Time to reenter the world, good buddy."

After turning east on Camp Street they bounced along the oft-repaired surface, passing quite a few mid-rise buildings being refurbished, transforming and gentrifying a declining area. More than a few had been renovated, a necessity after the devastation of Hurricane Katrina and subsequent storms. An occasional new edifice rose among them, with cranes and cement trucks restricting passage in an already narrow street.

"Okay, she's a looker," Mike admitted, "but who says she's not married?"

"Doesn't wear a ring."

"Maybe not while on duty."

At wide and busy Canal Street they merged with the late afternoon chaos of cars, trucks, taxis, and busses, the din amplified by billowing exhaust fumes. Myriad pedestrians crowded the sidewalks with some daring fools darting across that thoroughfare.

"Want me to inquire?" Armand asked.

Mike grimaced while scanning the towering office buildings and upscale hotels lining both sides of the street, terminating at the pseudo-Moorish architecture of Harrah's Casino. "Too many pressing things to attend to, with no time to divert attention to females."

"That good-looking gal," Armand said, "has a really nice figure, and is mature enough for a stud like you already on the wrong side of fifty. Being as she's brainy and personable, she just might go a long way toward inserting heaps of sunshine in your life."

Chuckling at Mike's pretended non-concern, Armand parked on the backside of their building. A huge parking lot took up the block on the other side of Iberville Street at the intersection of North Peters, which divided the contemporary architecture of the business district from the colonial ambiance of The Quarter.

Mike and Armand strolled into the alternate entrance to the shopping mall of Canal Place. They traversed the concourse flanked by upscale stores and a food-court offering a variety of cuisines, then crossed to the broad lobby of the office tower. While ascending in the elevator Armand commented: "That ole' gal's eyes like to sparkle every time she focused on you."

"Okay," Mike grumbled as he and Armand strode down the hallway, "I've noticed her attributes. But I'm not tripping over myself to get to her, assuming she's available."

"You just ought to, good buddy."

Mike growled inwardly at himself for becoming increasingly aware of attractive women. Up to six months ago he'd been oblivious to all but those so overblown sexy a blind man couldn't help but notice. However, he restrained yearning for any of them, in spite of their voluptuousness.

But things were changing. And yes, he found Kaylee attractive. Was the memory of Arlene fading into the past? Or was it a spike of testosterone production?

#   #

Chapter Twelve

Mike nodded appreciation for the office assigned him, since it accommodated a decent sized desk and a four-tiered file cabinet, plus two straight-back chairs for visitors. And it had all of the necessary communications and technical equipment. It even had a window for sunlight to beam in and deter claustrophobia.

He dropped into the swivel chair and glanced at Armand, who lingered in the doorway. "Wonder if any of the staff came up with any revelations."

"I'll check with them," Armand said and left.

Hearing footsteps after a few minutes and expecting them to be Armand's, Mike's brow arched in surprise when he glanced up to see Kaylee in the doorway. "Got to thinking," she said, "about some things you discussed with Kenman and wondered if you guys are being straight up with me."

When Mike didn't reply, though his eyes narrowed, she added: "You needed to have gotten a heads-up to speak that knowingly about some of those things. So, I came here hoping to be assured you guys aren't holding back info—shafting me."

Mike had all he could do not to snigger at the suggestive reference. "We haven't dug up anything near as much as you folks have, considering the size of those envelopes Lieutenant Montrose burdened us with. Have you looked through them?"

"Not yet, but I intend to."

"You should, and get a grasp on the case before venting on us."

"Okay, I'll accept at face-value that y'all are not handing me a crock. I'd sure appreciate you passing on whatever you come up with, even if it's a duplication of what my people gave you . . . make me shine."

"You do that without help." Then Mike gulped, surprised he'd said that.

Her eyes sparkled as she studied him.

Trying not to reveal his attraction for her, he leaned back in his squeaky chair to feign nonchalance. "What else can we do for you, sergeant?"

"The name's Kaylee. You have any objection to dealing on a first name basis? No? Good. It'll make it easier if we eliminate formality—simplify our relationship."

The word; *relationship*, resonated in his hypothalamus, the brain's control center for sex drives. His dark eyes searched her handsome face.

"I wasn't in it from the start," she said, "so am less familiar with the case than y'all. However, I have the same reports in the car they gave you. Plan to spend the night studying them, so's I'll be up to snuff when we discuss things tomorrow."

"Your husband is going to love that. Hopefully you'll fix his dinner before you bury your nose in paperwork."

"Divorced three years now. Don't have any motivation to indulge myself with a fancy meal any more. So I'll have plenty of time to peruse that stuff over a frozen meal rendered gourmet in a micro-wave."

Armand stuck his head in the doorway and his brow arched upon awareness of Kaylee. He struggled not to grin. "Nobody appears to have made any dramatic discoveries. We're still on square one."

"Told you," Mike said to Kaylee.

She pursed her lips and nodded while turning to exit. "See y'all in the morning."

He watched her leave, aware that she dressed conservatively, probably to play down her charms . . . while he doubted those garments were obtained at bargain marts.

Recalling her car, he chuckled at her attempt to mask affluence. She told him she'd shed her husband. Still he remained irresolute whether to pursue her. Okay, with Arlene dead nearly two years he had every right to pursue some company.

# #

Chapter Thirteen

   Mike drove the black SUV to his hotel, resigned to the pokey
pace of commuter traffic. Remembrances of Kaylee muddled his
thinking. Things were a might less confusing when he was married and
not interested in other women.

   He smiled as memory flashed back to when he met Arlene, soon
after relocating to Baton Rouge to attend law school at Louisiana State
University. Only a few months earlier he'd taken advantage of the few
openings in the Louisiana State Police.

   After a year of studying jurisprudence, he decided he didn't like
law any more than he did engineering, which he'd studied previously.
But being happy in police work, he switched his major to criminal
justice, and upon completion achieved assignment to the Investigations
Bureau.

   He grinned as he recalled that day, while chatting with a group
of fellow students on the campus of LSU, he met Arlene. She studied
government as an undergraduate student. Immediate attraction resulted
in their dating and having some good times together. Within months
they went steady, and married after Arlene graduated. Four years later
they were blessed with Miriam.

   With Arlene at the State Transportation Department, those two
civil service salaries provided them a comfortable lifestyle. In time both
rose to executive level with attendant monetary rewards. Those were
good and happy years. And tears welled in his eyes.

   Holy shit! Mike jammed on the brakes. Thrust forward, he
thumped against the steering wheel. Grasping the wheel he jerked

himself upright then wrenched the steering wheel to avoid crashing. That big-ass pick-up truck suddenly appeared—squealing out of a blind turn.

"Swerve, dumb bastard!" he'd yelled, his eyes wide with fright—his heart pounding. But the goddam thing bore down on him at full-tilt—with a big-ass steel bar for a front bumper. With limited space on the roadway, he wrenched his steering wheel hard-over and careened between two parked cars—barely squeaking through to bounce onto the sidewalk. God almighty! he barely veered out of its path . . . didn't want to get crushed.

The som'bitchen thing roared past, missing his tail-end by a fraction of an inch. He panted residual panic while shuddering at awareness of its capability of crushing his car, especially at that speed. Goddam if he hadn't almost gotten killed.

Was it out of control, or was the stupid bastard asleep—maybe drunk? Why was it coming at him at full tilt? Didn't the driver see him—realize how close he came?

Generally only cops applied pushbars to the front of their vehicles. Was that guy a cop? If not, why have a steel bar for a bumper? The som'bitch had swerved around the next corner and disappeared, leaving Mike to glare at an empty street. He blinked repeatedly while hyperventilating. And he couldn't stop wrestling with whether it had been intentional. It sure looked that way. But why? Did that yahoo intend to ram him?

Cursing the asshole, he thanked God there weren't any pedestrians about. Imagine if it had been earlier when people streamed out of the surrounding office buildings filling up the sidewalk. Exhaling gratitude, he backed off it—careful not to nick those parked cars. After emerging fully into the street, possible because of a lack of traffic, he sped to the cross street the pick-up truck had turned onto.

Despite the sparse traffic there, he failed to spot it. The som'bitch probably sped off and turned onto one of the cross streets to avoid detection. But which one, and in which direction? Seething with residual anger, he accepted the futility of searching for that reckless asshole . . . in spite of yearning to put a hurting on his ass.

So he resumed his course to his hotel, while running that incident over and over in his head. No matter how many times he analyzed and re-analyzed it, he concluded that someone intended to take him out.

But anyone who'd try something that rash would have to know where and when to intercept him. Okay they might have spotted him leaving the office building, and have known that he stayed at the Grand Southern Hotel on Carondelet off Poydras.

But had they then waited along the route to waylay him? Naw, no matter how many times he ran everything through his analysis chamber, he refused to characterize it as intentional. The odds against success had been too great.

However, if that driver hadn't intended to harm him, why hadn't the guy stopped to ascertain if anyone had been hurt, instead of speeding off? And to where in hell had it disappeared? True, hit-and-run incidents occurred all too often, especially when the drivers were drunk.

Obsessed with a need to be certain, he sought to recapture in memory the moments before the near-collision—focusing on just before he turned into Barrone Street. Yeah, he remembered two men in a sedan, with one of them talking on a cellphone.

Not that it perked his interest at the time. Everybody you passed nowadays, riding or walking, gabbed away on those things. Had they shadowed him and communicated with the driver of the SUV? Had he been set up?

Why? No question that no love existed between him and a lot of local cops since that exposé a year ago. And some of those yahoos had the poor judgment to try something that outrageous. Had they tried to settle the score?

Or had it been people involved in the assassination at Belmonde's? Yes, it just might have been thugs employed by Brent Kenman, resulting from fear he'd put in the slickster's ass. Or was it simple coincidence and he was reading too much into it? But memory of that big-ass steel beam for a front bumper, refused to fade out of mind. You don't rig something like that without a purpose.

If the slaughter at Belmonde's had been the work of redneck racists those ole' boys just might have the gumption to take him on. But even those mooks had to know that killing him wouldn't preclude the investigation. There's no end of agents in the department to take his place and pursue those som'bitches, as well as hunt down their employers.

Naw, he doubted anyone in the NOPD would attempt to kill the director of state investigations, considering he and his staff were no closer to identifying any of the shooters, much less the instigators of that heinous assassination. And nobody with half a brain expected his demise to cancel the investigation.

No, he refused to believe his visit to Kenman's office had spooked that iceman into ordering a wild-ass rubout. The shrewd som'bitch had too many smarts to try something that drastic, knowing damn well they had nothing on him.

Despite lack of high regard for the NOPD, especially District Commander Shayde, he refused to give credence to their folks taking it upon themselves to eliminate him . . . accepting it as a stretch to do anything that outrageous.

However, the locals did have a bone to pick with him because of his corruption exposure last year. Just maybe one or more sought revenge for the indictments of their buddies. Hell, every police department in the country had yahoos who'd resort to the ridiculous, for whatever purpose. Authority sometimes had a way of corrupting judgment. Was something going on that he'd better stay alert to, if he wanted to go on living?

#   #

Chapter Fourteen

"You look like you've been here awhile."

Mike glanced up and shrugged to Armand peering at him from the doorway. "Got in real early and been poking through this pile of confusion the locals burdened us with."

"God a'mighty, if I hadn't seen you leave last night I'd wonder if you spent the night here. Doubtful you'd be here all this early had you gone with that lovely sergeant."

"Not sure if I'm ready to start up with someone yet."

"You'll sure know after you've dipped your stick."

Mike chortled. "Can't deny it's been a while." He reflected on telling Armand about that near-collision last evening, but vacillated. Nothing about what occurred could be conclusively characterized as premeditated. He had enough things to explain without having to reassure folks he wasn't paranoid.

"Anything interesting in that stuff?" Armand asked. "Didn't have a chance last night to read too much of it."

"Read a bunch of it before falling asleep last night, and a bunch more this morning. Haven't stumbled on anything to bring joy to my heart."

"Where do we go from here?"

"In a whole new direction. You mind assembling the staff ?"

Armand nodded and left to execute Mike's request. Not too many minutes later he stuck his head in again. "They're all headed for the conference room."

Mike pushed himself up to trundle down the hall to gaze at their sleep-lined faces. They clutched mugs of coffee—making him wish he'd brought one. "Okay, folks, we spent a lot of time in that restaurant yesterday—only to come away empty."

"No surprise to me," came from Nelda.

"It occurred to me," Mike said, trying not to expose bristling at her remark, "while going over everything that we hadn't investigated the help personally."

"Nor, it appears," Gustave said in his condescending manner, "have the locals. Didn't happen upon anything informative while browsing that pile of confusion."

The others averted their eyes rather than admit they hadn't read the NOPD reports, or at least much of it, which they all had copies of.

"Just as well," Mike said. "Compiling the case ourselves assures us of accuracy of detail. So I'd like y'all to dig deep into the lives of those employees, leaving nothing uncovered, to see if you can find a connection to those assassins."

"Heap of folks are employed at that restaurant," Nelda said.

Armand nodded agreement while pushing his glasses up on his nose. "A dozen or more in the dining room and fifteen in the kitchen . . . plus the owner, a couple of managers and the bar help."

"Divvy them up," Mike said, "and put every one of them under a magnifying glass. I'd like y'all to probe into their bowels, get so intimate you learn what they had for breakfast on that fateful day."

"And how well they've been eating since," Julie Provenzano added, evoking nodding.

Mike pointed a finger of approval at the man. "Record every damn thing about those folks, including employment records, financial conditions, domestic situations, and especially run-ins with the law.

71

Take note of any infractions, even traffic violations."

"I'll run them through NCIC," Armand said.

Mike bobbed his head in approval of checking with the National Crime Information Center, a database of criminal records that the FBI maintains to aid local, state, and federal law enforcement. "Run them through the state police files also."

"The local PD," Gustave said, "just might have compiled useful data."

"If they had," Armand commented, "why didn't they share that with us?"

"Local cops are considered our best informational sources," Chi Chi said.

"Not this bunch," Mike said. "I've tangled with them before."

"The NOPD is as good as any other big city bureaucracy," Nelda said.

"Okay," Mike said, rather than generate contention, "we'll conference again before lunch to see if we've combed out something useful."

#   #

Chapter Fifteen

"My damn belly button is knocking against my backbone," Nelda said, as she plopped into a seat at the conference room table.

Chi Chi started to respond, but compressed his lips when he spotted Mike and Armand entering.

"Gustave, you want to start?" Mike asked.

"Mine were mostly dining room help," Gustave said. "Two traffic tickets within the last year—both paid. No vagrants or outstanding warrants."

"Pretty much the same for me," Julie said, "even with a couple worked in the kitchen. One had a misdemeanor arrest for disorderly conduct—nothing promising."

Nelda sucked her teeth. "I didn't raise a damn thing. Truth be told, I feel like I wasted my damn time combing through that shit."

"Nobody with anything serious," Chi Chi said. "One female with a felony arrest, buttoned for beating up on her boyfriend's other girlfriend. Then I had a guy had his license pulled for DUI. Probably tools around now without one. Didn't come across anything indicating anybody was into something."

"I got a hit," Armand said. "One of the galley assistants, by name of Toby Avezzano, got himself convicted for hijacking a truck some eight years ago and served four before being paroled nearly a year ago."

"He steal that truck alone," Julie Provenzano asked, "or have accomplices?"

"A gang of five," Armand said. "One beat the rap. Another got

73

a walk for flipping on his buddies. Avezzano and two others did time."

"That sounds mob related," Julie said. "Want me to take it from here?"

"What's so damned mob-related about stealing a damn truck?" Nelda asked. "Home boys steal anything with wheels every damn day of the week."

"When gangs rob trucks," Julie said, "they consider the disposal of the loot beforehand, considering that a truck is difficult to conceal, especially with a bolo out on it, knowing they'll have the police breathing down their necks. That's why truck robberies are generally mob related."

"Roger that," Chi Chi said. "They can't risk sitting on it too long."

"Where do we take it from here?" Mike asked Julie.

"We check out the guys got collared with him," Julie said. "With five guys to go on we'll likely find one is connected, or associated with someone who is. It might help if I have a talk with this Avezzano."

"Planned for Armand and I to lean on him this afternoon," Mike said. "However, we'll avoid any direct references, just make him nervous, while careful not to broach the subject of his conviction. Meanwhile you dig into that hoist and trace his cohorts for a mob-lead. Then you and I will visit him tonight, after he's had a few hours to stew. Hope your wife doesn't mind you working late."

"Junie's a cop's wife who understands the time demands. Yeah, I'm into your scheme, boss, of letting him stew all afternoon after you guys visit him . . . long as you don't leak the reason for your interest in him."

"Why all the damned subterfuge?" Nelda asked. "Shake the sucker when you go to that classy-ass restaurant and convince that fool to spill his damn guts."

"Others there might have a connection with the shooters," Chi Chi said. "They report our leaning on Avezzano and he might not last long enough to extract info from."

"Besides," Mike said, "we don't want the word getting back to the locals that we're focusing on anybody in particular . . . have them fouling things up."

"Whatever," Nelda said. "Can we go get ourselves some damn lunch now?"

"Name your sandwich," Mike said. "I'm buying. I'll send one of the clerks out to get them. After lunch, I want y'all to swap files and go through those people again, but dig deeper. There might be more than one of them with a mobster in that woodpile."

"Since Avezzano has a record," Julie said, "the FBI has a sheet on him."

"I can work through some old buddies," Nelda said, "to see if the NOPD has info on the guy, without letting the cat out of the bag to get back to their brass."

"It'll be appreciated," Mike said. "Meanwhile, why don't y'all order yourselves some lunch."

"No offense, boss," Chi Chi said, "but I'm not into tuna, chicken salad or bland cold cuts. Anybody nearby serve rice and beans?"

"They do downstairs at that food court on the mezzanine level," Armand said.

"Good as any Cajun or Creole restaurant in The Quarter," Julie said.

Nelda chuckled. "Believe that those folks can slow-cook kidney beans with ham-hocks and the pot spiced with onions, peppers, garlic, and bay leaves. Yes, lord, makes you hope heaven is good as that is."

"Sometimes they stew up those red beans with that sausage they call Andouille," Julie added.

"Sometimes," Gustave said, "they substitute turtle or alligator."

"I'll settle for rice and beans with ham-hocks," Chi Chi said. "Don't need nothing exotic."

"Personally," Gustave said, "I opt for Chinese sweet and sour chicken."

"Give me a muffaletta anytime," Julie said.

Mike salivated for that huge round loaf of focaccio bread stuffed with prosciuto, sausage, two kinds of cheese, olives and capers, and oozing with an olive oil dressing.

"My suggestion," Armand said, "is that y'all go down to the food court to stations with every kind of food y'all desire. Bring your receipts back so Mike can reimburse you."

"You guys not joining us?" Julie asked.

"Armand and I need to poke around at Belmonde's," Mike said, "to see if any others might have been complicit, like that Avezzano."

"Abstain from having luncheon there," Gustave said, "unless you don't mind decreasing your net worth."

#

Mike stretched his legs as far as the passenger seat of the SUV permitted, to relax since Armand drove. The case wore on him, wearied him. But he jerked to attention when they reached the bottom of the garage ramp and Kaylee Boyle pulled up in her Cavalier. "Y'all going somewhere special," she called to them through her rolled down window.

76

"Oh shit," Mike groaned. "How we going to shake her?"

"Why do we need to? You can use some pleasant company."

"Don't get cute. We can't have her privy to what we're up to."

"We can do this without letting the cat out of the bag."

"How do you suggest we lean on Avezzano without her realizing it, and leaking it back to Sebastian Shayde?"

"You entertain her," Armand said, adjusting his glasses, "while I chat with Avezzano. Y'all might find some common ground."

"Stop playing cupid."

"Well?" she called to them. "What's it going to be?"

Mike sighed resignation and waved her to join them. He watched her park across the street then assessed her as she crossed to them. No denying she had a nice figure and that it raised his carnal thermometer. But he shook off those thoughts, still not comfortable entertaining that kind of indulgence, as if it depreciated the memory of Arlene.

"Going anywhere special?" she asked after climbing in the back.

"To lunch," Mike replied as Armand pulled into traffic.

"Where y'all going you need to drive there? This area is loaded with great lunch places. There's no end of them all along Decatur Street. Oh, and that food court—"

"Belmonde's," Mike said.

Kaylee exhaled. "We needing to pay for it?"

"Cops take a free meal," Armand said, "it's called graft."

"Yeah," Mike said, "we're state employees and don't go on the pad like city folk."

Kaylee twisted her mouth in annoyance as she watched them exchange amused glances. "Hope to hell y'all don't find fault with a discount, considering that prices at that place are out of sight."

"You volunteered to join us," Mike reminded.

"Yeah, stupid me."

#   #

Chapter Sixteen

Mike held the door while waving Kaylee then Armand in. A surprised Emil Gasse hurried over. "Why didn't you call and let me know you were coming? Mon dieu, won't have an available table for at least an hour."

"Not a problem," Mike said. "We're here basically for information."

"Plenty of nearby places," Kaylee said, "to grab a snack."

"Any objection to eating at the bar?" Emil asked.

"Won't be the first time," Armand said.

"Doubt it'll be the last," Kaylee added.

"It will," Mike said, "if those assassins pay us a visit." Memory of that pick-up truck with the scary pushbar-bumper made him hope those shotgun-wielders didn't show up for an encore.

"Lunch is on the house," Emil said.

"No way!" Mike shot back. Armand started to comment, then shrugged and nodded support, while Kaylee wrinkled her face in disappointment.

"I'll join you in a little," Emil said. "Can't leave the lectern at the moment, with patrons waiting to be seated and more expected."

Mike led the way, down the hallway opening onto the small dining rooms with every table occupied—the place abuzz with convivial repartee. The bar covered much of the rear wall, enhanced by that deadlight with a large B etched into its frosted glass. A scattering of patrons collected there, drinking and socializing while waiting for tables.

Three contiguous stools remained unoccupied. After mounting

one, Armand perusing the menu, then rubbed his hands together in anticipation. Kaylee drew breaths at the realization that lunch could cost a few hour's pay. "Wish I'd had better sense than hitch a ride with y'all. Been better off if I'd had me a salad in one of the fast-food joints."

"Like to start with a drink?" asked the bartender with a close-cropped beard on his friendly face.

"What I'd really like," Mike replied, "is for you to tell us what you remember about the afternoon of the assassinations."

Armand flashed his credentials so the bartender understood the reason for Mike's inquiry. "The world exploding," the man replied, directing their attention to the replaced square of frosted glass. "Glass flew everywhere. Good thing Mister Boheemer asked for Kalamatas olives, which I keep in the frig under the bar."

"Did you happen to get a peek at any of the shooters?" Mike asked.

"Stooped just as that window exploded . . . then all but crawled into that little frig."

"That's using your head," Kaylee commended.

"By the time I came up for air," the bartender said, "the thing was over."

"Glad you survived," Mike said, "but we have a dire need for witnesses capable of identifying those shooters."

"Doubt anyone on this side of that wall saw any of the shooters," the bartender said. ". . . Or tried to. Our world exploded in chaos and we were all too scared to do anything but hunker for cover."

"Y'all used your heads," Kaylee said.

"Since we're not going to get any useful information," Armand said, "we might as well get to ordering." He continued to rub his hands together, his eyes sparkling as they rippled across the menu. "Okay, I'll

79

start with the Turtle Soup au Sherry, and cap that with Pan-fried Redfish Meunière, accompanied by a chilled glass of Sauvignon Blanc."

Mike and Kaylee gasped while totaling the prices of Armand's extravagance. "I'll stay in the appetizer column," Mike said. "Make mine the house-cured Salmon Gravlax served with Louisiana crawfish pâté and sliced vine-ripened tomatoes dressed with citrus herb vinaigrette."

"And to drink sir?"

"Cold bottle of Abita." Mike had become fond of the locally brewed beer.

"I'll follow his lead," Kaylee said, "by ordering an appetizer. How 'bout the Fried Green Tomatoes with two Remoulade sauces?"

"Quite ample," the bartender assured. "It's served with garlic bread."

When Kayle nodded, happy to hear she'd have enough food, Mike commented: "No kissing you this afternoon."

"I don't remember inviting you to."

Armand searched their faces for promising signs. But she remained passive as she turned to the bartender and ordered carbonated water.

#   #

Chapter Seventeen

Mike sighed contentment and wiped mouth and hands with his linen napkin. "Time to get to work. Why don't you two re-interview the dining room help? I'll take the kitchen. Hopefully we'll get a heads-up about what motivated those assassinations."

Armand cut his eyes at Mike but didn't vocalize his vexation for being shunted away from questioning Avezzano . . . having anticipated the challenge of eliciting relevant information from that source.

Mike ambled into the kitchen and chatted with the closest employees. He tried not to distract anyone, aware they were busy—harassed actually. Order slips and smoke trailing from the many pots and pans clanging and banging while noisily transferred from stoves to counters monopolized attentions. Nevertheless, he talked to a few before approaching Avezzano to allay any suspicion that he went there specifically to grill that person.

An unshaven guy with a potbelly, Toby Avezzano wore his collarless white baker's jacket half-open, exposing a soiled undershirt. He screwed his chubby face up and shook his head to Mike's question. "Didn't see no more than nobody else."

"Even though you were closest to the shooting?" Mike gestured to their proximity to the frosted glass.

"Didn't want them seeing me looking too hard and get my ass shot off."

"You don't strike me as a guy shakes in his boots when he sees a gun."

"I ain't no hero. And those guys was real scary-looking."

81

"One of them aimed his shotgun at you?" Mike asked.

"At all of us. Three of them covered us while two eyeballed people on the other side of the window. Didn't know why in the beginning—thought it was a damn hold-up."

"And now. What have you concluded?"

"A rub-out."

"Describe how it went down."

"Didn't the others do that already?"

"I'd like to hear your version."

"Hey, I wasn't paying no whole lot of attention to them guys at the window, only to the hoods was pointing widow-makers at us. Didn't the others you been talking—"

"Where were you when they came in?"

"Right here—baking the bread and rolls in the oven."

"Describe the shooters."

"Big-ass shotgun muzzles powerful enough to blow your ass through the wall."

"What did the men holding them look like?"

"Like mean-ass guys in ski masks and dark jackets, or sweaters, or one. Don't ask me what colors."

"What did the two at the window look like?"

"Like the others, with ski masks, dark jackets or sweaters, and shotguns."

"You can do better than that."

"You kidding? You ever had the barrel of a big-assed shotgun pointed at you?"

"Doesn't mean you can't describe the guys holding them."

"Hey, I'm telling you what I saw, considering I was scared shitless. They had instant death shoved in our faces."

"Enough of the frightened act. You don't look all that faint-hearted."

"Why you leaning on me?"

"I'm leaning on everybody in my quest for some decent descriptions, so help me out here, being as you were closest to the shooters."

"Okay, okay. One was a fatso, who stood right near me. The other guy, a lanky sucker that towered over everybody else, reloaded and fired the third volley."

"So you were close enough to the chubby shooter to smell his body odor."

"And his sickening-sweet after-shave." Avezzano gasped, then blinked. His jaw hung slack, exposing his realization that he'd let something slip.

"Describe him," Mike said, pretending unawareness of the slip.

"Didn't dare stare at him. No reason to anyway, with that mask on and all."

"What else do you remember about him?"

"Nothing. Nothing. Not a goddam thing."

"If you're holding out you're going to be in a world of hurt."

"Why would I? Don't need no grief over this. Those guys rushed in here and pushed heavy metal in our faces. Why am I getting leaned on for that?"

"Sounds like you've been leaned on before."

"Who the hell hasn't? When you're a young guy you think you're a wise-ass. Eventually a cop leans on you. It's—whatta' you call it—the right of passage or something. Every smart-ass kid goes through—"

"And as an adult?"

83

Avezzano blanched and averted his eyes. "Think I'd be sweating my ass off here for chump change if I was into something?"

Mike nodded to him and strolled away to talk to others in the kitchen. After a quarter of an hour he felt he'd taken enough time to allay any suspicions that might evolve from his chat with Avezzano. Entering the dining room, he sidled alongside Armand and whispered: "He's edgy—and ripe."

"Super. What's our next move?" Both glanced to be certain Kaylee wasn't in hearing range.

"Tell Julie I'll pick him up behind the office at eight. Emil told me that Avezzano works from ten in the morning to seven in the evening. We'll give him time to get home."

Seeing Kaylee approach, they lapsed into complaining about the difficulty of eliciting pertinent information. She nodded. "Sure doesn't sound like any of these folks anticipated that shooting, much less were involved in any way."

"Probably suffer nightmares," Armand said.

"Hey, you guys have already done all this," Kaylee said, "as have our dicks."

"Where do you suggest we look for answers?" Mike asked.

"I'll get heat from Shayde if you repeat this, but I'd be poking into Kenman's affairs. If he was the prime target, how come the guy shooting at him aimed so high he knocked out two ceiling fixtures?"

"Good to hear that you're not parroting Shayde," Mike said.

"Some things are obvious. It's possible to mistake Darby Williams for Kenman, his being almost as white as any of us." Then she gulped and glanced at Mike's swarthy face. He gave no indication of offense.

"Taking out Darby Williams," Armand said, "eliminates

84

competition for Willis Hoke."

"Which barely existed," Mike said. "Next question is, why'd they take out Antwan Croix and Jerome Sessy, since neither could be mistaken for white?"

"And neither contested Big Willie in the primaries," Kaylee added.

"The tall guy," Armand said, "reloaded to take out Sessy, which discounts the guy getting in the way of a stray bullet."

"We need to pursue that trend of thought," Mike said. "But for now, let's go back to the office so I can drop you two off and read through the rest of those reports from the NOPD in hopes of finding direction, if not answers."

"Need to finish them also," Kaylee said. "Fell asleep last night about halfway through that boring pile."

#

Mike drove back, double-parking temporarily on Bienville behind One Canal, to let Armand and Kaylee out. She lingered at the side of the car until Armand was out of earshot.

"Word is that you're widowed about two years. Told you yesterday that I'm divorced. So we're two single people. Anything wrong with us having dinner?"

"Not a thing. Like to get to know you, but I have things on tap for tonight."

"Besides reading boring reports?"

"It needs to be done."

"Anything you keeping from me about the case?" When he shook his head, she asked: "So what's occupying you tonight—another woman?"

"Haven't been in town long enough to hook up with anyone."

She twisted her face, embarrassed for having broached the subject. "Whatever it is, I guess you don't want to share it with me."

"Like I said, I'd like to have dinner with you, but it's not going to be tonight."

Kaylee grinned to mask humiliation for having made the overture, as well to conceal exasperation at his response. She waved goodnight and moved off to her car.

# #

Chapter Eighteen

Mike bumped through the narrow streets of The Quarter en route to the office. He'd had a hamburger with fries for dinner at Café Anthony on Bourbon Street, in the heart of The District. People of all ages, sizes and races, mostly tourists, milled noisily through those streets in search of the uniqueness of New Orleans.

Sure he could have gotten a burger closer—even in that food court—but he enjoyed the ear-splitting, tinny jazz played in that gin mill. It blocked out all the sadness and mental anguish that haunted him since losing Arlene, then his daughter, Miriam. Yes, and it temporarily relieved the angst derived from work-related responsibilities that weighed heavier with each passing day. Memory of his goof in Shreveport grated in his gut.

Thankfully, that brass and percussion clamor diluted the bitterness that festered in him toward that lying bitch for threatening to torpedo his career and terminate his position with the AG's office . . . earned by long years of application. But it didn't annul the recurring recollections of Kaylee suggesting having dinner.

No matter how much he tried to convince himself that he'd be better off avoiding involvement with the honey trap, her face persisted in popping up on his mental monitor. Yes, she was outspoken, while she comported herself with propriety. No denying she'd inject cheerfulness in his life. But was he ready?

He distracted himself from thoughts of her by gazing at his surroundings of small restaurants and dreary stores while creeping along narrow Iberville Street. They sold everything from inexpensive Creole and Cajun fast-food to used furniture, dilapidated antiques, second-hand clothing, inexpensive shoes and sandals, wild-ass costumes, cheap-ass jewelry, as well as a variety of voodoo paraphernalia.

Approaching Starbuck's at the corner of Iberville and North Peters, he spotted Julie hunched over and pacing while squeezing a coffee container, exhibiting that pugnacity of street hoods . . . indicative of the reason he excelled at apprehending hoods. Upon identifying the SUV, Julie chucked the container in a waste container and climbed in.

Mike took Canal, despite the vehicles competing for the limited space, since it figured to be less hectic than traversing the narrow and crowded streets of the Quarter at night. The headlights of endless vehicles plus illumination blaring from stores and saloons almost blinded him. People spilling into the streets added to the pandemonium.

"Confirmed the address with Avezzano's parole officer," Julie informed. "Also got a heads-up that he'd followed the straight-and-narrow since getting out, with less than three years to go."

Mike nodded as he followed Julie's direction to turn east on Rampart Street, the northern boundary of The Quarter. Many of its weathered buildings were boarded up. Frame constructed, they suffered from aging and neglect which rendered them vulnerable to the ravages of storms long before Katrina wrecked them. Many have since been crudely patched, while too many were boarded up and abandoned.

Following Julie's advice, he turned north on Esplanade Avenue, lined by mostly two storied Victorian-styled houses, the remnants of a by-gone age grown shabby. Much of the neighborhood deterioration could be traced to the absentee landlords converting their dwellings to multi-family rentals, while stinting on maintenance.

"Tell me something about yourself," Mike said.

"Became a state cop twelve years ago, after finishing college.

88

Before that I did four years in the Air Force."

"Then you put time in the Investigative Bureau before Jace brought you aboard."

"Yeah, a happy circumstance that allowed me to move back to Naw'lins, where I was born."

"Married, right? Got kids?"

"Believe it. Nice Italian girl I met in Baton Rouge. American, that is, with grandparents from Cosenza in Calabria, not that far from Catanzaro, where my grandparents come from. We got two daughters, seven and one."

"Now you make me feel bad for pulling you away from your baby."

"No sweat, chief. Kids are great, but I can use the respite on occasion."

"Tell me about it. I had a daughter."

Julie averted his eyes. He, like everyone else, heard of the tragic death of Mike's sixteen-year-old.

Mike tooled up Esplanade, into an area called Tremé, once a red light district called Storyville, now the rundown abode of jazz musicians determined to attain success along with monetary reward. He followed Julie's direction to park in front of an old two-story frame house with the attic dormer adding a third floor. It cried for repairs and looked like it hadn't been painted since Huey Long was governor. Shabby might be construed as complimentary.

Inquiring at the front door, they learned that they had to climb an outside stairway in the back, three stories up to the attic. Mike frowned when learning those apartments had no bells. They'd simply have to climb up there to learn if Mister Avezzano was home.

After clomping up that creaky wooden stairway both hoped to

89

hell the guy was in and not let their exertion be in vain. Arriving at the object door, they leaned on the wall, one on each side as they caught their breaths. Mike reached out and rapped on the flimsy door.

"Yeah—who's there?"

"Police," Julie called out. "Open the damn door so we don't have to kick it in."

The clicking of locks ensued, and a second later the paunchy, unshaven guy in soiled undershirt peered out. His eyes widened as he recognized Mike, afterwhich he opened the door fully, puzzlement contorting his face. "What's it now?"

"You want to answer our questions standing out here," Julie asked, "so your neighbors can hear your business?"

Avezzano stepped aside and waved them into a skimpily furnished interior. Mike had to apply effort to not to express appall at the trashy place with furniture a second-hand store couldn't sell. The bed in the corner with its rumpled bed covers hadn't been made.

"What's this about?" a female voice railed them.

Mike glanced at the dumpy woman standing in the archway of a tiny kitchenette littered with dishes and cookware.

"Stay in there and mind your own goddam business," Avezzano barked at her. She glared at him for a moment before disappearing beyond a limp curtain. Then he turned back and waved his two visitors to take seats.

"We're hoping we won't have to stay long enough to sit," Mike said. He didn't relish dropping into the folds of unkempt upholstery littered with discarded clothing.

"But that depends on you," Julie said, relieved that they remained standing. "We're out of here if you answer our questions without any dodges."

90

"What the hell I got to hold back about?" But Avezzano's blinking and eyes dancing from one to the other of his questioners revealed insecurity.

"You weren't smart enough to volunteer pertinent information when interviewed at the restaurant," Mike said.

"Whatta' you mean? I answered all the questions, both to you and to the locals. Told y'all everything I know about what I saw of them shooters and all."

"I traced a couple of the mugs you did time with for that truck hijacking," Julie said. "One of them worked for Little Lenny. So I'm connecting you there."

"No way! Yeah, I teamed up with them guys back then to knock over a truck."

"Oh sure," Julie said, "just that once."

"Swear to God. Seeing those street hoods throwing money around made me want some of it. But I swore never to get involved with double-crossers like that again."

"Lived a saintly life since then," Julie commented, sarcastically.

"Swear to God—been clean since I been out. Ask my parole officer. No way I wanna' go back. You think I'd be holding down a crummy job like mine if I had something going? Think I'd live in a dump like this? I been clean—swear to God."

"I connect you to any of your old crowd," Julie said, "and your freedom ends real quick, to serve the years you have left."

"Hey, whatta' you guys leaning on me for?"

"Identify the chubby guy," Mike said.

"I told you, they was wearing ski masks. Ask any of the others working in the kitchen. They'll tell you the same."

"But they only shrunk back from the shotguns," Mike said.

91

"You worried that if the chubby guy recognized you he'd off you to keep his identity secret."

Avezzano blinked and shuffled in a tight circle. "How'd you know that?"

Mike stifled grinning at that ruse working.

"You got you two seconds," Julie said as he pulled a cellphone from his pocket. "Only as long as it takes me to get your parole officer on the line."

"Once he dials," Mike said, "it'll be too late. You'll be on your way back."

"Whatta' you saying? I been toeing the line, for Christ's sake. I didn't violate any of the rules of my parole."

"Times up," Julie said. He started to punch buttons.

"Okay! I'll give you what I got. Actually I ain't sure of the guy because of he was wearing that ski mask. But his being chubby and the way he moved, with that funny-ass walk like an over-age toddler, and bouncing his head around and all."

"Give it all up," Mike commanded, "like recognizing that sweet odor."

Avezzano blinked repeatedly while prattling: "His goddam aftershave. It was sweet enough to make you sick. You shoulda' heard him squeal like a fat fag when the tall galoot reloaded and plugged all them mullenyams."

"Give us a name?" Julie snapped.

"Swear I don't remember his name, or where he lived, or nothing. Swear to God. Yeah, I remembered him as a guy went out with my cousin in Memphis."

"Stop stalling," Mike growled at him.

"Hey, if I saw the hump twice it was a lot. Left Memphis nearly

92

ten years ago and come down here, so never saw him again."

"Tell us what you remember about him," Julie said.

"Like I said, I ain't positive that's him. It's just that the fat fuck moved like that guy and wore that same sick-smelling aftershave."

"What kind of work your cousin do?" Julie asked.

"Waitress—in Memphis anyway—in a ginmill."

"Give us her name and how to contact her," Mike said.

"Lenora Avezzano. But relatives said she had enough of fatso but couldn't shake him, so moved to New Jersey somewheres to get away from him."

"That won't do it," Julie snarled.

"It's what I got—swear to God."

"You don't want to finish out your time in stir," Julie said, "you're going to have to come up with better than that dodge."

"The damn truth, guys. Hey—I know. I'll give you the names and telephone numbers of a couple, three relatives in Memphis might have her address and all. I don't. Swear to God."

Mike handed him a notebook and pen. "You better hope those names and numbers bear fruit."

"They don't," Julie said, "your ass is going to pay the price."

"Hey, whatta' you guys want from me? I'm being straight with you and giving you everything I got. Jeezus, don't let my name slip in none of this. Don't want that faggy-smelling gorilla thinking I finked him out. He'd do me sure."

# #

Chapter Nineteen

Mike wiped the morning puffiness from his eyes while glancing up when an excited Julie Provenzano bustled into his office waving a sheet of paper. "Tracked down Avezzano's cousin to Asbury Park, New Jersey. Her phone."

"Good work." Mike dialed, then clicked his phone on speaker. "Let's get lucky and catch her at home this time of day."

"She ought to be," Armand said, tagging behind Julie. "A ginmill waitress doesn't make all that much money in daytime, especially in the morning."

"Besides," Julie said, "she hung with a mobster. That pretty much indicates she works at night. Those guys rarely see the sunshine."

The three of them stared hopefully at the phone as it droned three, then four times. They brightened at the click of it and the sleepy voice that answered.

"Lenora Avezzano, please," Mike said. "This is she? Super. Hadn't expected to be that lucky to catch you at home this time of day."

"I work nights. Was sleeping."

"Sorry to have awakened you. This is Mike Molino of the Attorney General's office in Louisiana. Yes, that's right. I'm hoping you can help me locate a man who may have valuable information for us. That's the problem—I don't have a name. He's a chubby guy that you dated in Memphis, who wears a sweet-smelling aftershave."

"Who the hell told you that?" Her voice lost the sleepiness—dripped with resentment and resistance.

"That's not relevant. We know you hung with the guy, and

we're asking you to identify him."

"What if I don't?"

"Then we'll have the Asbury Park police make your life miserable. Believe that they will. Cops work together. You'll spend a lot of time in the interrogation room there. They hassle your boss you'll more'n likely lose that bartending job."

"Hey! I need that damn hustle."

"Then cooperate, or face the consequences."

"Why in hell you leaning on me?"

"You haven't seen any pressure yet, lady, and won't if you cooperate."

Quiet ensued. But after a few seconds she asked, "What's he done now?"

"Not so much what he's done as what he knows about what's done. So tell us his name."

Another pause, then: "Chucho Banzini."

"Chucho?" Mike asked.

"Yeah, it's what I knew him by. He fit it. Hey, you find him, you don't mention me. Skipped out of Memphis because that fat weasel didn't understand the word *quits*. Ain't anxious to have him following me to New Jersey, screwing up my life."

"Promise, but I need to know where I can contact him."

"How in hell I know after all these years?"

"Help me, I help you by keeping your name out of it."

"Try Memphis. He's likely still around there—his stomping grounds. What'd he do anyway?"

"Thanks very much for your help." Mike clicked off and leaned back in his chair. "Now we need to find Chucho Banzini of Memphis."

Julie chuckled. "Doubt his goombahs seek advice from a guy

they call Donkey."

"At least it identifies the guy we're looking for," Armand said.

Nelda stuck her head in the office. "Parked your squeeze from the PD in the reception area. Told her you're in conference."

"She's not my squeeze."

"Whatever. You want me to pass her in?"

"Just a minute." Mike turned to Armand and Julie. "Get a description of this guy from the Memphis police and ask them to check whether he's in town. If so, have him picked up. If not, have our state police out of Baton Rouge put out a six-state APB on him. Make it innocuous, like for questioning in a capital crime."

"I take it," Armand said, "that we aren't sharing this info with that good-looking sergeant."

Mike cut his eyes at Armand but didn't bother to answer. As they left he asked Nelda to send in Sergeant Boyle. Then he stared at the ceiling while reviewing what he'd learned, accepting that while it wasn't case-breaking it offered them their first ray of light. No way in hell he'd share that with the locals . . . trust them not to somehow screw it up.

"Hi." Kaylee leaned against the doorjamb. "Any reason for parking me outside? You guys got a secret meeting going?"

"Don't your bunch ever have meetings?"

"Too many. But my concern is whether you're keeping me in the dark. An important promotion is hinging on accomplishment with this assignment."

"Doubt that we've uncovered as much as y'all, given your head start. You got anything we can use?"

"Let's not turn this into some kind of game. I'd like to believe that y'all are playing this straight and keeping me in the loop."

"Why wouldn't we?"

96

"Hey, it's no secret that there's no love lost between your bunch and ours. Besides, you're obviously not all that happy about having me around."

"Actually, I've been wondering how we might get better acquainted." He blinked, surprised by having made that impulsive admittance.

"Could've fooled me by the way you've been practically avoiding me."

"You always paranoid."

"That your take on me? . . . Not as observant as reputed to be."

"I'm aware of you—noticed you the minute you walked into Montrose's office."

She grinned crookedly while continuing to lean against the door buck. "Then why don't you realize I'm outgoing, not inhibited? Don't hide my feelings or deny an interest in someone, like you do."

"Didn't realize I did. Didn't realize you didn't."

"I'm the one proposed we have dinner. Remember?"

"Sorry, have been disconcerted by aspects of the case, as well as personal things. Why don't we do lunch?"

"We had lunch yesterday, at Belmonde's. Can't afford it twice in the same year."

"That was Dutch. I'm inviting you to be my guest this time."

"Have a meeting at headquarters this afternoon that rules out lunch."

"Hey, I try."

"Try again some time. Need to get back to my office. Anything I can take with me to show I'm abreast of all that's happening?"

"Nothing for the moment. But anything we get will be shared with you."

"I'm holding you to that, and reminding you I can be vindictive. Talk to you later." She turned toward the hallway.

"Want to do supper?"

She paused and half turned. "But not Belmonde's—right?"

"Can't afford to spend a week's pay taking you to dinner, so I'm thinking on something affordable. And I intend to pick up the tab, just like on a real date."

"Sounds good, long as it's no bargain-basement eatery."

"Tell you what: I'll think of something real nice and call you about five to tell you where to meet at seven."

"I'll be waiting for that call. You do have my cellphone number?"

He nodded and followed her with his eyes until she disappeared. Then he chuckled, surprised at himself for having made that overture. Damned if he didn't still have the gumption to come onto a gal.

Nelda leaned into the doorway. "You getting sweet on her?"

"I'm hoping that's not why you stuck your head in here."

"Not that dumb. That reporter, Edmund Knuth, is on the phone for you. Answered it because Corine is on a break."

He picked up the phone. "What can I do for you, Knuth?"

"Any chance we can meet for lunch?"

"Just blew a lunch date."

"Good, then you can take one with me."

"You can't talk about whatever it is on the phone?"

"It's better discussed in confidence, Director, and you'll want to hear what I've got to say. How's the Crescent City Brew House on Decatur at twelve-thirty suit you?"

"Twelve-thirty works for me. So does the Brew House."

#   #

98

Chapter Twenty

    Kaylee knocked before entering the spacious office of District Commander Sebastian Shayde. Its starkness of oyster-colored walls, broken only by two elaborately framed portraits of black deputy superintendents of the past in full uniforms laden with decorations, consecrated a chamber glorifying African-American success in the New Orleans Police Department.

    She frowned upon discovering visitors occupying two of the four leather-padded chairs in a semi-circle facing Shayde's impressive desk. Breathing deeply she masked her dislike of Brent Kenman and pudgy Nicholas Boheemer.

    It pricked her concern that Sebastian Shayde spent so much time with them. Okay, she knew he had boundless ambition, so probably sucked up to Kenman because the guy had heavy political juice. However, it mystified her that Sebastian didn't connect those movers-and-shakers with engineering that atrocity, or, at least, considering the unlikelihood of Kenman walking away unscathed when professional killers announced their intent to take that ole' boy out.

    Did Sebastian suffer some kind of denial—a refusal to consider them dirty—unless provided with irrefutable proof. Wouldn't surprise her, knowing how stubborn he could be. Compressing her lips, she condescended to nod to the two visitors before slipping into the end chair, leaving an empty one to insulate her from Kenman—indifferent to how he interpreted that.

    "What have you to report to us, my dear?" Shayde asked.

    "Can we keep this in-house?" she asked as she pretended

unawareness of his lustful examination.

"These gentlemen share our concerns in this matter." Shayde said. "They've paid their dues, suffering trauma for having been there and shot at, besides having a stake in the political fallout."

"Impeccably stated," Kenman commended.

"Therefore," Shayde continued, "they deserve to be privy to whatever surfaces. Which brings us back to your progress report with respect to the folks at the AG's office."

Why, she wondered, didn't Sergeant Patty O'Shea, lead-investigator of the case, and Lieutenant Jesse Montrose, the commander of detectives in the district, attend a discussion of the Belmonde's case? How do you exclude those two but include these two? Damned if outsiders should be privy to reports.

But she sighed and relented, having better sense than butt heads with the district commander—certainly not when angling for a promotion. "They've only just gotten their investigation up and running, having started a good two, three days behind this department, consequently haven't accumulated near as much as our folks."

"They're busy interviewing folks, including everyone at Belmonde's," Kenman remarked, "as well as myself . . . as you know."

"Without turning a rock our people hadn't already," Kaylee said, modulating her voice so as not to sound confrontational or reveal disdain for the egotist.

"An indication of their level of expertise," Boheemer commented, smirking.

Kaylee shrugged—having decided to refrain from vocally responding to the chuby buffoon, propped up in the chair in expensive suit and tie. She'd heard he'd inherited a bundle. But it's doubtful he'd have much political juice without Kenman's tails to hang onto.

100

"How do we know you're being completely candid?" Kenman asked, as his eyes boldly examined her from head to foot.

"Don't appreciate the implication of your guest, sir," she said to the district commander; having decided not to butt heads with the powerful politician.

"Let's focus on the positives," Shayde said. "You're in line for a good appointment, having passed the lieutenant's exam. You do what we need done and you'll be rewarded."

"Out of the rat squad," she said, "to hunt bad guys, not cops."

"Prove that you deserve it," Shayde said, "by sticking that good-looking nose of yours in to learn every detail Molino stumbles onto."

She suppressed scowling, unhappy about having to betray Mike, having found herself attracted to him and having committed to dating him with the hope of them getting better acquainted. Accepting the need to respond, she said: "There's only a half dozen of them in that office and not all of them are working the case, versus the resources this department has brought to bear. Doubtful they'll uncover anywhere near as much as our people."

Shayde sniggered. "Molino is eager to put a hurting on this department and will dig deep, requiring we exert every effort to prevent that bastard humiliating us again."

Kaylee again suppressed a grimace as she wondered why a man as bright as Sebastian Shayde didn't have the good sense to endorse the exposure of corruption in the department a year ago instead of nursing a grudge against the person who did. And you'd think he'd appreciate investigators of other agencies joining the hunt for those assassins.

Basically Sebastian proved himself a dedicated cop, without a single bad mark over a long career with NOPD. Fact is, he'd earned a reputation for exemplary law enforcement, especially in supervisory positions. His fault, as she saw it, was his stubborn insistence to defend the department against attacks by outsiders whether or not the aspersions were qualified. A damn fool in that regard—devoted to the sanctity of the blue-line.

Just as obviously, ambition motivated his cultivating political influence. Overly cocky at times, he'd brag-assed how he had the *slick* to *play* the power brokers. A few times she'd had to stifle characterizing it as *sucking up* and *ass kissing*.

Anyway, she wondered why he didn't distance himself from these two, considering they raised hackles in the minds of any thinking person. Sure as hell they qualified as implicated in some manner in that atrocity at Belmonde's . . . if not as the prime suspects.

"Why don't we simply discredit Molino?" Kenman said. "That way we throw a roadblock in the way of credibility if they happen to stumble onto anything."

"Yeah, utilize the media to keep the heat on him," Boheemer said. "He's been ducking that Shreveport scandal, thanks to the on-again-off-again media attention, with only the tabloids publicizing it. We need to get the syndicated publications involved."

"Then let's apply pressure," Shayde said, "to heat up interest in the scandal by splashing it on Morreau and hopefully inducing him to discard his flunky."

"Rattle Birch Murdock's cage as well," Kenman said. "Being he's running scared, he'd sacrifice Molino in a heartbeat."

Shayde nodded enthusiastically. "We'll continually fuel those stories until they splash a big yellow stain all over Molino."

"Sergeant Boyle can contribute to destroying his credibility," Kenman said.

Her eyes snapped to him. "How exactly—"

102

"Publicize his hitting on you," Kenman said, "insulting a fellow law enforcement officer and violating the code of respect for fellow officers. Hell, call it sexual harassment. It'll reinforce the public's opinion of him as incorrigibly wanton."

"The simple fact that he hasn't hit on me," Kaylee said, "denies me making that kind of accusation." She held her breath, hoping they didn't somehow learn she'd accepted to have dinner with him.

"You can claim he came onto you," Shayde said. "Back it up by accusing him of being unnecessarily handsy."

"And what happens to my ass when his people support his refuting it? False accusations can get me in a world of hurt."

"Your word against his," Kenman said.

"I'd have to have been alone with him to make that kind of claim. To date that hasn't happened. His people are always around and will sure as hell support his denial of that charge."

"Don't tell me he hasn't given you a once-over," Kenman said. "Claim he insults you by the way he ogles you."

Kaylee sniggered. "Unlike you, sir, that man has eyes only for clearing this case."

Kenman scowled, but her continued talking denied him an opportunity to rebut. "He sure isn't chasing my skirts. Tell you true, doubtful he's chasing anything except those assassins."

"We'd like your cooperation," the district commander growled.

"Are you saying I should tell bold-face lies?"

"Make it happen," Shayde said. "You're an attractive woman. Rub up close to him and encourage him to—"

"Hold on now. I'm no damn street skank. I'm a goddam cop, same as—"

"Cops serve as decoys," Shayde said. "They lure Johns into

103

offering money so we can bust them."

"I've passed that stage," Kaylee said. "Have a gold shield, goddam it, and am not about to prostitute myself."

"Think team player," Shayde said. "Just hang close enough so he'll reach for you. Then you make it public. That's all I'm saying."

"I'm as much a team player as anyone else in the job. But I sure as hell am not about to make false statements that can bounce back and bite my ass."

"We're here to back you up," Boheemer said.

"Big deal. You two aren't even cops. And, I assure you, I intend to conduct myself according to the highest standards of a law-enforcement officer." She breathed deeply to control rising anger.

"Just stay alert," Shayde grumbled. "You get anything, cause anything to happen, you get on this bandwagon, be a team player."

"You got it, captain. The smallest impropriety gets reported to you. But it has to be something real, not fabricated."

Kenman rose while saying: "Considering he's been widowed two years, he's got to be aware of an attractive woman like you, sergeant."

Kaylee clenched her teeth. Sure she appreciated flattery, but preferred to hear it from someone other than that cozener.

Boheemer followed Kenman to the door and nodded when Kenman said: "We'll stop off at the Times-Picayune on our way back to the office to light a fire under the smear campaign of Molino."

"You still need me?" Kaylee asked Shayde as the visitors reached the door.

"Hold on for a minute," Shayde said. He'd risen and hurried to see his guests out. After closing the door behind them, he turned to Kaylee. "Looking at you reminded me of what I've been missing."

104

"That's it for me," Kaylee said as she rose.

Shayde remained with his back against the door, blocking her exiting. "What's gotten into you Kaylee? We were tight. I mean tight."

"You mean I was your plaything until your roving eyes happened onto new."

"Aw, come on, sweet thing. We can get past that, a foolish deviation. Men wander. You're used to that. Your husband wandered."

"And I divorced his cheating ass . . . like I dumped yours."

"Come on, sweet thing, let bygones be bygones."

"I foolishly succumbed to you, though aware from the get-go that you only wanted a white plaything. Tell you true, it didn't surprise me that you wandered off to pursue that cute little Latina to spice your life with variety."

"Yes, Kaylee, I strayed. But I adore you and want us to make another try."

"Not in this life." She reached for the door handle, but he blocked her effort.

"Best you get your head straight, woman, you want to get that promotion to lieutenant and out of PID."

"Oh, is that it? I'm mired in the rat squad as a sergeant unless I drop my pants for you again."

"Don't sound so crude, damn it. It's not feelingless like that. I want to renew our thing, not just jump in bed with you."

"We never had a thing—never had a chance to have a thing."

"What in hell you call it then?"

"You scored because I found it beneficial. Did what I had to after passing the sergeant's exam higher than most who got promoted before I did."

"Don't make it sound so crude and unfeeling."

105

"How else can you describe it, since I didn't get promoted until you had this booty? We sure as hell didn't have a romance."

"But we could have. No reason we can't have one now."

"No way! . . . especially with your jealous wife suspicious of every female comes in contact with you."

"Leave my wife out of this! You want—"

He tensed from the rap on the door. Pulling it open he confronted Lieutenant Jesse Montrose. It surprised the lieutenant to be responded to so quickly. Then his brow knit as he glanced from Shayde to Kaylee and back to Shayde, both near the door.

"Am I interrupting anything? I can come back later." He'd heard the rumors, like everyone else in the department.

"No. No," Shayde said. "We just finished a meeting."

"A meeting? Did it have anything to do with Belmonde's?"

"Some other things," Shayde said, "not concerned with that investigation."

Montrose's eyes narrowed with suspicion. He searched Shayde's face, but refrained from getting into a pissing contest with the district commander. It could only damage his career—since Shayde was rumored to be in line for promotion to deputy superintendent.

"What do you need me for?" Shayde asked, impatiently.

"We picked up a six state APB put out by the state cops for some Italian-sounding guy." Montrose consulted his note pad. "Banzini. Think it could have originated with Molino?"

Shayde turned to Kaylee. "You hear anything about this?"

"Never heard that name."

"See what you can find out," Shayde said to Montrose. "Run the name with the FBI. Let's see what comes out of the woodwork."

#   #

106

Chapter Twenty-One

Mike nosed into the desultory traffic of North Peters Street to bounce on the oft-patched pavement while passing grotto-like stores and eateries that attracted tourists searching for the mystical soul of New Orleans.

He paid little attention to his surroundings, consumed with speculating whether Knuth had something to share, or schemed to milk information about the investigation. Mike conceded that the guy had sources to verify whatever he expounded; justification for attending the meeting.

Nodding to that, he followed along in the snail-pace of traffic on the narrow street shaded by the three and four storied brick buildings enclosing it. Some dated back nearly three hundred years. The most pretentious had narrow balconies enclosed by decorative wrought iron railings gracing the upper floors. Referred to as galleries in New Orleans-speak, they were remnants of colonial France, enhanced by the subsequent influences of colonial Spain. Their sidewalks, referred to by locals as banquettes, were slabs of quarried rock that survived since the eighteenth century, when Lafitte the pirate roamed offshore.

Parked cars along both sides of the narrow street left barely enough roadway for traffic to snake between, creating a lethargic file. But folks in the old section accepted that everything had its own tempo, a kind of easy shuffle, to the tune of a muted wail.

Mike noted in his rear-view mirror a dusty pick-up truck that followed him from the time he pulled out of Clay Street to turn north on Bienville. He breathed relief to see a standard front bumper, not a steel pushbar. Yes, and he conceded it could be going to Decatur Street for any number of reasons, including grabbing lunch at one of the many eateries along that popular thoroughfare.

He sized up the two glum-faced guys in the cab. Both wore workman clothes and needed shaves. Their unsmiling and bored demeanors reminded him of undercover guys he'd worked with in the major crimes division, disguising themselves as workingmen and grouchy from the boredom of stakeouts. Could those two be cops? Why else did they tail him? Or did they?

Deciding to give them the slip, he turned onto Decatur and increased speed as much as traffic permitted, then hung a left onto Saint Louis, where lighter traffic allowed him to rev it up a notch. He wheeled a right at the next corner, and tooled down Chartres Street while constantly checking his rear-view mirror. With no pick-up truck in sight, he took another right at Toulouse and headed back toward Decatur.

At that corner he searched traffic in all directions but didn't see any sign of that dusty truck. Okay, he gave those guys the benefit of the doubt that they had coincidentally been on the same roads as himself, en route to a delivery or some maintenance chores. He chuckled as he wondered if he looked that glum when on a stakeout or while tailing a skel. Yeah, he'd smile occasionally next time.

Still, he pondered whether some of the local boys in blue just might be champing for payback for that hurting he'd put on nineteen of them last year. Authority is at times distorted, to the degree that occasionally a cop takes it upon himself to punish a wrongdoer, or to even the score when someone antagonizes him or her. Many believed they were justified in protecting groups or organizations they aligned with, even to the extent of exacting vengeance.

It wouldn't surprise him if Shayde put a tail on him to learn with whom he interacted. But he doubted if Shayde put a hit out on him. For all his arrogance, Shayde had earned his reputation as the consummate law enforcement officer.

No questioning the guy's ambition, which he wore for the world to see. Hell, everybody had a right to climb to the next rung and the one above that, ad infinitum.

Tooling along Decatur he grinned sardonically at the circus of milling tourists, sidewalk performers and hippie-like artisans. A mule-drawn buggy waited at the curb, its handler hawking sightseeing tours of The Quarter. The high-pitched melody of a calliope from the paddlewheel steamer a block away on the Mississippi punctuated the touristy hilarity amplified by street vendors and sidewalk entertainers.

He parked in front of the Crescent City Brewhouse, in spite of the signs restricting it. Placing his AG card on the dashboard he hoped none of the parking commandos ignored the placard and ticketed him. Sure he could beat the rap, but preferred to avoid ruffling any more feathers—in this town.

He searched around while climbing out, but didn't spot that dusty pick-up or anything that pricked his suspicion. Scoffing at his paranoia, he scanned the mid-rise Jackson Brewery diagonally across the street, the weathered riverfront structures beyond that, and the boxy warehouses in the other direction. On his side of the street the stores flanking the Brewhouse, exhibited interesting wares behind wooden-paned display windows; their creaky doors so warped by humidity they barely closed.

The double doors of the Crescent City Brew House had been propped open because of the balmy weather. So he sauntered in to inhale beer and fried foods while delighting from immersion into that happy drone. The cacophony of voices at the crowded bar on his right throbbed in his ears. Beyond that he saw the huge copper vats where they brewed their own beer. On the other side, along the wall left of the bar, diners filled up the stools at the five hightop tables.

A never-ending buzz emanated from the crowded tables in the large room beyond. Cellphones penetrated the pulsating drone of voices while intermittent high-pitched laughter pierced all of the other noises. The activity of waiters and waitresses bustling to serve the lunch-crowd added to the pandemonium of midday revelry.

Mike worried how long he and Knuth might have to wait for a table. He didn't want to spend too much time here, what with all the things needing his attention, considering the time limitations. Then his head jerked in surprise when he spotted Knuth waving to him from one of the hightops.

Had the guy gotten lucky, or used reporter juice to obtain it? Whatever. He approached and accepted Knuth's handshake before straddling one of the stools. "Love this place," Knuth said.

Mike nodded, but before he could elaborate, a harried waiter asked if they wished to order. Both opted for a schooner of the dark beer. Then Knuth expressed a desire for a shrimp po'-boy, dressed. Mike dittoed the order before leveling suspicion-slitted eyes on Knuth. "Hope you didn't bring me here to pump me for a story."

"Why are folks cynical of the press—considering that the media keeps society apprised of what is happening in their world. Without us, the average citizen wouldn't have a clue as to all the ways the politicians and big business rips them off."

"Nor have their opinions shaped by the very politicians and business tycoons you mentioned," Mike rebutted, snickering, "who use the media to convey what they want disseminated to the public."

"Polemics aside," Knuth said, "I'm yearning to discuss

something with you that's been weighing on my mind . . . a theory regarding that slaughter at Belmonde's."

"Why didn't you mention it when we bumped into each other at the cophouse?"

"Didn't expect to encounter you then, consequently wasn't prepared to go into this at length."

"Into what exactly?"

"By my reckoning," Knuth said, "Jerome Sessy was the prime target, not Darby Williams."

Mike's eyes widened as he tensed with attentiveness.

"I've also concluded," Knuth went on, "that the assassination was at the behest of the Russian mob."

"What in hell brought you to those conclusions?"

The waiter returned to serve them each a frosty beaker of house-brewed dark beer. They clinked glasses before tasting the heady beverage. Knuth leaned toward Mike to speak confidentially, in spite of the surrounding din reducing probability of being eavesdropped.

"About a week ago I dropped into Damian's Place on Bourbon Street for a clandestine lunch-meeting with an informant. You might remember that particular joint—just west of Dumaine Street—the unofficial frontier separating the straight Quarter from the gay Quarter east of there."

After Mike nodded, Knuth continued. "My contact selected that particular place since he doubted we'd encounter any of his homophobic coworkers there. As it happened, while waiting for him I spotted Big Willie Hoke's son, Loren."

Mike's eyes widened with surprise and interest, then narrowed as he wondered why that was relevant. He knew of Damian's and that it attracted straights as well.

Knuth twirled his hand as he continued. "Antsy and concerned because the guy I expected hadn't shown, I thought about probing Loren for a comment with respect to the prospects of his father being a shoo-in in the primary. But it wasn't a compelling subject, already talked to death on TV. Besides, I wasn't all that anxious to rehash the untimely demise of Darby Williams. Nor did Loren Hoke's sexual preferences dawn on me."

The waiter delivered each of them a long loaf of crispy French bread loaded with spicy, pan-fried shrimp topped with lettuce, tomatoes and dressed with an abundance of mayonnaise.

Mike groaned approval upon taking a bite.

Knuth chewed on his with relish before speaking again. "Frustrated me when my guy didn't show. It denied me that promised heads-up about a lot of money changing hands in the process of awarding contracts for the planned municipal building extension, which I anticipated as an incredible exposé, putting another feather in my cap."

Mike bobbed his head in acknowledgement, without that gesture interrupting his taking another bite from the succulent sandwich.

Knuth groaned his delight of his po'boy, which bulged his mouth while informing: "When the guy never showed, I assumed he got cold feet, or leaned on—maybe bought off with a piece of the pie he'd planned to expose. With nothing better going for me, I decided to approach Loren Hoke for an interview to justify the time spent there."

Mike inhaled patience as he wondered where in hell Knuth was headed.

"Just as I made my way around diners crowding tables and chairs, a Hard-Faced guy sat at the young man's table. Loren Hoke glared at the guy, apparently annoyed by the audacious intrusion. But Hard-Face didn't seem put off, and dropped a newspaper on the table

112

while gesturing for Loren to read it."

Knuth took another bite before continuing. "It took coaxing by Hard-Face before a reticent Loren picked it up and opened it. The young man's eyes bulged with mortification. He clapped the paper closed. Hard-Face smirked triumphantly as he handed Loren a few pages of white paper with something typed on them. Appall etched Loren's face as he read then reread them, all the while shaking his head in negativity."

Mike chewed his po'boy while remaining attentive, though unsure what he was being told or how it might be related to the Belmonde's case.

Knuth chewed and swallowed before continuing. "I squeezed past the young man but failed to catch a glimpse of whatever intimidated him. Nor was I able to hear what they discussed."

Mike grimaced impatience, then took another bite and chewed ecstatically. Oh well, the sandwich was worth the time he spent listening to Knuth, even if he wasn't particularly interested in Loren Hoke since he didn't associate the guy with the case.

"But I was aware of Hard-Face leaning toward the young man and addressing him in a sibilant whisper too low to overhear," Knuth said. "The man's adamancy cowed Loren, who clutched the newspaper and the typewritten pages, even after Hard-Face left.

"Since I could always corral Loren Hoke, and milk him about what made him look like he went into shock, I tailed Hard-Face. Expected the guy's identity to clue me to why he approached the son of a state senator, who happened to be the leading nominee of his party for candidate to run for the governorship."

# #

Chapter Twenty-Two

Mike stuffed in the last bite of his po'boy while wondering where the chronicle was leading.

"Shadowed Hard-Face east on Bourbon," Knuth said, "then across Esplanade into Fauborg Marigny. There the guy ducked into a dingy tavern on Pauger Street, a place I remembered from an old investigation as a hangout for Russian mobsters."

Mike nodded to that while chewing and groaning ecstatically.

"Waited a few minutes before entering," Knuth said, "to avoid appearing to have tailed the guy. Even so, the half dozen or so growlies there eyed me disdainfully—as I imagine they did any stranger. In spite of that, I nonchalantly bellied up to the bar and ordered a bottle of beer."

Knuth sniggered. "Bartender made no effort to hide resenting me. Anyway, while paying for the beer I glanced around and spotted Hard-Face at a table with a gangster I recognized as Igor The Terrible. That erased doubt that I needed to know more about why that bunch made contact with Loren Hoke."

Finishing his sandwich, Knuth washed it down with beer before continuing. "Decided not to loiter too long in that dive, but waited until I'd gotten a block away before cellphoning my office to have someone work up a profile on Loren Hoke. Next day, when I went in, I learned Loren was employed at Trans-Oceanic Exchange Bank."

Mike's brow arched at that revelation as memory struck regarding Jerome Sessy having been the general manager of the New Orleans branch, one of the skyscrapers on lower Canal.

"Reviewed the information compiled about Loren while in a cab

114

on the way there," Knuth continued. "The kid earned a reputation as an egghead at the University of Chicago, where he majored in finance. So it came as no surprise that he worked in one of the largest financial institutions of international dealings."

Knuth paused to drain his beer. "Talked my way through half a dozen low and middle-level managers without explaining my mission to get a sit-down with Jerome Sessy. That ole' boy was the only African-American in the state enjoying a position that lofty—in the banking industry any way."

Mike peered back into memory, for information about TOEB, which handled sixty percent or more of the international banking for New Orleans, as well as a dominating percentage of the commerce along the Mississippi River, an area that comprised roughly a third of the USA. Helluva' important bank!

"Consequently," Knuth said, "I felt ill at ease mentioning having observed Loren Hoke with a Russian mobster. As expected, Sessy didn't readily accept my assumption that mobsters recruited him to launder mob money. Yes, Sessy admitted that Loren was in a position to move capital, situated as head of the division that handled international transfers. But he refused to believe the young man abused his privileges by implementing anything that abhorrent. Besides, he pointed out, the Hoke family had money, didn't need to resort to gangster activities."

Knuth sighed. "Sessy finally acceded to investigate discreetly, concerned with the reputation of the bank, but leery about intimidating the senator. Yes, he assured me of an exclusive of whatever surfaced."

Knuth shrugged. "Accepted that arrangement, certain Sessy would report to me whatever transpired. Hell, the guy had a lot to lose if money were laundered in the bank he managed and he wasn't forthcoming. As it turned out, he ended up dead a few days later, depriving me of that verification."

Knuth wiped his hands and face with his napkin. "Have since learned that Loren resigned from the bank. As it stands, I lack sufficient justification to run a story that destructive of character . . . certain to bring Big Willie down on me with both feet. So I'm approaching you since the AG's office has the capability to discreetly investigate the allegations. You then owe it to me to feed me the thing exclusively."

"Agreed," Mike said. "We'll explore all possibilities— covertly. I'm sure as hell no more eager than you or Jerome Sessy to make an enemy of Big Willie."

"Using every resource at your disposal," Knuth said.

Mike shook his head. "Can't let too many people in on it. Everything in government gets leaked eventually, and I'm not anxious to explain why I'm investigating the senator's son . . . on the basis of some improbable claim."

"Dig and you'll sure as hell find probable cause."

Mike ground his jaw but decided against discussing his reluctance—and his fear of that state senator of Shreveport coming at him with all guns blazing. The scandal that presently harried him would expand and eventually crush him, regardless of whether it had legs. Politicos of Big Willie's stature could have anyone taken down.

Snorting to thoughts tumbling in memory, Mike decided against confiding in Knuth that they tentatively identified the shooters as Italian-Americans. Hell, the ski masks those Rambos wore eliminated certainty that it had been Banzini. True, those guys made derogatory references in Italian. But that may have been intentional by the Russians to confuse identification. And it might have been a chubby Russian wearing that after-shave Avezzano recognized.

Without knowing squat about the tall guy, they had no way of

116

determining his ethnicity . . . or that of the others for that matter. Besides, Mike damn sure didn't want the word getting out and spooking Banzini before he had a chance to take that donkey into custody, so he damn sure wasn't going to divulge anything to a reporter.

"Let's keep in touch," he said.

#   #

Chapter Twenty-Three

     Mike pulled into traffic to head back to his office. He repeatedly shook his head but couldn't dispel the confusing parts. Spotting a large SVU behind him, he scanned its bumper and exhaled upon seeing nothing out of the ordinary, certainly no steel pushbar.

     Still, he continually checked his rear-view mirror until that vehicle turned off. At intervals he checked out everyone around him but didn't see anything threatening or suspicious. No vehicles appeared to tail him. God, he hoped he wasn't getting paranoid.

     No matter how he characterized that incident last night, he couldn't dismiss the probability that it intended to take him out—aware that rogue cops were capable of outrageous acts. Nor dared he dismiss the possibility that audacious gangsters had the balls to attack police officers. Hell, judges and assistant district attorneys had been taken out on occasion. Besides, based on what Knuth divulged, the business now appeared to take on implications beyond political connivance. No predicting the audacity of the Russian mob.

     More importantly, no way he wanted Big Willie on his case, especially at a time his reputation was already in tatters. Yes, he'd be wise to avoid aggravating the State Senator Hoke, knowing if he didn't he'd get stomped on for scandalizing the man's son without validation.

     But, and it was a big-assed but, he had to consider Knuth's information indicating that the Russian mob was out to gag Sessy, resulting in Darby Williams getting caught in the crossfire. True, all of the descriptions they received pointed to Italian-Americans. However, that didn't rule out the Russians, since there were numerous incidents of

118

the two mobs working reciprocal arrangements to confuse the cops. Inability to show motive hampered convictions . . . letting hoods get away with crimes.

And Knuth's theory sure laid credence to the outrageous act of gunning down three black men—to make sure they got the right one—two of which qualified as among the most important people in Louisiana. Then it baffled him that one of the shooters mentioned Kenman by name.

Goddam! Kenman admitted he invited Darby Williams to lunch there . . . but denied including Jerome Sessy and Antwan Croix. God a'mighty, this business is getting more confusing by the minute.

With that matter tumbling around in his temporal lobe, he entered the AG's office complex—and stopped short upon encountering Kaylee waiting for him in the reception area, her face drawn. He gritted his teeth to stifle revealing annoyance at having to deal with her when he wanted to delve into the case.

But he waved her to accompany him to his office and take a chair. "Something wrong?" he asked as he sat behind his desk and thumbed through messages, trying not to expose angst to get rid of her.

"My bosses ragged me something awful for lacking info about that APB for some guy with an Italian name." She checked her notepad. "Banzini."

Mike blinked, unprepared to hear about that so soon. But he feigned a confused expression and shook his head.

"You saying you have no knowledge of a bolo put out by the state police?"

"They don't run every damn thing they do past me. Thank God. Besides, I don't ramrod the state cops."

Kaylee's sigh attested to her relaxing. "Want to share with me

119

where you've been all afternoon? I've been waiting here most an hour."

"Lunch with an old buddy—male. You want to be bored with the details and learn why we're anxious for the Saints to make it to another super bowl—or whether this year's draft-picks will improve the Hornets and—"

"Not particularly. Okay, have to go—am late to meet with and instruct folks taking over for me in PID. But I waited to talk to you face to face."

"Glad you did. Can't deny I like looking at you." He surprised himself for that boldness, realized his old glibness was coming back.

She tried but didn't succeed in suppressing a gratifying smile as she rose and turned to leave. "Don't forget supper," she called from the doorway.

Oh shit. He didn't admit he had. Too damned many things rattling around in his head. He sighed relief when she left, freeing him to dig into proving or disproving Knuth's theory, without anything leaking to the NOPD. Later he'd make up his lack of candidness with her.

#   #

120

Chapter Twenty-Four

   Yawning, he leaned back, taking a break from browsing the
NOPD reports. He'd been disappointed to find nothing implicating
Russians. Nor did it indicate how in blue hell the Russians expected
Sessy to accompany Darby Williams to meet with Brent Kenman at
Belmonde's—at that precise time! That question haunted him—if
Knuth's premise was correct: whatever impelled Kenman to get in bed
with the Russian mob?

   Was it possible that Kenman had nothing to do with the rub-out?
Then why was he there at that specific time . . . lined up in front of that
window with only Williams invited as his guest? Had the Russians
learned about the meeting and took advantage of it by going there to
light up Sessy? Then why did they claim to be hunting Kenman?

   True, Kenman admitted he'd arranged the meeting with Darby
Williams, but claimed he hadn't anticipated Jerome Sessy attending.
Even if invited, doubtful Sessy wanted his endorsement of Williams
advertised, since it was sure to provoke some of the bank's accounts, as
well as a few of those corporate moguls serving on the bank's board. So
it stretched credibility that he'd publicize his political preference.

   Hell, half of the bank's Louisiana clients were conservatives
who backed Willis Hoke. More than a few might not welcome a black
man into the governor's mansion, while pretending to commend the bank
for appointing a black manager; in an attempt to herald liberalism.
However, they'd more than likely be pissed if Jerome Sessy openly
endorsed Darby Williams . . . Even those who claimed to have voted for
Obama. Racial prejudice wasn't erased by that election despite the

121

propaganda circulated.

Sessy's presence there that day had to have significance other than support for Darby Williams. Okay, according to Knuth, it had to do with money laundering. The sudden resignation from the bank by Loren Hoke supported that supposition. Yes, Knuth said he'd called the bank and discreetly checked that out . . . though without getting particulars about what motivated the young man to quit.

Still, it required stretching the imagination to suspect Kenman setting something like that up for the Russian mob. No denying the man was ambitious and devious, but it'd take a hard sell to convince Mike that he served organized crime. Dammit, not one good reason materialized in his muddled thinking for hiring killers to take out any of those three victims.

However, he didn't doubt for a minute that those assassins went to Belmonde's at that precise moment for the specific purpose of blowing those three men away. That means they'd been apprised of that meeting beforehand, or have set it up. No matter how he turned it, Kenman came up tainted as suspicious. What was his connection with the hit-men? What was his motive? And how does Mike prove it?

Why was Antwan Croix killed? The guy was an assistant campaign manager for Darby Williams. Why hadn't Josh Bigelow, the campaign honcho attended that meeting? Why his assistant?

Intrigued, Mike phoned the Darby Williams campaign office, hoping they hadn't as yet closed down. He perked when a gal answered. She told him that Mister Bigelow was busy on another line, with a second and third caller on hold, and that if he left his name and number Mister Bigelow would return his call in just a little.

Mike did so, then ground his teeth when he hung up, having had his fill of leaving messages and waiting for return calls. Hell, since the guy was busy on the phone, Mike figured he'd catch him there and be able to converse privately, as opposed to over a line that could be bugged. He didn't doubt for a minute that the NOPD had techies who could secretly accomplish it. Besides, it wouldn't surprise him if Josh Bigelow refused to discuss anything confidential over the phone. So he hurried down to his car.

He figured the fastest way, considering most of the narrow streets in damn-near medieval New Orleans were one-way, was to circle his building and take Iberville to Wells, which dumped him onto two-way Canal Street. But he found that wide thoroughfare choked with late afternoon traffic.

He anguished with the possibility of the guy leaving early, considering he didn't have no whole lot to do without a candidate. Hopefully those three calls proved long-winded and kept the guy there for a while. Maybe it'd make sense to call and let him know he's on the way there. Goddammit! He gnashed his teeth for not having brought his cellphone. Christ, he never went anywhere without it—his connection to the world . . . couldn't believe he didn't bring it.

After an aggravating period of time, he finally traversed the few blocks to turn into Tchoupitoulas, a one-way street headed west. Encouraged by having only four or five blocks to go, his buoyancy tapered to pessimism when traffic crawled because construction vehicles intermittently blocked the narrow roadway. Many buildings were still undergoing hurricane repairs, with a few getting facelifts.

The pace of traffic and the obvious lack of parking spaces induced him to pull into an empty spot at the curb a block before the target building. He trotted the rest of the way to the first floor office of a recently refurbished edifice that served as campaign headquarters for Darby Williams . . . or did. The sign had been taken down.

123

"Sorry, sir," the gal at the front desk disinterestedly informed, "Mister Bigelow left for the day."

"Thought he was busy on the phone."

When she shrugged without bothering to explain further, Mike asked: "Can you give me his home phone?"

"No, sir. Leave your number and Mister Bigelow will call you tomorrow."

Mike clenched his teeth, hesitant to identify himself as with the AG's office, not eager to start any rumors, with no telling where this gal's loyalties lie. But he wasn't happy about anguishing all goddam night with a wild-ass supposition. And he doubted Josh Bigelow's home address or telephone number was listed in the local directory. VIPs concealed that kind of information to avoid being harassed.

A black woman with the busy air of an executive emerged from a back office to collect papers from the reception desk. Mike flashed his credentials to her, using his body to block the receptionist from seeing them. "Any chance I can have a minute of your time?"

"May I ask about what?"

"Confidential. Please, ma'am, one minute." He wanted as few people as possible privy to things. God knows how many ears Shayde or Kenman had. And he damn sure didn't want rumors getting back to Big Willie.

She shrugged and waved him into an inner office. It didn't surprise him that she caved so easily. More than likely she'd been interviewed a number of times by the city police, even possibly by state investigators.

"We've received information," he confided, after she closed the door, "concerning the assassination of Darby Williams and Antwan Croix that could scandalize the reputations of those men."

124

"Oh, God, no!"

"Can't get into specifics, ma'am, but I need to run it past Josh Bigelow before any of it goes public, requiring I catch up to him this afternoon."

She rubbed her forehead, stunned by the revelation, and obviously indecisive about giving out proprietary information.

"It's imperative," he repeated, "that I converse with Mister Bigelow to prevent unfounded rumors casting shame on the memories of dearly departed Darby Williams and Antwan Croix."

She sighed concession, then jotted down the man's home address and phone number. "But don't expect to catch him there for a few hours. Mister Bigelow has, since that awful tragedy, stopped at Big Al's on Bourbon Street on his way home."

When Mike looked askance at her, she explained: "He and Darby Williams had been close. Consequently Mister Bigelow mourns that man's passing by drowning himself in loud and brassy jazz."

"Thanks," Mike said, without commenting on the seeming aberration. Hell, he did the same thing. Trotting back to his car, he pulled open the door to discover his cellphone on the floor. He slapped his forehead as admonishment for not having searched for it. Still shaking his head, he pulled into rush-hour traffic.

Office workers swarming out of surrounding buildings joined construction workers finishing for the day to fill up the sidewalks and spill into the street. A press of cars and trucks transformed that thoroughfare into a morass of vehicular and pedestrian confusion.

With Tchoupitoulas a one-way going away from The Quarter, he had to drive west to Julia Street, a one-way headed north, and take that to Carondelet, a one-way whose sluggish traffic flowed east, and became Bourbon Street after crossing Canal. He gritted his teeth while poking

125

along behind a choke of vehicles, all too often blocked by happy hour celebrants spilling recklessly into the roadway. He feared that by the time he arrived at his destination Josh Bigelow will have had his drink or two and left.

After crossing Toulouse he again ignored parking restrictions by pulling up to the curb in front of Big Al's. And again he relied on his placard on the dashboard to exempt him from getting ticketed.

Loud and raucous music emanating from the gin mill enveloped him on the sidewalk. People dawdled there, with some gyrating to the loud music. Many clutched Styrofoam containers of beer and applauded three black teenagers taking turns doing their shuffle and passing the hat for spectators to reward them.

Mike dropped a quarter in it, despite considering them too amateurish to deserve even that much. He'd seen some really good hip-hop artists on these sidewalks. Those three didn't qualify.

#   #

Chapter Twenty-Five

Mike pulled open the door and recoiled into his shoulders, assailed by the penetrating wail of a trumpet accompanied by a howling trombone and the frenetic banging of drums and cymbals—a cacophony that gave loud a new meaning. Blinking against the din he penetrated the semi-darkness crowded with bodies, most transfixed by the loud jazz.

While acclimating himself to the clanging and booming vibrations he searched for that particular face. A few black ones were sprinkled among the white ones. He accepted that New Orleans still had places that mostly whites patronized, and others that mostly blacks did, while the majority had mixed crowds. Separation of the races was voluntary, no longer an imposed injustice.

Ah, he spotted Josh Bigelow, a big man with a full head of graying hair, which lent him more the appearance of a poet than a political strategist. Sitting at the back end of the bar, on the stool furthest from the music, the guy nursed a squat glass of amber liquid. He looked spaced, like his mind drifted in the waves of that clamor. Mike hoped he hadn't become stupefied by noise and booze to where he couldn't comprehend and converse.

Mike touched his shoulder and Josh flinched, like someone unexpectedly awakened. Annoyance contorted a mature face etched with grief. Recognition relieved angst and elicited a smile. He extended a hand to be shaken. "What in hell brings you to this joint?"

"To rap with you, good buddy," Mike yelled to be heard above the din.

Josh's eyes narrowed with questioning. Mike decided against

mincing words. "Following up a rumor accusing Loren Hoke of laundering money for the Russian mob."

Josh's jaw fell. Turning away, he downed the liquor in his glass, then signaled one of the bartenders for a refill. The man poured a twelve-year old single malt scotch, then turned questioning eyes to Mike.

Needing to retain lucidity, Mike decided against swilling bourbon, so ordered a bottle of beer. He gestured that he'd pay for both drinks. Josh clinked his squat glass against Mike's bottle; appreciative like most men to receive a free drink.

"Forgetting my manners," Mike shouted into Josh's ear, "I should have started the conversation by expressing my condolences over the untimely loss of Darby Williams, knowing you two were good buddies."

Josh bobbed his head in acknowledgement.

"Having done that," Mike said, "I'll reiterate my remarks regarding the rumor that Loren Hoke laundered money for the Russian mob."

"Where in hell you hear that kind of slander?"

"Is it true?"

Josh clamped his eyes closed, as if lanced by pain. Reopening them he moaned: "We competed against Big Willie but we're still in the same party."

"I'm aware of that."

"Then you'll appreciate that I'm not about to malign the senator's only boy. Nor am I going to impair the father's run for governor. Fact is, I'll support it."

Mike hunched acceptance of Josh Bigelow's declaration.

"Two, three times since that atrocity at Belmonde's," Josh said, "I've checked Big Willie out and concluded he had no part in it."

128

"Never suspected he did."

"Willis Hoke doesn't know about those rumors," Josh said, "and I've vowed not to break the heart of a man who's served the people of Louisiana all these years."

"I know you're hanging out in this raucous place," Mike said, "hoping it'll drown out the sorrow in your heart for Darby Williams."

"How in hell you know that?"

"It's the same way I've mourned my wife and my baby girl the past two years."

"Oh, God! Yes. You have my condolences. Forgive me for forgetting. Sincerely, Mike, I feel for you."

"Thanks. Back to Loren: What's his story?"

"What's done is done and I'm not crucifying anybody. Darby's dead. Let all the scandal mongering die with him."

"Three men have been ruthlessly murdered. It didn't happen without intent, nor was it devoid of purpose—and certainly wasn't accidental."

"Been thinking about nothing else. Wish to God I had answers for it."

"I plan to get some, Josh. My job is to root out those ruthless killers, and I promise you I will."

When Josh didn't respond, Mike said: "You can help me and help yourself, by telling it from your point of view, to prevent it being spun into sensationalism."

"You think I'm going to say anything that scandalizes the party?"

"This isn't about party, Josh. It's about the murder of three really good men."

Josh hung his head, didn't respond.

129

"We've already learned that Loren resigned from the bank," Mike said.

Josh again clamped his eyes closed and again grimaced pain.

"We're also aware," Mike said, "that Loren is a closet homo and had meetings with an emissary for Igor The Terrible, a kingpin in the Russian mob."

"Holy shit! How in hell you find all that out?"

"Why not enlarge on it . . . fill in the blanks?"

"No way, considering what it would do to the boy's daddy, not to mention the devastating affect it will have on Loren . . . an innocent who got duped."

"Whatever, Josh, the truth has to come out."

"Man, you can't muddy the personal waters of folks—AG's office or no."

"Come on, Josh, we're past that now. This thing will get told depending on who spins the information that surfaces."

"Oh God!"

"You want to help Loren and his daddy you have to help the truth get out. You don't and it'll likely be distorted eight different ways to hell and back."

Josh averted his eyes and swallowed his drink. Banging the empty glass on the bar got the bartender's attention for a refill. Mike held his hand over his bottle to indicate he didn't want any more. When Josh got his refill, he stared blankly into it.

"It gets told," Mike said, "your way or the imprecise way of things learned in bits and pieces. I'm doing everything I can to delay Edmund Knuth from going public with partial accounts and aspersions."

"Should've realized your source. Jerome Sessy told us about their talk. How damn much y'all know?"

130

"Most of it, with a need to fill in the gaps."

Josh wagged his head in uncertainty. Then his shoulder slumped in concession. "Yep, Loren is a closet homo. And, yes, the boy involved himself in laundering money."

Mike nodded to that, not surprised that Knuth's information played out.

"But it isn't as simple as it sounds," Josh said. He compressed his lips and swiveled his eyeballs around, obviously searching for how to approach the subject.

"Don't even think about spinning it, Josh."

"Mike, you need to understand what'all happened, like a bad dream that came screaming out of a dark night."

"Just tell it," Mike said. ". . . But straight out without putting a slant on it."

Josh grimaced his reluctance as his aging face took on deeper lines of anguish. Mike patted his back. "It's only a matter of time before reporters and scandalmongers start their talk-fest. So why not tell it the way you want the world to hear it, rather than letting it end up with a lascivious spin."

"Easy for you to spout that rhetoric."

"Because I lived it . . . made the mistake of not confronting rumors in Shreveport when they first raised their ugly heads."

"Oh, Jesus! Almost forgot about that, Mike. How you faring with that?"

"Not as well as I would if I'd faced it head on. That's what you need to do."

Josh breathed deeply as he turned pain-filled eyes to Mike. "Okay, Darby received a call from Jerome Sessy asking for a confidential meeting, assuring Darby that he had information capable of

131

dramatically affecting the primary."

Mike leaned closer, not wanting to miss a word.

"We'd been fighting an uphill battle against Big Willie," Josh confessed. "The senator simply had the edge statewide, with Darby leading only in New Orleans. Primary day kept drawing closer and we needed a miracle bounce to pull the thing out. So we met with Jerome Sessy, to be shocked by the revelations he revealed."

Mike denied himself taking a swig of beer, anxious to hear what they discussed.

"Sessy told us how that reporter, Knuth, approached him with the wild accusation that Loren Hoke was in bed with the Russian mob. Sessy didn't want to believe anything like that about Big Willie's boy, even though he personally supported Darby in the race, as one black man exhibiting his pride for a deserving black candidate. True, he didn't do it openly since it behooved the manager of an important bank to conceal political preferences . . . not that the whole damn world didn't assume who Sessy and ever' other successful African-American backed."

Nodding to his statement, Josh continued. "But Sessy had no option but investigate a disturbing rumor, considering his position, which is when he happened upon Loren processing the transfer of fifty million dollars to confuse both its origin and its end destination. When confronted, Loren broke down and cried, but refused to explain why he'd done what he had. He quit, there and then, and left the bank."

Josh sipped from his squat glass before continuing. "Jerome understood his obligation to report the thing to the feds and the banking commission. But he wanted unimpeachable evidence to avoid Big Willie accusing him of playing politics. No denying the thing helped Darby, therefore was sure to be considered partisan. However, if Darby exposed it without substantiation it'd likely boomerang against him."

Mike grunted agreement to that, aware of how Hoke-backers would spin defense of the senator by maligning Darby Williams as malicious and spiteful since he was losing.

"The three of us," Josh said, "talked it to tatters and came to the conclusion that we didn't dare go public with something that volatile without validation. Man, we needed to be concerned that the public not perceive it as mud-slinging to discredit our opponent. There were already too many attack-ads circulating. Besides, it could be a scam, to make Darby publicize something to end up backfiring on him."

#   #

Chapter Twenty-Six

Josh took a big swallow and shook his head. "Deciding we needed the protection of Loren's confession, I went to his apartment that evening and found him sitting in the dark. Lord God, that boy was despondent—on the verge of suicide. No, he wasn't amenable to enlightening me. But I persisted, reminding him that I and his daddy were in the same party and shared the hope of wresting the governorship away from the incompetence of Birch Murdock."

Josh shifted on his stool and shook his head, dejection shading his face. "Took a heap of talking before Loren finally broke down and admitted he'd laundered money for the Russian mob—twice. The first time for five million dollars and caught in the act the second time trying to launder fifty million. Loren said he was thankful that Jerome Sessy walked in on him in time to cancel out the attempt. He realized now that they'd never let it end, but rather pressure him into becoming part of a criminal conspiracy—with no end."

Josh sipped his drink. "Asked him if he wasn't concerned now that he'd enraged the Russians. Hell yes, he said, but what could they do beside kill him—which he considered a benediction by putting him out of his misery and shame . . . hopefully before he was indicted and that scandal got splashed onto his daddy."

Josh took another sip. "Asked him how he got inveigled into doing something that outrageous? Loren only muttered that he'd prefer not publicizing something that shameful. Despite my doggedness, he hung tough. To break the impasse, I told him his sexual preference wasn't a secret. Shocked, the kid barely got out the words to ask how I

134

knew. Had tears in his eyes when he stammered how he'd never been involved in anything like that before, despite years of yearnings."

Josh shook his head in commiseration. "Told him that his hanging out at Damian's Place raised a few brows, being that it's common knowledge that closet types go there because they haven't the balls to go a block farther east to a gay bar and let themselves go."

Josh took another sip. Then he again shook his head in commiseration for the confused young man. "Loren burst into tears while admitting he'd suffered those yearnings from late boyhood, and most painfully during his college years. But he'd resisted every excruciating desire. Yes, he went to Damian's, but never took it any further."

Mike grimaced sympathy for the young man, while impatient for Josh to connect everything to the case.

"Told him to get it off his chest," Josh said. "But Loren hung tough for a good while. Took doing before he conceded that it all happened so damned unexpectedly. He'd attended a function for a friend displaying at Rory's Gallery in the Warehouse District, where he met Ion Karlovy, a Hungarian Adonis. Ever' gal in the place swooned over that blonde gladiator."

Josh again shook his head in sympathy. "Poor guy said he suffered yearning more than ever, and said he stayed only as long as courtesy required. But he said a week later he ran into Ion while sipping wine and viewing artwork at Adele Bessant's showing at Gordon's Gallery. Ion shocked Loren when he invited him to sail on his boat on Saturday. Loren accepted, thrilled to be befriended by the Adonis. Of course he'd fantasized about romance with the hunk, but never really expected it to happen . . . doubted he had it in him to indulge in something like that."

135

Josh sipped half of the remaining booze. "Said they sailed Ion's thirty-foot sloop on Lake Pontchartrain, then anchored in a remote cove to have lunch. Ion suggested they take a dip first. Since neither brought bathing suits they skinny-dipped. Loren admitted desire burning within him, but invoked self-control. Besides, he feared the Hungarian Adonis angrily rejecting any overtures and thereafter scorning him, and possibly even publicly denouncing him."

Josh breathed deeply before continuing. "Loren struggled to admit he'd been flabbergasted when Ion suggested they eat without bothering to towel off or dress, commenting how he found men desirable when sparkling with water. The Adonis broke out a bottle of Syrah to drink with their sandwiches. Loren said they finished one bottle of that delightful red wine, then uncorked another, all the while chatting like good old buddies.

"At some point Ion moved close to Loren and told him he found him attractive. Pressure expanded in Loren's head, blocking his ability to think, or even to respond. No, he'd never expected to have an affair with Ion . . . in spite of fantasizing it. He had no ability to resist the man caressing his naked torso and cupping his breasts. When Karlovy slipped his tongue in Loren's mouth, Loren surrendered to the desire that haunted his body for so many years."

Josh shook his head and sighed before continuing. "Loren bemoaned his bad luck when Karlovy left for Budapest the following day on pressing business. The boy said he expected Ion to return as quickly as possible, to resume the tempestuous affair, believing Ion fell as much in love with him as he did with Ion."

#   #

136

Chapter Twenty-Seven

Josh ordered a refill. Mike again held his hand over his barely touched bottle. After Josh took a long swig he continued. "Loren said he suffered two weeks of waiting for a phone call or e-mail, neither of which he received. He refused to accept that Ion moved on to some other vulnerable conquest . . . Didn't want to believe he'd served as a convenient plaything . . . used and abandoned."

Josh paused to wag his head in empathy. "He said despite despondence he lunched alone at Damian's to brood over love lost. A stranger stunned him by sitting at his table, ignoring his objection. The smirking intruder had the unmitigated nerve to drop a newspaper on the table and tell Loren he would find page four especially interesting. Loren glared at the paper, but refused to touch it. The man persistently gestured to the newspaper, threatening that the only way to get rid of him was by opening it to page four. Anxious to free himself of the pest, Loren did, and gawked at the array of photographs of two naked men clipped to the page."

Josh paused for a deep breath. "Loren said it took a moment to recognize that they were of he and Ion Karlovy, with each photo depicting the Hungarian's organ inserted in a different part of his anatomy. They left nothing to the imagination."

After again wagging his head, Josh continued. "The interloper introduced himself as Arik Choskova and told Loren the only way to avoid exposure required he transfer five million dollars to an account in Nashville, without any chance of it being traced. Loren adamantly refused.

"The man laughed at him as he threatened exposure of his homosexuality to scandalize him as well as embarrass him socially and probably forcing him to leave the bank. His father also will suffer the scandal—that disgrace possibly influencing the senator to withdraw from the primary and abandon the pinnacle of a long and successful career.

"Loren bowed his head, more concerned with how it impacted on his father. He cursed Ion Karlovy for suckering him. But he took refuge in Arik Choszkova assuring him it was a one-time only arrangement. Upon execution of the task, the Russian promised to deliver to Loren all of the photos and negatives, and leave him alone. Accepting his lack of alternatives, Loren succumbed—this one time."

Josh again sighed his sympathy for the young man. "Loren said it took enormous willpower to overcome his reluctance and his fear of consequences. But he did it and breathed easier, believing the threat of scandal had been averted. Still, he writhed in angst for days while waiting to receive those damning photos. When, after a week, they hadn't been delivered to him, he returned to Damian's, in hopes of encountering that Russian to demand he fulfill his promise.

"Sure enough, Choszkova appeared, grinning as he dropped a sheaf of papers in front of Loren and instructed him that this time they wanted him to transfer fifty million dollars—to a bank in Turkey.

"It did no good to remind the smirking bastard that he had been promised a one-time arrangement. Choszkova replied that Loren had violated banking laws, so either did as bid or faced imprisonment, as well as the ruination of his father's political career.

"His options preempted, Loren went back to the bank and had just gotten started with the transaction when discovered by Jerome Sessy. Shamed beyond description, he simply quit and walked out. He

138

has since locked himself in his room, preparing himself mentally for when the feds came to arrest him—or the Russians to kill him. He even contemplated suicide since he believed he lacked any other way to solve his dilemma."

#   #

Chapter Twenty-Eight

"Let's cut to the chase, Josh. How'd those buttons expect Darby and Sessy to stand in front of that window at Belmonde's . . . at that precise time?"

When Josh's eyes clouded with confusion, Mike asked: "Why did Darby meet with Brent Kenman, the opposition's campaign manager?"

Josh clamped his eyes closed and wagged his head before relenting to explain. "Reported everything that transpired to Darby. All of us had misgivings, based on having reduced Big Willie's lead in the last few days. Didn't overtake him or nothing like that—just narrowed the gap. Looked like the beginning of an upward trend. That's why we were concerned that if the Loren thing had been cooked, and we went public without proof positive, we'd come off as slanderers and blowhard idiots, assuring Hoke's victory on primary day."

Mike nodded to that rationale.

"Deciding to work it real careful like," Josh said, "we phoned Kenman and laid it out to him. The guy was speechless. After a few seconds he said he'd get back to us, and to please keep a lid on it until then, in deference to Senator Hoke, a fine man who didn't deserve that kind of shock or scandal. The next day he called to invite us to luncheon at Belmonde's, but only on the condition that everyone privy to the info attended. Hell yes, we had misgivings, knowing Kenman to be conniving and ruthless."

Mike snickered as he recalled the guy lying that he only invited Darby Williams.

140

"Relieved our angst," Josh said, "when Kenman claimed he'd discussed the matter with his candidate and they were prepared to withdraw from the primary, but only with absolute assurances that the scandal never gets aired. That blew our minds. Hell, it assured Darby's nomination—with beating Murdoch a slam-dunk."

"Why then didn't you attend ?"

"Minutes before leaving for Belmonde's we received a call from Len Brachter in Monroe. That good ole' boy said he'd corralled a couple of heavies who wanted to talk perks before committing the millions they had at their disposal. They intended to fly in within the hour. No way we dared neglect Kenman and his intent to concede the race. On the other hand we couldn't postpone a get-together with those contributors, considering that Hoke dropping out was still wishful thinking. Even if he did we still had a hard election campaign ahead and needed ever' dime we could get."

Josh compressed his lips and shook his head ruefully. "I stayed to entertain the visiting politicians, which saved my ass from getting blown away—while condemning Antwan who went in my place."

"I find it hard to believe," Mike said, "that people like Kenman and Boheemer have stooped to cold-blooded murder to advance their agendas."

"Take their backgrounds into account, Mike. When Kenman was a city prosecutor, with a chance to run for the state senate, his main backer, Judge Boris Pierny, ended up on the wrong end of a hit and run. While never proven, a whole bunch of folks suspected it was a cold-blooded murder."

When Mike shrugged concession to that, Josh reminded: "The two times Boheemer had opportunities his sponsors ended up dead. Both incidents were suspicious. So don't put it past either of those

141

slicksters to resort to homicide to further their careers. Hell, they'd been the victims of it."

When Mike hunched concession, Josh downed his drink. Nodding, he said: "That's the entire story."

"Now we need to connect the dots," Mike said, gazing contemplatively into the musical din. "We need to present irrefutable proof that Kenman engineered the assassination of those three notables."

Josh hung his head. "No way I can deny it's important to get to the bottom of this, for Darby's sake, for Jerome's sake, and Antwan's, who was a valued associate." Then he gazed sadly into the musical din. "Darby was a damned good man, who deserved to be the first black governor of Louisiana."

When Mike nodded, Josh reminded: "Hell, he was mayor when you investigated crooked cops here. You'd never made a case against them without his cooperation."

"Believe that I'm aware of that and grateful to Darby. I'm not questioning his credentials. My job is to present evidence the prosecutor can use to convict his killers."

"You're right, Mike. I was wrong not to expose that mess. Okay, count on me for any help you need. Solving that crime in cahoots with y'all will better serve me than getting spaced in this noisy dive."

Mike realized he'd gotten so entranced by the story he'd become oblivious to the clamorous vibrations of jazz. A different realization dismissed that. "Aren't you afraid of being killed—having the same information the others were murdered to hush?"

"Considered that probability, but I'm not going to get all het up over it. They come after me, they come after me. Isn't much I know to do to defend against professional killers."

"Man, you have to have some concern."

142

"Hell, I don't have idea one who they are. Doubtful I'd be aware of them if they occupied the next stool."

"Then you never sought police protection."

Snickering, Josh shook his head. "No telling whether some in the NOPD were involved with that hit, considering the depth of corruption in New Orleans."

"You got that right. But you need to consider protective custody."

"Not a chance, Mike. I'm not about to let any thing or any body cage me."

Shrugging acceptance, Mike patted his shoulder and said: "Take care, good buddy." He turned into the vibrations of frenetic music to head for the door.

#   #

Chapter Twenty-Nine

Mike wagged his head while trundling out of the saloon, trying to sort everything that buzzed in his brain. The thing finally made sense. But how do you prove it beyond a reasonable doubt?

He chuckled, momentarily diverted by the circus of sidewalk-revelers. It never ceased to amuse him to see milling tourists gawk at amateurish entertainers.

Many of those visitors were fascinated by craftspeople displaying an array of primitive products that ranged from paintings and sculptures to knitted goods and far-out garments as well as a variety of hand-made jewelry. Some of the wannabee artisans—longhaired and unwashed—many decorated with metal objects piercing parts of their bodies. More than a few had part or all of their upper torsos covered with garish tattoos.

He also found amusing the many spectators with their fists wrapped around large containers of beer—a staple in The Quarter referred to as a *big-ass beer*, and legal to tote around only in the streets of that area. More than a few yelled raucously while others jerked to the music that throbbed in frenetic waves from the surrounding watering holes, either unaware or unconcerned that competitive rhythms emanated from adjacent establishments.

Horse-drawn wagons clip-clopped down the street, their headway hampered by swarms of rubbernecking tourists wandering into the thoroughfares. Car horns of bumper-to-bumper traffic pierced the dissonance of human babble, amplifying the unbridled revelry.

Snickering at his surroundings, Mike slipped behind the wheel and tucked away his AG placard, relieved not to have gotten a ticket . . . not anxious for more contention with the locals. While starting the motor he noticed the time as a quarter to seven. Oh shit! He'd promised to meet Kaylee somewhere at seven.

He slapped his forehead as he remembered he'd told her he'd call her at five to tell her where. Oh, man, he faced the daunting task of explaining that he'd forgotten they'd planned to get together . . . for their first date. Oh, Lord, he hadn't even thought about a place to take her.

While nosing into traffic, he grimaced at the realization that his goof probably blew his chances with her. Dammit, he'd gotten a yearning for that gal, as well as the gumption to pursue her. Wagging his head, he cursed the slow headway in that choke of traffic exacerbated by throngs of celebrating pedestrians spilling into the road, oblivious to vehicles as well as to horse-drawn carriers clip-clopping along.

It took a few minutes to reach Saint Peter Street and hang a left, where traffic moved at a slightly better pace, despite it being narrowed by endless parked cars. But it headed away from the river, toward Rampart and out of the crowded Quarter. Memory prompted his eyes to dart to the rear-view mirror. No big-ass pick-up trucks or any kind of suspicious vehicle. He hoped he wasn't becoming paranoid.

Dammit, he scoured his brain for a way to explain to Kaylee what delayed him, without exposing all the information acquired. He finally had his hooks into a case and wasn't about to let the locals unravel it. True, it had confusing aspects, with none of it substantiated, but he still had no intention of letting it get leaked to the NOPD.

Not only didn't he trust them, but halfway suspected one or more of having a part in those assassinations. A gal that bright wouldn't let him get away with alluding to things. She'd quickly sniff out being stonewalled and sure as hell burst that infatuation-inflated balloon. Any hope of a relationship appeared to have withered on the vine.

Hell, he'd finally felt ready to pursue a gal, maybe even establish a relationship—after nearly two years of widowhood. And here he ruined the chance to start up with a gal who turned him on. Kaylee sure as hell fit the bill with respect to the female he wanted to be involved with. But he hesitated calling her, expecting her to be pissed and doubting she'll be receptive. And no, he wasn't about to share any of what he'd learned. So how does he explain not calling earlier?

Yes, he expected her to be loyal to her bunch. Cops are committed—have to be to do that job. But having investigated their locals, he didn't have a whole lot of faith in their not fouling up the investigation—inadvertently if not intentionally. Not that there weren't a lot of good cops on that force. Lieutenant Montrose certainly qualified as a dedicated law enforcement officer. O'Shea, however, as far as Mike was concerned, waited for the jury to report in.

Overall they suffered the problem of many major-city forces, of too many good cops failing to oppose or challenge the corrupt practices and misdeeds of the violators. The bad guys disregarded oaths to serve the public weal, concerned only with personal considerations or self-aggrandizement, as well as abusing authority to inflate ego.

More than a few sadists got away with pummeling people because other cops didn't want to contravene the blue-line credo by reporting the miscreants. Agh, so much for that bit of dogma, which didn't solve his dilemma.

Sucking up courage, he took out his cellphone and dialed. He held his breath while it rang. Then, after an icy hello, he said: "Hi, Kaylee. It's Mike."

Click! He flinched and shrunk into his shoulders. Okay, he didn't expect her to gush hospitality, so accepted that it wasn't going to

146

happen. However, he couldn't just quit on her . . . didn't want to. Sucking up another lungful of resolve he pushed redial.

When she answered he spoke quickly. "Give me a chance to explain how I got caught up in things. Just didn't—"

"Spare me the bull, Director Molino. Why didn't you simply straight-out tell me you'd rather not see me socially." Click!

Oh shit. He stared at the cellphone as he contemplated whether to subject himself to further abuse. Dammit, he had to work with her, be in her company every day. No question that he needed to make it right —and the sooner the better. Hell, he'd taken worse grief along the road of life, so grimaced and punched the redial button again.

"Hey!" he yelled when he heard her phone click off the hook, and without giving her time to speak. "At least let me explain before hanging up again."

"Explain what?"

"How I lost track of time while chasing my tail all over town trying to scrape up some semblance of direction to point this damn investigation. But I'm still drowning in a case where every damn clue leads to stagnation. You have to understand that, being as your bunch suffer the same damn malady."

"That's why you're calling two hours late?"

"Hey, I've been chasing down a whole lot of vague leads and—"

"Accomplishing what?"

He cringed, aware of the subdued interest in her voice. "Spinning my damn wheels. But I have to keep trying—don't have the right to throw up my hands and quit. You ought to understand being—"

"Okay, you're busy. Call me in a month or so when you have some free time."

"Hold on! Don't hang up!"

147

"Why the hell not?"

"Give me a break here, girl. I'm not running some kind of game at you."

"Fine. You're forgiven. Happy?"

"You're a cop and know what it's like. Hell, it's not too late to meet somewhere."

"For me it is. I showered and changed into something comfortable. Not in the mood to dress and contend with the hustle and bustle out there."

"Another time then. Please! I'll keep the next date, I promise."

Silence. He forced himself to breathe while waiting for a reply, but got only more silence. "Hello."

"Tell you what."

He sucked in breath, grateful for that note of possible reprieve. But long seconds elapsed before he heard her voice again. "Pick up a couple of sandwiches and a bottle of Muscadet and we'll dine here at my place."

"Muscadet?"

"That's what I like. You don't want to make any concessions, then forget about it."

"Hey—you want Muscadet, sweet darlin', you got Muscadet. Where the hell do you live anyway?" He held the phone between his shoulder and head as he jotted down the address, steering with his knees—a practice he'd condemn someone else doing.

#   #

Chapter Thirty

    Mike chafed at the realization that even the damned trolley clanked past him as he inched along Saint Charles Avenue. He grimaced concession to all the swank hotels and tony restaurants along both sides of the avenue as the reason for all that pedestrian and vehicular traffic.

    Finally he passed into a residential neighborhood, as upscale as the commercial, but the glut thinned a little. Checking numbers on the multi-family edifices interspersed amongst manses, he spotted her address on a modern three-story building. It had a colorful cloth awning sheltering its entranceway and more of the same covering balconies with iron railings on the second and third floors. Damned if he didn't wonder how a sergeant in the PD earned enough to live in the Garden District, in that level of luxury.

    Finding a place to park became a new quest, with every legal spot occupied. Passing the next cross street he pulled to the curb in front of the impressively steepled Episcopal Cathedral, with signs clearly prohibiting it. But he left his AG placard on the dashboard and hoped for the best.

    After being rung in, he entered into a wide courtyard, with a number of outside stairways to apartment balconies. Tired after a long day, he searched for the elevator, refusing to climb three flights, lugging two packages.

    Exiting onto the carpeted landing of the third floor and nodding approval of his surroundings, he sought and found her apartment. After ringing the bell he mused about the way this ole' gal lived, in digs high on the proverbial hog, but drove around in an inexpensive Chevy. Sure

149

made him wonder if she intended that car to conceal her extravagant lifestyle. When he thought about it, this lady had flair in an unpretentious way. Yeah, that's one of the things that attracted him.

He received another pleasant surprise when she answered the door, wearing silky blue pajamas, with her light brown hair let down and brushed out to soften and enhance her features. His lips pursed involuntarily into a silent whistle when she waved him into the beautifully appointed abode that could have been taken from the glossy pages of one of those decorating magazines.

She relieved him of one of his packages and led the way into the kitchen, where they placed both on an island dining counter. She beamed approval upon removing the two bottles of Muscadet from one of the bags—a generous touch. Then she expressed additional delight when she unwrapped the two sandwiches of crisply fried oysters with celeriac remoulade on French bread, accompanied by a side of onion straws with a honey-mustard dip.

He'd moved close behind her to gaze over her shoulder, hopeful and impatient for her sign of approval. She swiveled around, gently grasped his chin, and drew his head down to plant a light kiss on his mouth. Mike rocked back on his heels, stunned by that expression of gratitude. Damned if this gal didn't take a forthright approach to things.

She uncorked one of the bottles and poured the wine into two stemmed goblets already set out on the dining bar, along with decorative paper napkins and stylish stainless steel utensils. They clinked glasses and sipped. Then she gestured him to sit on one of the high stools as she pushed one sandwich to him and kept one for herself; centered the onion straws and dip between them.

And she wasted no time in biting into it, then groaned her delight.

"Guess I did good," he said.

"You did well enough to erase your earlier neglectful behavior."

"It wasn't neglectful. It—"

"Eat. No shoptalk. This is off-time."

He grinned, and did as instructed—savored the oysters and the wine. To stimulate conversation, he asked: "You a native—live in New Orleans all your life?"

She nodded. "Born in the Gentilly section."

He reached back in memory to recall that part of town as middle-class.

"And you?" she asked.

"Lake Charles—a lot of years ago when it was a country-bumpkin town."

After another bite, he commented: "Never before met anyone with your name."

"Result of a compromise. My mama wanted to name me after my grandma, and my daddy wanted to name me after his granddaddy. So they combined grandma's name, Kay, with granddaddy's name, Lee. Glad they didn't join it the other way."

Finished eating, Kaylee rinsed the dishes and silverware and placed them in the dishwasher. She sponged off the dining bar, then picked up her wine glass and the other bottle of Muscadet, which she had opened, and led the way into the living room.

Mike dutifully followed along with his goblet. She dropped down on the comfortable sofa and patted the pillow next to her. He didn't hesitate to sit beside her. And both sipped their wine. Mike fingered the lapel of her silky pajama blouse.

"You always entertain your men like this?"

"Only the ones I want to seduce."

She chuckled at his startled reaction. "I told you I'm not inhibited. I've always had the gumption to go after what I wanted."

151

She ran her silky hand down the side of his face, transmitting affection. His breath caught, but he forced himself not to tense or withdraw. He hadn't enjoyed those sensations with anybody except Arlene since the day he met her. He never wanted to.

But he knew he had to put the past to rest and not dwell on Arlene. A future had blossomed, and he needed to accept this new burst of joy.

Kaylee smiled kittenishly as she leaned into him, ran her hand under his chin and drew his head down until their lips met, gently and exploratory—steadily increasing in passion. Her boldness inspired him to slip his hand inside her pajama top and cup her breast. God, it had been so long. And he quivered as a new beginning blossomed.

#   #

Chapter Thirty-One

"You looking chipper this morning," Nelda said.

Mike stopped short as he entered the reception area, stunned.

"You looks like you found you some loving last night."

Mike sputtered but failed to find words of response, so waved offhandedly at her and continued on to his office, his face distorted by confusion. What in blue hell did she discern that prompted her to draw that conclusion. Did his skin or eyes mirror the song in his heart? He chuckled at realization of the probable cause.

"You grinning like a hound dog found meat on the bone," Armand said as he followed Mike into his office.

Mike's mouth moved but he vacillated sharing his revelation. He hoped Armand didn't linger so he could call Kaylee . . . had all he could do to contain himself during his drive to the office. But he'd refrained from doing it while driving, preferring to wait until he lounged in his swivel chair—undistracted and able to luxuriate in their intimacy.

"The locals located that blue delivery van used by those gunmen," Armand said.

Mike jerked to attention. "Really? How in hell'd you learn that? Don't tell me the locals shared that news."

"Not hardly. Chi Chi's been monitoring the police band and overheard a cruiser reporting spotting one under the Saint Claude Avenue Bridge that crosses the Inner Harbor Canal."

"Kudos to Chi Chi." Mike bounded out of his chair. "Let's get us a look at it before they tow it away."

"Hope you're taking me along?" Chi Chi said from the doorway,

153

having tagged along with Armand.

Mike stared at him while considerations swirled around in his brain. He pointed a finger at Chi Chi and instructed: "Team up with Nelda—who knows this city intimately—and follow us in a separate car. But keep a distance so the locals won't spot you, while remaining available if needed."

Armand drove the SUV, since he had more familiarity with the city, with respect to which streets would be less trafficked at that hour of the morning and allow them to make good time getting to their destination; eager to get there before the locals towed that vehicle away. Mike nodded approval of the other SUV following at a distance.

Armand tooled up North Peters for a block, before turning right on Bienville, a street flanked by older buildings, a few in the process of rehabilitation. Most reflected the devastation of Katrina and subsequent storms, as well as dereliction due to those residents lacking the funds for adequate maintenance.

They took Rampart east, into a shack-town of single-story shotgun houses mixed among two-storied rickety survivors of the past century. A few had been rehabilitated to some degree. Most looked decrepit. The cloud-blanketed sky added gloom to the depressing neighborhood.

Mike anguished at being delayed by traffic, a conglomeration of aged and battered vehicles, most of them commercial. All moved unhurriedly, worrying him that they wouldn't get there before the NOPD transported that van to their garage to comb it for clues. He knew damn well that bunch wasn't about to share with him . . . any more than he was with them.

After a number of cross streets Rampart became Saint Claude Avenue and angled through an area with many of the buildings boarded

154

up. Junky storefronts proliferated. Laundromats and check-cashing stores, interspersed with bars, convenience stores, luncheonettes, pawnshops, storefront churches, beauty parlors, and an occasional gas station with antiquated pumps; one with pumps removed and graffiti-covered plywood over what were once windows and a door.

Approaching the steel girder bridge that crossed the Inner Harbor Canal, they passed a partially boarded-up store with the word SUPERMARKET crudely painted above its rickety door. Armand drove past it and down a ramp alongside the bridge, with weathered houses lining the other side of the ramp .

At the underside of the bridge Armand pulled up behind an unmarked black Impala parked alongside a police cruiser. Ahead of them, in a dead-end, they spotted the blue delivery van abandoned behind a burnt out vehicle.

Mike accompanied Armand in greeting Patty O'Shea, who ambled around from the front of the unmarked black sedan. "What the hell you two doing here?" O'Shea asked. "But then, I doubt you'll admit to tapping the city's police band."

Armand chuckled. "A friendly pelican dropped the news on us that y'all found that blue delivery truck around here."

"A shame it is," O'Shea responded, "that the bugger hadn't dropped a bit more on you. That aside, let's hope Shayde doesn't hear that you learned about it and blow the little cool he's got left."

"And you?" Mike asked. "It doesn't bother you to have us horning in?"

"I've no objection, laddie, to a cop doing his job. On the other side of the coin, it wouldn't surprise me a bit if one of those at the station house had a mind to take out a certain chief investigator of the AG's office."

155

"You one of them?" Mike asked. His mind flashed back to the pick-up truck with that killer bumper, then to the dusty one that followed him briefly. For the thousandth time he considered sharing those experiences with Armand.

"Not so long as you're not on my case, which is doubtful, seeing as how I avoid giving any reason to the rat squad to scrutinize me."

"Keep working with a clean slate, the way you have," Armand said, "and you'll never worry about being the subject of investigation. What's the story here?"

O'Shea gestured to the blue vehicle. "One of the boyos in the cruisers spotted the damned thing and called it in."

"Has it been examined yet?" Mike asked.

"Haven't had half a chance," O'Shea said. "Got here only a minute or so before you. Chatted a bit with the uniforms who found the thing—dumped here yesterday according to a couple of the home boys."

"And only discovered today?" Mike asked, his voice vibrating with incredulity.

"This isn't exactly a neighborhood cops pick to coop in, laddie."

"I'd think you'd have had the cruisers searching everywhere for that thing," Mike said, "considering you had little else to go on."

"You suggesting we don't do our job?" O'Shea asked.

"No, he's not, Patty," Armand said. "Mike's as upset as you and I for failing to make any progress in finding those killers. We're all frustrated."

"Well, laddie," O'Shea growled, "don't harbor too much hope that it'll reveal anything useful. Like as not, that bunch cleaned that truck proper like."

"Still," Mike said, "there might be something telltale in it."

"It'll be examined by CSU people after taken to the garage,"

156

O'Shea said. "We'd rather no one rummages about in it and contaminate any evidence that might be there."

"Which findings," Armand said, "you'll share with us."

"That's up to District Commander Shayde. Suck up to Lieutenant Montrose and you might get lucky."

"Those uniforms canvas the area?" Mike asked.

"Aye, and encouraged two homies hanging about to admit being fearful of messing with it because some tough goes by the name of Jamie Blue Boy claimed it as his. After a bit of pressure those lads admitted that more than likely we'd find Jamie Blue Boy hanging around that store up on the corner, which is where I was planning to go when you two arrived. Care to accompany me?"

Mike and Armand nodded as they turned up their jacket collars against the onset of a light drizzle.

\#   \#

157

Chapter Thirty-Two

Mike hunched against the weather while trudging along with Armand and O'Shea up the hill then around to the side of the partially boarded-up market on the corner. They approached four young men huddled under the overhang of its eave.

They leaned against sheets of plywood covering what once was a plate glass window. O'Shea pointed out the chap in the red knit hat as the one described to him as Jamie Blue Boy.

The four young men straightened up, spooked by the approach of three men in suits and ties . . . appeared ready to scatter.

"The first of you runs," O'Shea called to them as he brandished his Glock, a large semi-automatic pistol, "will get two or three slugs up your asses."

The four young men cowered against the graffiti-covered plywood, blinking indecision while glancing to each other for direction, uncertainty flickering in their eyes. They glowered at the cops.

Mike flashed his credentials, annoyed that O'Shea hadn't identified himself. Of course, the homies made them for cops, but procedure and the Supreme Court required they make that known.

"Only one of y'all we're interested in," Armand said, "is Jamie Blue Boy."

"Who?" the young man with the red knit hat asked. He and the others stared blankly at the questioners then at each other.

"You know who you are," Mike said, gesturing to his red knit hat, "and know who we are—and know goddam well we know who you are."

158

"Aye, James," O'Shea said, "t'is yourself we've a need to converse with." He shooed the others away with a wave of his gun.

They shuffled about, reluctant to separate. But after Jamie Blue Boy nodded consent they tromped off into the drizzle—glancing back at intervals but never faltering in distancing themselves from the fuzz.

"What y'all want to rap with my po' ass about?"

Mike snickered at his surly attitude and his bobbing his head side-to-side to affect bravado, the tough-guy act to mask trepidation.

"Listen carefully," O'Shea said as he holstered his pistol, "for I'm only going to explain the ground rules this one time." His forced grin conveyed nothing of friendliness as he waved his big fist in the youth's face. "We're after asking you a number of questions, and any time we think you're not being truthful I'm going to plant this in your ugly puss."

The young man's eyes bulged as they focused on his huge knuckles.

"So don't lie too often," O'Shea said, "or your friends won't recognize you thereafter. Nor will you have a pleasing appearance to attract the prettiest lassies."

Jamie Blue Boy hunched against the plywood, his posturing less truculent.

"It's that blue delivery truck you've staked out as your own," O'Shea said. "Tell us all about its coming to be parked there and you won't have a bit more to do with us."

"One of the homies found that bucket, man. I ain't got thing one to do with it."

O'Shea's fist smashed into Jamie's face. The young man bounced off the graffiti-covered plywood boards and staggered as he struggled to stay on his feet. Blood oozed from his lower lip.

159

Mike jerked erect, having never expected the detective to actually get violent. He'd thought O'Shea's threats were meant to scare the young man into cooperating.

"I'm going to ask that question again," O'Shea said, his fist inches from the young man's face.

"Let's not leave ourselves open to brutality charges," Mike said as he shouldered between O'Shea and a cowering Jamie Blue Boy.

O'Shea snickered. "Sure and I'm glad I don't work for the likes of you, Mary."

Mike ignored the remark as he addressed Jamie Blue Boy. "You want to save yourself an ass whupping, you'll tell us every damn thing you know about that van."

Jamie shook his head, as if he didn't understand, his eyes still blank. He spit a blob of blood.

"Oh there's a pile of shit," O'Shea said, waving his fist as he tried to shoulder past Mike. But Mike blocked him from executing the blow.

"Get smart," Mike growled at the youth, "before you get your face smashed." Jamie's smirk induced Mike to scowl before stepping aside and joining Armand under the eave to escape the drizzle.

O'Shea brandished that cocked fist, a grin on his meaty face. Jamie drew back against the plywood. "Yo, man, I gets worse if I rats out my boys."

"Our only concern," Armand said, "is about the people that abandoned that van. Your boys can't get in trouble for that."

"Don't take too much time deciding whether to comply," O'Shea said, his fist inches from the youth's face.

"Yo, man, I wasn't the one spotted it."

"Tell us who did," Armand said. "Then tell us why you staked it

160

out for yourself, like your aces claimed."

"Which one of them fools been blabbing their damn mouth?" Jamie demanded.

"Now I'm running out of patience, boy," O'Shea growled. He tapped his fist against the youth's cheekbone.

"Was Jackarando, man. Jackarando found that bucket."

"Then why isn't he hanging about?" Mike asked.

"Jackarando told me to keep anybody from taking it or any of its parts. Said he'd get it painted so we could sell it and split whatever we got for it."

"Then why are you loitering nearly a block away?" O'Shea asked.

"Man, my ass got bored hanging around there baby-sitting that raggedy-assed bucket, so I made a deal with two homies to guard it for a split of my take."

"Enterprising," Armand said, chuckling.

"Bullshit," O'Shea said as he cocked his fist. "I'm giving you half a minute to concoct a better story than that."

"That's the damn truth, dog. Knocking out my damn teeth ain't gonna' change one damn thing."

"Where can we find this Jackarando?" Mike asked.

Jamie waved his arms. "He roams, man . . . taking care of business in the 'hood."

"You know well as I do," Armand said, "his boys know where to contact him."

"Jackarando got him a whole lot going. Hard to say where he be at this minute. That the damn truth."

"Not only do I want to know where to find him," O'Shea growled, "but I want a really good description of him. It's that or you

161

end up with a broken face."

"Jackarando a badass. You knows him when you sees him. He bad as he is big, dog."

"Call me that again," O'Shea growled, "and I'll be after breaking your face."

"Okay, man, no offense. Just trying to explain how that cat big —did some boxing—can whup my ass. I sure ain't looking to be messing with him."

"Real smart," Mike said. "Mess with Sergeant O'Shea instead."

The Irishman grinned, savoring the prospect of battering the youth. Jamie tried to back away but the plywood restricted his movements. He held his hands in front of his face, his eyes imploring the burly detective. "I swear, man, I ain't got clue one where that cat be at this moment. My man in the 'hood somewhere, roaming 'cause he got him a whole lot of shit going."

"Give us a description of that badass," O'Shea said. "And I do mean a good one."

"He big, man, and wearing one of them wooly African caps. You know, man, a whole bunch of colors like Rastas and folks wear. Oh, yeah! My man got him a badass black leather jacket that is boss, with straps on the shoulders like soldiers has."

O'Shea waved Mike and Armand to accompany him down the ramp. "I'll radio those that patrol this area to be on the lookout for that so-called badass."

"Gonna' get some gum," Armand said as he headed for the market door. He lingered inside until O'Shea had gotten beyond hearing range before he called Nelda on his cellphone and explained who and what to look for.

#   #

162

Chapter Thirty-Three

Nelda scrutinized her surroundings, her face grim with determination as she U-turned and drove back up Saint Claude, the windshield wipers swiping away the light rain. She compressed her lips to suppress revealing pride for having been anointed to collar the quarry . . . by the Director of the Investigation Division.

Hunched forward over the wheel, she examined the few young men and the one female they passed. Chi Chi also scrutinized those hurrying along the broken sidewalk with their necks pulled into their shoulders against the drizzle.

Some took shelter in doorways of ramshackle buildings. A few of those puffed on cigarettes. Occasionally two or three shared one, savoring it to the smallest butt.

Nelda scoffed but otherwise ignored them, having no intentions of wasting time on weed-heads, or any other damn thing to distract her. Yes, Lord, she'd locate that badass and prove that Nelda Washington can be depended upon—yes, and that women cops are as capable as men.

"Why don't we question some of these studs?" Chi Chi asked. "One of them might know the whereabouts of this Jackarando."

"That's what I'm talking about," Nelda said, sucking her teeth in criticism. "You brag-assing about growing up in yo' barrio, but didn't learn shit in that Bronx except to waste your damn time grilling innocent residents."

"They're homies, woman."

"Man, they don't know no more about where that badass is than

163

you do."

"What are you talking about? You think homies don't know their turf?"

"Look to me like a pack of unemployed po'asses with nothing better to do than mope around in the damn rain . . . without the brains to get out of it."

"So who we looking for?"

"Some one of them simple-ass gangbangers able to impart useful damn info."

She slowed as they approached a Laundromat partially boarded up with plywood dabbed in colorful graffiti murals. She inched up on two guys snuggling close to the limited overhang of the eave for protection from the rain.

"That's what I'm talking about," Nelda said. "See they has those bandanas hanging from their belts."

Chi Chi blinked realization. "Gang ID."

"You do recognize badasses. Yes, Lord, those cats swaggers when they walks, believes they bad, and knows everybody else in the 'hood who's bad."

Smugness twisting her face, Nelda parked. She and Chi Chi climbed out to see the two young men start to hurry off in opposite directions. "Hold up!" Chi Chi commanded as he grabbed the one that passed closest to him. But the big guy spun around and wrapped Chi Chi up in his muscular arms, wrestled him around and thrust him against the building before turning to flee.

Nelda abandoned pursuing the other guy to aid her partner. She thrust a foot between the husky guy's sneakers, tripping him to flop on his belly and splash water up from the wet sidewalk. He tried to scramble back to his feet, but Nelda kicked his legs out from under him.

"Stay down, you simple ass," Nelda growled, flashing her shield. "We the po-lice."

He ignored her as he struggled to push himself up from the pavement. Nelda kicked one of his arms out and he flopped onto the trash-littered and rain-soaked cement again.

Chi Chi lurched over to the prone guy and kneeled on his back, mashing the hump into the moisture while twisting his arms behind him. After a moment of futile struggling, he squealed: "Okay, bro', y'all hurtin' my ass."

Nelda pulled Chi Chi off him, then took the mook's arm to help him up. He slipped on the wet concrete, struggled to stabilize himself. Nelda slammed him face-first against the building.

"Hey! Y'all hurtin' my ass."

"Yeah, baby," Nelda said, "but it 'bout to get worse less you tell me the damn truth as to where I can locate Jackarando."

"How the hell I know," the guy said, his face contorted in pain.

Nelda twisted his arm and again mashed his face against the building. He screeched. "Talk, fool!" she commanded. "And best you don't 'diss me with no lies, or I will break both yo' damn arms."

"My man hanging at that luncheonette on North Clairbourne near Desire."

"How I know you not bullshitting me, fool?"

"No jive, mama. It the damn truth. Hear what I say? I left main man ten minutes ago rapping with he aces."

Nelda released him. "We don't find yo' main man where you telling us, we coming back to find and bust yo' ass for assaulting a po-lice officer."

Then she waved Chi Chi back to the car. He climbed in while swiping the rainwater off his face and watched her zip down one street

165

and up another.

"Damn, mama, you bad."

"Best you learn to be just as bad 'fore you gets yo' ass whupped."

"Cat took me by surprise."

"You needs to anticipate to prevent street mutts kicking yo' ass."

#   #

Chapter Thirty-Four

Nelda slowed as she turned onto North Clairborne, a street flanked by ratty shotgun houses in disrepair, like all the other streets in that area. She parked across the street from a shabby luncheonette alongside a small warehouse with a rickety overhead door, and directed ChiChi's attention to four men huddled under the narrow overhang outside of that seedy eatery.

"Take the right side. I'll take the left. That dude in the leather jacket with epaulets and wearing that colorful cap, is our man. Let the others book if they wants."

As he unlatched the door to climb out, she scored him with: "Use some damn smarts this time."

He averted his eyes while nodding.

She drew her Glock semi-automatic after getting out of the car and held it against her side to conceal it in the folds of her raincoat as she crossed the street. Glancing to her right, she made sure Chi Chi covered that position.

And she permitted herself a grin when she saw that he kept his right arm pressed against his plastic slicker, gratified that Big Apple cops had as much street smarts as those in the Big Easy.

The four young men became attentive to the approaching bureaucrats and tensed to split. Nelda raised her piece. "Any one of you dumb asses moves, I'll blow away your damn manhood." She held her shield out in front of her with her other hand. "Just so y'all know, we the po-lice."

They stared dumbly at her, then at Chi Chi, who also aimed a pistol at them. Stymied, they shrunk back against the wall.

"Onliest one of you I wants to rap with is Jackarando," Nelda said. "The others got yo'selves traveling papers."

They shuffled in place, shrugging to each other and staring blankly at the black pistols with their seventeen round magazines chambered with forty caliber bullets. She sniggered as she addressed one of them. "You always wear that rastaman cap, believing it makes yo' sorry ass look bad?"

The subject scowled objection to the uncomplimentary question. When he projected disdain for the weapon, Nelda sniggered at his bravado. "Where you get that badass jacket, Jackarando?"

Accepting he'd been identified, he forced a grin. "I yo' man, sista'. Can be yo' daddy. What you wants?"

"Show some damn respect, fool, 'fore I puts a bullet in yo' ugly ass." She waved her weapon at the others. "Walk while y'all able."

They shuffled in place for a few seconds, until Jackarando bobbed his head , after which they split, hunched against the light rain. Nelda and Chi Chi cuffed the surly young man, ignoring his objections and demands for an explanation. They shoved him into the back seat of their SUV. Nelda got behind the wheel, with Chi Chi beside her.

He called Mike on his cellphone. "Hey, boss. Collared the mark. Sure thing, we'll meet at Saint Claude and Congress."

"What this about?" Jackarando demanded, sitting awkwardly, with his hands cuffed behind him. But they ignored him while turning up one street and down another.

Arriving at their destination, they pulled to the curb. Chi Chi climbed out, opened the rear door and pulled Jackarando out. Nelda joined them in standing next to a light pole near a weathered two-storied frame building that tilted from age and neglect.

168

"Why we doesn't stay in the damn car instead of hanging in the damn rain?" Jackarando grouched.

Nelda and Chi Chi ignored him as they searched up and down the street. A minute later they waved over the black SUV. Mike and Armand climbed out, their suit collars turned up against the rain, which increased in velocity.

"You got you a badass name, homie," Mike addressed the scowling prisoner.

"And a badass cap," Armand said, hunching against the decreasing temperature.

"Why in hell we standing in the damn rain?" Jackarando demanded, glaring at Armand and Mike. Water rilled down his face.

Nelda prodded him with an elbow in his side. "These men want to know how you came by a name like that."

"My daddy give it to me." He sneered and rolled his shoulders defiantly.

"Isn't every father names his big strapping boy like that," Armand said as he swiped rainwater from his glasses while pushing them back up on his nose. Then he obeyed Mike's gesture to bring the hood along with them into the partial shelter provided by the lee side of the derelict house.

Jackarando bobbed his head in appreciation of getting out of the downpour. "My daddy a longshoreman and say the most bad cat on the docks called Jackarando."

"That why he gave you that name?" Nelda asked.

"Nobody, but nobody," Jackarando said, "mess with that dude. Even white folks walk careful around him. And that back in the days when white folks mess with black folks whenever they wants. So my daddy name me Jackarando so nobody mess with me."

169

"Smart man," Mike said. "And I'll bet he had the good sense to cooperate with the police whenever they asked him for information."

Jackarando dipped his shoulders in a noncommittal gesture.

"You answer our questions honestly," Armand said, "and we going to let you go about your business."

"You don't," Nelda said, "we going to find a reason to drop yo' ass in a jail cell."

"What y'all want to know?"

"Who abandoned that blue delivery van under the bridge?" Mike asked.

"Shi-it. Y'all mess with me, chase my boys' asses away, cuffs my ass, then makes me stand in the damn rain—and that's all you shaking me for."

"That's it," Mike said.

"Some ginny boys left it there, man."

"Be more specific," Armand said. He again wiped rain dapples from his glasses before pushing them up on the bridge of his nose.

"Two ginny boys drove it there," Jackarando said, "late yesterday."

"And just walked away?" Nelda asked cynically.

"Two other ginny boys in a black Buick picked them first ginny boys up. Seeing those ginny boys drive off in that big-ass Buick you knew damn well they wasn't coming back. So I staked that sucker out for my damn self."

"Describe them," Mike said.

"You know, man, ginny boys."

"Were they tall, short, skinny, fat?" Nelda asked.

Jackarando rolled back his eyes to scour memory. "One was tall. He one of them came in that big-ass Buick, but not the driver.

170

Sucker wore glasses."

"Describe the others," Mike said.

"All them ginny boys was hefty, but one looked like he ate him a whole lot more spaghetti than the others."

"What makes you think they were ginny boys?" Mike asked, his eyes boring into the homie to discern every expression—identification being essential.

"Man, I'm wise to the difference between ginny boys and micks, or ginny boys and Polacks, or ginny boys and spics. They sho' wasn't brothers."

"Try using a less offense way of referring to people," Nelda said. "They have a way of describing yo' sorry ass you wouldn't like."

"Don't bother me none," Jackarando said, "like it do my man here." He dipped his head toward Mike. "I'll call y'all Eye-talians if that make you feel better."

"I'm not Italian," Mike said.

"Damn! You fooled me. I thought you was a ginny boy."

Mike exchanged glances with Armand; both expressing disappointment in the reliability of Jackarando's identifications. Mike then instructed Nelda and Chi Chi to return to where they waited before, in case they're needed again.

To Armand he said, "Let's get back to the van and see if there's anything there more informative than what this mook has to offer."

Nelda uncuffed Jacarando, then joined Chi Chi in the car. Jackarando glowered at the two cars driving away and abandoning him in that remote place in the rain.

#

"We're not certain," Mike groused, "if the assassins were Italian or Russian, based on the crude descriptions of Jackarando."

171

Armand looked askance at him. "What makes you think they're Russian?"

"Met yesterday with Knuth, who fed me a theory that suggests Russians were the assassins—or, at least, benefited from it. Later I hashed it all out with Josh Bigelow, Darby Williams' campaign manager who backed up much of what Knuth fed me."

"Glad you shared that." Resentment edged Armand's voice.

"Didn't have a chance this morning. Before I even poured a cup of coffee you surprised me with the news about finding that van."

"How 'bout during that drive to the bridge?"

"Caught up in the anticipation of learning something from that vehicle. Besides, I'm not all that eager to spread the word, good buddy. It's complicated and involves Big Willie's boy, Loren. Can't let that howling cat out of the bag until we verify it to prevent running afoul of Big Willie and getting snake-bit."

"Hear you, but I'd be a sight happier if you kept me in the loop."

#   #

Chapter Thirty-Five

"You're a helluva lady, and one damned good cop," Chi Chi said as Nelda U-turned their car. "Look my way any time you want a partner."

"Thanks, man. It hasn't been easy. Some guy cops are still skeptical of gal cops, like we can't hold our own or something."

"You ain't alone, sister. Whitey still ain't comfortable with those who ain't. Don't let it get you down."

"It doesn't anymore. But I had to prove myself in the cop world."

"No question that you succeeded."

"Yeah, man, the hard way. I got forty-three hard years on this black ass. Coming from a poor family back in Fredericksburg, Virginia made my damn hill higher and harder to climb."

"When'd you get on the cops?"

"Went into the army when I finished high school. No way my family could afford to send me to college, even if I'd had something like that in mind."

"You wasn't the only one was poor, sister."

"After two years in the Quartermaster Corps I transferred to the MPs. Knew I wanted to be a cop, even back then. Lord, it took doing to get accepted in those days."

"How'd you end up here, with the AG's office, in New Orleans?"

"Was stationed near here when I left the army after eight years. Got accepted by the NOPD because those folks was hungry for blacks as

173

well as women back then. Being both and having that MP experience got me accepted . . . damn near recruited."

"You left the New Orleans force?"

"Had me a yearning to be a detective. But getting plainclothes duty damn near turned me off. Man, I didn't dig those stings in vice or narcotics. And believe I resented serving in vice, where I had to pretend to be a damn whore."

"Always wondered if that was demeaning."

"Believe it. Besides, I don't condone entrapment. The rotten-ass brass didn't give me any hope that I'd get my shield all that soon, in spite of the busts. So when Armand recruited me, I jumped at the opportunity."

She chuckled ruefully. "Yes, Lord, I yearned for dignity and to be with folks who wanted me around. Been divorced twelve years now and don't have no other family hereabouts."

"What happened to your old man?"

"He didn't have enough sense to bring his parts home without sharing them with every skirt along the way. Fool never learned the word: fidelity."

"What kind of work did he do?"

"A tough-ass drill instructor—one hell of a soldier."

"Just not a husband though, hunh? Like me. Gotta' admit I was pitiful."

"Meaning you sneaked around and cheated on your wife."

"Getting a little strange occasionally didn't seem like cheating or nothing."

"Shi-it. She'd strayed, you'd have had a damned conniption."

Chi Chi shrugged and gazed out the window, didn't respond.

Nelda read his face and changed the subject. "What drove you

174

to wear blue?"

"Power, man. Ain't every Puerto Rican got a legal right to wear heat."

"So you saying it bites your ass to be a minority. What are Puerto Ricans anyway . . . white, black, or otherwise? You'd never convince me you're not a person of color—got you something mixed up in there with that Spanish blood . . . or Irish . . . or one."

"In New York there are three races: white, black, and Puerto Rican. That last classification has nothing to do with being white, black, or any shade in between. If you or your parents came from that Caribbean island you in a class by yourself. And it ain't complimentary —not in the damn Apple anyway."

"Where a Puerto Rican boy get an Irish name?"

"My grandfather, an Irish seaman, jumped ship in Puerto Rico. The other ancestors are from Spain, with some dark blood mixed in. But you can see that."

"And the establishment keeps bullshitting us that prejudice is dead in America." Nelda chuckled as she flagged her head in criticism.

"We elected Obama," Chi Chi reminded.

"Praise the Lord. But we need to make more progress."

"Whatever we are racially," Chi Chi said, "we have to be somebody, do something with our lives so we can have pride. I chose to be a cop. Okay, no denying I dig the authority. But it makes me proud to help protect society."

"I know, man. Me too."

#   #

175

Chapter Thirty-Six

Mike's brow wrinkled upon spotting two additional unmarked cars when Armand drove down the ramp alongside the bridge. They parked behind them just as Lieutenant Jesse Montrose got out of one, along with two white detectives. Kaylee Boyle and a black detective climbed out of the other.

All wore slickers and rain hats and hunched into that raingear, as much against the chill as the precipitation.

Mike and Armand joined them at the flatbed truck where two men in coveralls attached chains from their winch to the blue van in preparation of loading it for transport to the police garage to sweep for evidence. Everyone nodded salutations to each other. Mike winced and shrunk into his collar when Kaylee cut cold eyes at him.

Oh shit! He never got around to calling her—with things popping all morning. Females expected to be called the morning after, especially after the first time, and after a melding of personas as torrid as they had.

"What are you folks doing here?" Montrose asked.

"They've likely hacked into police bands," O'Shea said. "But they're wasting their time as much as we are. Those assassins, no amateurs, like as not carefully cleaned that vehicle of all prints and any other clues to their identity."

Mike and Armand hunched their shoulders, their suit collars pulled up. Mike glanced at Kaylee, who'd averted her eyes. He grimaced as he accepted that this wasn't the time to explain that he'd intended to call her but got caught up in this business.

176

"Care to share a bit of what you've learned while cruising, with regard to locating that Jackarando?" O'Shea asked.

When Armand shrugged, O'Shea chuckled. "You two been driving around with your windows open?"

"Sure looks like they been standing in the rain," the black detective said.

Lieutenant Montrose trained narrowed eyes on Mike and Armand. "True, you didn't learn anything?"

"No more than Patty, here," Armand said.

"We got out to interrogate a few homies along the way," Mike said, "hoping someone would give us a heads-up."

"You mightn't have had to, Mister Holier-Than-Thou," O'Shea retorted, "if you hadn't blocked me from leaning on that skel."

"Be thankful I don't write you up," Mike growled.

"What exactly does that mean?" Lieutenant Montrose demanded.

"I don't condone brutality," Mike said.

Montrose peered questioningly at O'Shea. The big Irishman grinned and said, "I shook a mook, is all."

"This something needs to be written up?" Montrose asked Mike.

"Let's leave it alone," Mike said. He gestured to Armand and they climbed back in their car. As he did so he glanced to Kaylee, who'd turned her back to him. Okay, he'd call her later and somehow make up for his negligence. Dammit! He intended to call her . . . actually began to compose what he's say while driving back to his hotel last night. Yeah, he should've called her before leaving the hotel this morning instead of waiting until he got to the office.

"Glad you didn't pursue that business with O'Shea," Armand said while driving up the ramp. "He pushes the envelope occasionally,

177

but he's a good cop."

"Cops don't have a right to batter citizens."

"Can't deny that Patty is a thumper, but ask anybody and they'll tell you he's the guy volunteers to give blood when a cop is hurt. And he's the first guy through the door when taking out bad guys."

"He's also the bully gives law enforcement officers a bad name," Mike said.

#   #

Chapter Thirty-Seven

Mike strained not to yawn as he sat at the conference table with the other investigators, bushed after a few grueling days that hadn't yielded any appreciable results. Days hell! He hadn't enjoyed any real respite for the past six months or more, since he started on that drug case in Shreveport, which followed on the heels of a state-wide stock-investment swindle. Before that it was bank robbers, following on the heels of breaking up a ring of counterfeiters, which followed other cases, ad infinitum.

To top it off, he blundered into the debacle of his career, and returned to Baton Rouge with his tail between his legs because of a really dumb screw-up. Jace exiled him to this steamy city to unravel a mystery the locals failed to, in spite of having the benefit of home turf and a lot more manpower. But he needed to succeed to earn exoneration.

However, it being Friday, he hoped to spend some free time with Kaylee. God, that infusion of joy a couple days ago brought a smile to his being, ending a procession of gloomy months. How 'bout years?

But he hadn't gotten her on the phone, though he tried numerous times yesterday and today. Okay, she was being cantankerous by ignoring his calls when his name appeared on the ID screen. And she hadn't returned any of the messages he'd left.

Shaking those thoughts out of his head, he addressed his people. "I'm going to share information with you that cannot be divulged until we substantiate it. Those assassins went there by prearrangement to eliminate three men to prevent them from embarrassing Big Willie."

His minions stared quizzically at him, disbelieving he made that statement about something so obvious. Did he think they were stupid? But their jaws dropped when Mike related what he'd gleaned from Edmund Knuth, then Josh Bigelow.

"But you can't repeat any of this until we obtain proof positive," he cautioned, "or have Big Willie on our case. Nor do we need the locals leaking it."

"Problem with Knuth's premise," Armand said, "is that the Russians targeted Sessy, not Williams. But Kenman admitted inviting Williams to meet him there but denies inviting Sessy."

"Agreed," Mike said. "Besides, Josh Bigelow's explanation eliminates the Russians."

"While still implicating Kenman," Gustave said.

"That the reason," Nelda said, "we needs to take a magnifying glass to Mister Whitebread and his homies."

"And dig until we prove he engineered that desperate act," Julie added.

"We should have been shadowing his ass," Nelda said, "so we'd be there when he paid off those goons—giving us that proof positive."

"Nelda's got a point," Gustave said as he stroked his beard thoughtfully. "We really should have considered that and tapped his phones."

Armand snickered. "Doubtful we'd find a judge in this town with the courage to sign a court order to tap Kenman's phones."

"And don't dare do it without official sanction," Mike added.

"That's the problem, right there," Julie said, staring intently at the wall. "Kenman is a political powerhouse, not only in this city, but in the whole damn state, backed by Big Willie. We'd be biting off a whole bunch more than we'd be able to swallow."

"That's what I'm talking about," Nelda said. "Kenman about one slick cat. My man playing a bunch of ends against the middle."

"Kenman set up the meeting and profited by it," Armand said, "whether or not he used Russians or Italians to prevent Loren Hoke's antics from scandalizing his father."

"Willis Hoke has a long history as a moral person," Gustave said. "Sure he's ambitious, but I know enough about that man to believe he'd never condone anything like that, even to attain his ambition of getting to the governor's mansion."

"Good and well as that sounds," Julie said, "Big Willie gains more than anybody else in the state from that triple killing."

"As well he stands to lose more," Nelda said, "if that kind of dirt about his family gets out."

"I believe," Mike said, "it was done without his approbation."

"Second that," Armand said while pushing his glasses up. "Doubtful he'd react that desperately to the threat of scandal, being as humiliation isn't exactly a revelation in any part of Lu'ziana."

Gustave chortled while nodding. "Quite a few notables have had to weather such storms."

"Nobody, but nobody," Nelda said, chuckling, "did it better than ole' Kingfish."

"Big Willie," Mike said, "can always relinquish being a primary contender without losing his standing as a kingpin in state government."

"But Kenman might not remain a mover-and-shaker," Armand said. "This is his chance to grab the gold ring and become a political star and a king-maker."

"Always gets back to Kenman," Mike said.

"Perhaps," Gustave said while contemplatively stroking his beard, "it serves our purpose to have an in-depth conversation with the senator."

"Not our best option," Armand said. "We go off half-cocked and piss that man off, we'll end up with a whole lot of hostility backed by heavy political muscle."

"Plus an iron wall," Mike said, "bolstered by his political brethren as well as by folks of the NOPD."

"And," Armand said to Mike, "he'd put your ass in the proverbial sling—given that Shreveport debacle."

Gustave nodded. "We'd be best to back off until we have substantial evidence."

"Okay," Mike growled, "let's suspend the postmortems until Monday. Armand and I will pay a call on Brent Kenman this afternoon to rattle his cage. You people clean up as much peripheral work as possible before breaking for the weekend."

#   #

Chapter Thirty-Eight

Mike and Armand grinned lasciviously when Kenman's slinky receptionist waved them to seats in the ante office, close enough to her desk to savor her eau de cologne.

"We got lucky," Armand whispered while feasting on her delightful parts, "not to have Kaylee here to censure us."

Mike chuckled, pretending to share that amusement. He hadn't confided in Armand that he'd connected romantically and intimately with her . . . nor about her unwillingness to forgive him for failing to call her the morning after. No, he wasn't ready to divulge his relationship nor his frustrations with that cantankerous gal.

It didn't take a psychologist to judge her as aggressive and dogged. Doubt that anybody ever misjudged her of being reticent or demure. No sir, that ole' gal didn't figure to back off and probably didn't forgive slights. So maybe expecting to take the relationship to that pinnacle might have been a mistake.

He and Armand hunched acceptance of foregoing further ogling when after only a few minutes they were ushered into the richly appointed office of Brent Kenman. Both paused at the door with raised brows at sight of District Commander Sebastian Shayde and Kaylee Boyle, along with chubby Nicky Boheemer with his hangdog look.

Everyone greeted each other desultorily, though none of the four already there rose from their seats. Mike and Armand remained standing; hadn't been invited to sit. The lack of chairs to accommodate them didn't diminish the slight.

"Whatever brings y'all back?" Kenman asked.

"A friendly chat," Mike said, "with you."

Kenman gestured to those around him. "I've no secrets from these folks."

"Y'all interrupting," Captain Shayde said, "so say what's on your mind and get on your way. The less we suffer the presence of Molino the cop-basher, the happier I'll be."

Mike ignored that and addressed Kenman. "Our purpose in coming is to discuss in greater depth how all those bullets failed to blow your head off."

"That's blasphemous," Shayde barked, half rising out of his seat.

Kenman held up a hand to signal his intent to speak for himself. "I remind Director Molino he, not I, is the target of scandal."

"Expect your Shreveport impropriety," Captain Shayde said, "to be aired in the newspapers every damn day."

"And talked to death on radio and TV," Boheemer added.

"Those charges have not been substantiated," Armand said.

"He made his bed," Boheemer added, sniggering. "And slept in it with Melody."

Anger etched lines in Mike's face as he balled his fist. But Armand grasped his arm while admonishing them. "You folks obviously don't care whether he actually was dirty, but only in discrediting him publicly in case he uncovers evidence of any of you having as little as a pinky in that mass murder."

"Where in hell you come off saying anything like that?" Shayde demanded. "There not a shred of evidence even suggesting like that."

"Sure as hell defies credibility," Armand said, "that guys who quickly and calmly slaughtered three men missed the aforenamed mark standing directly in front of them. After clearly and loudly announcing intent to take that particular person out."

184

"Obviously," Boheemer said, "they mistook Darby for Brent."

"Not that hard to do," Kenman said, "being that you'd easily mistake him for white."

Boheemer snickered. "There's a whole lot of people in Naw'lins you can't tell is colored."

Captain Shayde laughed and slapped his knee. "Ole' Huey Long said there are so few pure white people in Lu'ziana you can feed them all with five cents worth of red beans and ten cents worth of white rice."

"All that racial stuff aside," Mike said, "a professional killer with a definitive target mistook his man for three other guys . . . Two of which were unmistakably black."

"Sure does stretch credibility," Armand said, "even if the shooters were color blind."

"Y'all believe whatever you want," Kenman said. "Just accept that we're going to publicize accusations of everything Mike Molino did to that innocent child."

"Perhaps," Mike grated, "you also need to publish that Mister Kenman invited those three victims to that location."

"Invited only one," Kenman corrected. "You spread that kind of innuendo and I'll sue the damn state for enough to finance two elections."

"This interview is terminated," Captain Shayde barked.

"Only if Mister Kenman says so," Mike countered. "His office."

"I'm going to concur with the district commander," Kenman said. "Good afternoon, gentlemen."

When Mike and Armand turned to exit. Kaylee rose and ambled toward them. "Y'all don't mind, I'll accompany y'all to the parking lot."

Shayde gawked and flailed his hands. "Why not wait for me?"

"Y'all are putting me to sleep rehashing the same business."

185

Shayde glowered at her but didn't vocalize further objection.

"You sweet on Molino?" Boheemer called out.

"If that's what you choose to believe," she replied.

Mike waved Kaylee and Armand through the door ahead of him. It pricked his curiosity that Kaylee abandoned her boss to leave with him . . . considering she hadn't answered his many phone calls. Damn if that's not one enigmatic gal.

While Armand went to get their car, Mike walked Kaylee to hers. He winced when she said: "Apparently you lose interest really quickly."

"Not true. I called—numerous times—without getting answered."

"Sure, after you got horny again."

"Not true. Give me a break here, girl. This case is weighing on me and may affect my future with the AG's office."

"Heard about it. You know that Shayde and Kenman intend to continually publicize stories with respect to your plaything in Shreveport."

"It wasn't like that."

"Having been through a really ugly divorce, I'm willing to accept that there are two sides to every story. My ex smeared me big-time, accusing me of bedding people I didn't even know."

"But my problem isn't in the past."

"We all make mistakes, get into bed instead of using our brains."

"Oh, they will, Mike. They spot you anywhere they'll spin it to sound scurrilous and it'll end up on the nightly news or the morning papers along with a lot of other damaging innuendos."

"You wheedling out of being with me tonight?"

"No, Mike. God sakes, I'm as anxious to be with you as you are

186

to be with me—maybe more—even if you were neglectful."

"I wasn't neglectful. It—"

"I believe you. Swear I do, Mike."

"Then let's get together and have a good time. Screw worrying about being seen together. Hell, it's Friday. Every watering hole in town will be crowded. Santa Claus can get lost in The Quarter."

Kaylee laughed.

"Half the celebrants," Mike said, "will be too bombed to recognize their own kin by nine o'clock. We ought to be able to lose ourselves in some noisy joint."

"I don't do joints, lover. This lady has graduated to class establishments."

"Name it then."

"Okay, meet me at eight at the Carousel Bar. It's in the Monteleone Hotel on Royal between Iberville and Bienville, in the heart of The Quarter. That place gets so crowded on Friday nights we'll be lucky to find each other."

#   #

187

Chapter Thirty-Nine

Mike and Armand trundled into the conference room to be confronted by Nelda holding up the newspaper. "Media is having a field day, boss-man, spouting off 'bout yo' hanky-panky in Shreveport."

"Folks all 'round town," Julie added, "are ranting that you defiled that child and blasting you as too immoral to be trusted to head up an investigation."

"No matter how many times they print that slander," Mike growled, "I never had sex with that kid. Y'all hear what I'm saying?"

"Be helpful," Nelda said, "if you tell it all and clean the air."

Mike's face hardened. "I made a dumb mistake, but didn't commit statutory rape."

"Did or didn't," Nelda said, "you got you double-trouble. They found a dark-skinned sister who got caught up in that roundup who claimed you didn't give her the leniency you did that light-skinned chick. Claims you discriminated against her by ignoring her pleas."

"If I did, it was inadvertent," Mike said, "being this is the first I've heard of that person."

"They come out of the woodwork," Chi Chi said, "trying to share some of the honey the scandal sheets spread around."

"Why not explain it," Armand said, "and clear the air. We're all friends."

Mike grimaced, then shrugged. "As y'all know, a group of states worked in concert to break up a dope distributing ring. One of the small-time pushers caught in the dragnet was a sixteen-year-old girl who reminded me of my daughter."

"An octoroon," Nelda said, "more white than black."

He grimaced and averted his eyes while conjuring up a picture of Melody, with her round face and dark hair. Her features and complexion barely hinted at African blood. His voice cracked when he said: "Miriam died of an overdose a few months after her mama was killed in a car crash. Can't tell you how that double tragedy all but crushed me."

He blinked back the tears and swallowed the knot in his throat while nodding to their murmurs of sympathy. "That kid, Melody, arrested my empathy, going to high school every day and bright as a sunflower while raising her little girl as a single mom. With few other sources of income, she'd succumbed to retailing in her school."

He glanced at their bobbing heads, with no one vocally commenting, so continued. "She had no sheet—in Louisiana anyway, reason I wanted to give her a new start and prevent her ruining her life— as well as save her from losing her baby if incarcerated. I was equally concerned for the baby being deprived of its mama."

Mike gritted his teeth as he forced himself to continue. "There's no way I can deny doing something stupid, as well as acting on the cusp of illegal by trying to shield Melody from prosecution."

"But rather than show some gratitude," Armand said, "that mercenary bitch caved to the barrel of money offered by the tabloids and told them what they wanted to hear . . . whether it was gospel or not."

Mike nodded, grinding his jaws. "Would she have reformed? In retrospect I have to admit I doubt it. And I sure ought not to have taken it upon myself to rehabilitate her."

"You made an effort," Gustave said. "Commendable."

Mike snickered. "Resulting in kicking up one big-assed hullabaloo. But, believe me, I never had any kind of sex with that kid.

189

Never even entertained it. Thought of her as the daughter I lost."

"But you didn't give a dark sister the same consideration," Nelda said. "She had her baby and didn't have any record either, and could have used a break."

"Didn't know about her."

"Surfaced recently," Armand said. "Like Chi Chi said: chasing a payday from one of those scandal sheets."

"Might have been created by one of those tabloids," Gustave said. "They're not above devious subterfuge."

Mike flagged his head side to side, a morose expression on his face. "It had nothing to do with Melody being almost white, or whatever else. Doubtful I even saw her as Melody. I was saving Miriam. It was dumb."

"But left yourself open to criticism by the black community," Nelda said.

"I remind you, Nelda, that Mexicans are not readily accepted as whites. Nor are Choctaws. I'm a product of both."

When Nelda started to retort, Mike held up a hand. "I know having dark blood is no defense against racial prejudice. Take it from me that I've never judged anyone because of race, religion or gender. In fact, I've been concerned my whole life with not becoming a victim of racial prejudice. I remind you that it's not only practiced against blacks."

#   #

190

Chapter Forty

Mike settled into commuter traffic to head for The Quarter and kill an hour listening to ear-splitting music before meeting Kaylee. Like Josh Bigelow, he used that cacophonous blare as a balm, to deaden mental and physical responses to those bugaboos haunting the deepest recesses of memory.

The booze expunged the residual pain by tranquilizing his brain. Clamorous music served as a narcotic to reduce to a state of inertia all the misery of torturous remembrances.

Actually, those life-shattering tragedies had been steadily diminishing in memory, requiring less palliation. Providentially, that plunge into ecstasy with Kaylee dispelled most of that lingering gloom. But he twinged with guilt, questioning whether he'd earned the right to lay to rest the memories of Arlene and Miriam?

He bobbed his head in affirmation of his right to find a life and to experience happiness again. No, he wasn't eclipsing recollections of his wife and daughter. Arlene and Miriam would always have a special place in his heart and mind. But he needed to open this door to the future. Yes, he had a right to do that since it didn't malign the past.

Impatient to be with Kaylee, he wondered why he hadn't made the date earlier in the evening. Then he could already be immersing himself in her aura and commingling their personas. He chuckled when it dawned on him that they were meeting in a public place, denying immediate gratification.

However, after dinner he anticipated returning to her place to experience again that rapture of two nights ago. No, he didn't want to

191

take her to his hotel room, or anywhere lacking the elegance of her apartment, consequently the romantic ambiance. Or was he still unwilling to bring a woman to his place . . . even to a rented hotel room?

Hopefully she'd picked a restaurant that served spicy Cajun food, in a noisy ambiance. With throbbing music in his ears and fiery Cajun fare burning in his throat he rarely conjured up those depressing remembrances of Arlene crushed in that tangle of wrecked vehicles—nor of Miriam, so incapable of facing reality that she escaped the pain and anguish by offing herself with an overdose of stupefying drugs.

He clenched his teeth, berating himself as a poor excuse for a father for having never realized his daughter experimented with narcotics. Experimented hell! After the fact he learned from her friends that she'd messed with the stuff for at least two years. Somehow it had escaped him. Damn! He thought he'd paid close attention to his daughter, been a concerned father.

Miriam had cleverly concealed it from him and her mother. And two caring parents failed to closely monitor their only child to prevent that tragedy in the making.

The flash of the traffic light to red brought him to alertness, to brake and avoid plowing into cross-traffic. He flinched at the sound of the car braking behind him. Memory impelled his eyes to flick to the rear-view mirror. Seeing two gray-haired ladies occupying it he chortled at his paranoia.

He relaxed and waited for the light to change. Memory of Wednesday night made him smile . . . at it happening so naturally. There had been a few friendly ladies since Arlene's death, but he hadn't been able to release himself to involvement with any of them. Yes, he had now. And no way in hell he'd consider it cheating.

No, he refused to let the thing with Kaylee stir up guilt. Hell, it

192

exhilarated him, propelled him into a rapturous orbit and brightened his outlook on life. Yes, time healed old wounds when it happened with the right one . . . made him glad he'd waited.

Even the time they spent together, including lunching at Belmonde's, while not intended as social, had been scintillating. Something about the short conversation he had with Emil Gasse that afternoon flashed in mind—persisted in roiling his memory synapses.

What in hell was it that Emil had failed to dredge up? Dammit, he should've gone back there and helped the guy mine it from the black hole of memory.

When the light changed, Mike hung a right and tooled down to Royal Street, then hung another right and headed in the direction he'd come from. After crossing Canal Street, Royal became Saint Charles, separated by the trolley tracks. Within a few blocks he pulled up to the entrance of the parking lot of Belmonde's. Damn it, the place was full, so he backed into the restricted area near the kitchen door, a loading zone, and left his placard on the dashboard.

He argued with himself that having driven that distance overruled concerns of bothering Emil during a busy time. So he entered the restaurant, to encounter a line of people waiting to be seated. Shit, it was a goddam circus, typical of Friday night. Yeah, and he'd bet there was a bunch more coming. It sure said volumes for the amount of folks in New Orleans willing to shell out big bucks to be seen taking dinner in the right places.

Shaking his head to reproach himself, he turned to leave, when he heard Emil's voice. "Mike. You came for dinner?"

Mike turned and flailed his hands as he sought to explain. But Emil spoke before he could. "You're alone—on Friday night?"

"Forgive me, Emil. I foolishly thought you'd have a minute to

193

discuss the case and satisfy my curiosity about a couple of details."

Emil gestured at the gathering patrons.

Mike held up a hand to forestall the explanation. But Emil again spoke before he did. "Actually, we've seated as many as we can accommodate at the moment. I'm harried and can use a break. We'll take a minute to chat." He whispered to one of his managers to take over at the lectern for a few minutes. Then he led Mike down the hallway to the bar.

They found only one stool available, despite a happy crowd bunched up at the rest of the bar. He and Emil waved each other to it. Mike accepted that Emil had no intention of sitting with a patron standing, so sat and ordered Knob Creek on the rocks. Emil gazed at the bottles behind the bar before deciding on a Kir Royal: vermouth cassis with champagne.

"I feel like one big damn fool," Mike said, "for bothering you on a busy Friday evening. But impetuosity drove me to see if you might help me understand the enigma of the prime target of assassins escaping death while those killers wasted three men easily distinguishable from the supposed target."

Emil sipped his drink and sighed approval. Then he stared at the square window with the initial B etched in cloudy swirls, as if trying to read something there. "It mystifies me also—has been buzzing in my head for days."

"Spit it out," Mike said. "Then we'll try to make sense of it."

Emil nodded. "One of my waiters claims that while on his way to work, late because of a dental appointment, he passed a Mercedes coupe parked a block or so down the street with two men in it. Believed he recognized Mister Kenman."

Mike's eyes widened.

194

Emil nodded. "Kenman and Boheemer soon after entered with Darby Williams and his party."

"Of course!" Mike exclaimed. "They waited for the other party to arrive so they'd come in together, it being the only way they'd get away with their ruse about expecting a reservation to be honored, when they hadn't made one."

"My thinking also in retrospect," Emil agreed. "They went to the bar to have a drink while I shuffled reservations to arrange a table for them."

"Placing them in the sights of the assassins. Did you go back with them?"

"Yes, of course. Considering who they were. And now I remember how Mister Kenman supervised who stood here and who stood there. Mister Sessy brought their attention to a banquette being vacated, and suggested they take lunch there by pulling a few chairs around it."

"But, obviously, they didn't."

"I tried to dissuade them—didn't want those chairs blocking accesses in that area. Considered myself lucky at the time, having the support of Messers Kenman and Boheemer. So I supported Mister Kenman when he insisted they have a drink at the bar while waiting for a table. Told them they were compliments of the house."

Mike bobbed his head repeatedly, to acknowledge what he was being told and to urge Emil to continue while he analyzed everything rippling through his cerebral cortex.

"He really took charge," Emil said, "directing Mister Williams and his assistant campaign manager next to him with Mister Sessy to the far end."

"He staged a goddam set-up," Mike said. "Were you there when

195

the shooting started?"

"Fortunately no. I had gone back up front to make arrangements to get them a table as quickly as possible."

"And you rushed back when you heard the shooting."

"I wouldn't use the word *rushed*, Mike. Frankly, it took effort for my curiosity to override my cowardice."

"Smart man. Thanks for that heads-up. It makes things as plain as the beak on a hawk. Now all I have to do is prove it."

"Not an easy task, Mike. Mister Kenman is shrewd and ambitious. Had the displeasure of being acquainted with him for quite a few years. Trust him about as much as I would a water moccasin. What's your next step?"

"Locate those shooters and convince them to give up their employer."

"Will that be easy?"

"Nothing about cop work is easy." Mike drained his glass and Emil signaled the bartender for a refill. But Mike placed his hand over the glass and shook his head. "I'll leave you to your work now. Shouldn't have come at this particular time. But I'm damned glad I did. Thanks."

"Any way I can help, Mike. Why don't you stay for supper? Doubtful I can arrange a table for you, but you can eat at the bar— compliments of the house."

"No way! Nothing on the pad. Got enough grief. But thanks a whole lot. You're a good guy, Emil. Anyway, I'm meeting someone at eight."

"Good to hear it, Mike. It's time for you to turn back on. Am I correct in assuming it's that lovely lady sergeant who accompanied you at luncheon."

196

"That was all business."

"But I dare say, tonight isn't."

"You'd have made a hell of a detective, Emil."

"I'm happy doing what I do. And I'm glad to hear you're coming out of your shell."

Mike patted Emil's shoulder, as friends do. He slipped off the stool and dropped a twenty-dollar bill on the bar.

"Oh, you've been drinking as my guest," Emil said.

"Not on your life, good buddy."

"One drink doesn't put you on the pad, for God's sake."

"It can be construed as graft," Mike said. "And I need to be careful."

"Some night let's go out for a drink."

"You got it, good buddy."

# #

Chapter Forty-One

Mike inched along Royal Street, narrowed by cars parked on both sides. Pedestrians loitered in front of crowded restaurants flanking the roadway, as did upscale stores exhibiting fine furniture, expensive bric-a-brac, and objects d'art.

It occurred to him to check his rear-view mirror. But with traffic going nowhere he dismissed concern that anyone might pull something, considering there weren't any avenues of escape. While crossing Iberville he spotted the colorfully illuminated facade of the Monteleone Hotel a few hundred yards ahead.

Grimacing concession, he surrendered his SUV to the parking valet, having decided that enough friction existed with the NOPD, without fanning up more by relying on his AG placard.

Though he'd never before visited the landmark hotel, he'd heard a lot about it from lavish-spending bureaucrats who claimed it had been the favorite hangout of celebrities such as William Faulkner, Truman Capote, and Tennessee Williams.

Immediately upon entering the vestibule, he found himself swallowed up by those surging in and out of the impressively refurbished lobby; probably heading to and from the variety of posh restaurants.

He spotted the Carousel Room sign on his right, prior to the lobby doors, relieving him of having to compete with the throngs traversing the busiest areas. So he climbed the few steps and pushed through the swinging doors to enter the darkened cavern—within which the swarm of revelers inhibited penetration. Their celebratory din

198

muffled the strains of piano music.

Shouldering among the happy crowd he searched over the sea of heads for Kaylee. Ah, he spotted her propped on one of the barstools. Damned if she didn't look like the duchess of New Orleans in a satiny black dress with barely enough material to qualify as de rigueur. Yeah! This lady had a talent for vamping.

It took persistence to work his way through the throng, then squeeze into the mob on the slowly rotating platform upon which the bar and its stools were positioned. Her eyes sparkled when she saw him, enthralling him; it having been a long time since he'd enjoyed that kind of esoteric exchange.

When he succeeded in weaving his way to her they grasped hands and grinned at each other. Beguiled by her faint perfume and her bold as hell blue eyes, it took restraint not to peel off that flimsy dress there and then.

She, however, pulled his face close to hers and pecked his lips. He blinked and glanced self-consciously around.

Kaylee laughed. "You're stodgy."

He made a wry face while trying to find words to explain his reservation about being demonstrative in public.

"Thank God that's not the case in private," she said.

He had to bend to hear her words in that din. Then he quickly averted his eyes to prevent torturing himself when glancing at the silky flesh of her cleavage. Gesturing to her half-filled glass of faintly colored liquid, he asked: "What are you drinking?" God, he needed to get his mind off sex . . . at least while they remained in public.

"A Vieux Carré, the renowned house drink—a masterpiece made with rye, cognac, vermouth, bitters, and Benedictine."

It tickled him that they audaciously named their house drink

199

with a term that meant Old Square, which was how the old timers referred to The Quarter. "Will they make it with bourbon?" he asked.

"Please, not bourbon. This is a class joint, Mike." Both chortled at the snobbery.

One of the bartenders leveled his questioning gaze on Mike and lip-synced the question: "A Vieux Carré for you also, sir?"

Mike shook his head and shouted: "Knob Creek on the rocks."

While the bartender poured his drink, Mike gazed beyond the bar area to where bodies occupied every comfy club chair surrounding sturdy tables. He not only doubted he'd get lucky enough to relax in that area, but would never even get a damn bar stool, with the revelers three-deep and still coming.

Then he wondered by what miracle Kaylee had gotten hers in this press. It amused him to imagine some moon-struck guy who'd been tossing them down for an hour surrendering it to her as an overture to making out. Poor sap must have kicked himself when she told him she waited for someone.

Mike accepted his drink from the bartender and clinked his glass against hers. He chortled at her typical Cajun and Creole toast of: "Laissez les bons temps rouler." He remembered it meaning: *Let the good times roll.*

After a long and satisfying sip he commented: "Real nice place."

"My favorite watering hole until my marriage went sour."

"You saying you didn't come here with guys who came on the scene after the divorce?"

"Didn't meet anyone I wanted to share my favorite place with."

"Then I consider myself honored. We planning to stay long?"

"Why? What's on your mind?"

"Taking up where we left off Wednesday night."

"We haven't eaten dinner yet."

"Hell, we can take sandwiches in like Wednesday night."

"No way, big guy. I have a very special place in mind with a romantic ambiance. You'll be amply rewarded after dinner."

Both chuckled at that prospect. But her cheerfulness dissipated upon hearing: "Hi, Kaylee," and seeing the couple muscling through the crowd to them.

She sighed acceptance, forced a smile, and told Mike: "Say hello to Jack Symmonds and his wife, Ellie. This is Mike Molino."

"The Mike Molino with the AG's office?" the guy squealed, raising his eyebrows in pretended astonishment.

"Lieutenant Symmonds is one of Captain Shayde's closest subordinates," Kaylee informed Mike.

"Sebastian will not only be surprised" Jack Symmonds said, "to hear that you're out with the infamous Director Molino, but he'll likely be insanely jealous."

His wife, Ellie, tugged at him while scolding him. "Decorum, Jack. You really need to learn to be discreet." She flicked goodbyes with her fingers while pulling him away to melt into the crowd.

"Bad luck," Kaylee said. "Didn't want word getting back."

"Why the hell not? You ashamed to be seen with me?"

"Of course not, Mike. But there's a lot of acrimony in the department toward you. Being seen with you will have reverberations, especially dressed like this."

"I like how you're dressed. Besides, it's too late to change whatever will result, so relax and have a good time." He waved the bartender for refills, then asked: "What was that reference to Sebastian Shayde all about?"

Kaylee averted her eyes as she sipped her drink. "After passing

201

the sergeant's exam I sucked up to Shayde to expedite that promotion. Obviously Symmonds mistook that for something else. As you're probably aware, Shayde is married, to a possessive lady who can be belligerent."

Watching Mike chuckle gratified her that he'd accepted that explanation. She hoped he'd leave it alone so she needn't divulge her intimacy with Sebastian. No way she'd risk anticipating Mike's reaction to her having shared a bed with a black man. Racial prejudice and demeaning attitudes weren't rampant anymore, but weren't dead either.

#   #

Chapter Forty-Two

Mike and Kaylee swayed together while singing along with the unseen pianist, mellowed by the booze and inspired by the lilting music. Running his arm around Kaylee's waist he held her against him, though he remained standing while she sat.

Kaylee's blue eyes sparkled. "Glad to see that it only takes three drinks to dissolve your stodginess."

"Yeah, from stodgy to horny. Let's get out of here."

"Hey, we haven't had supper yet."

"Take a few of those olives with you if you're that hungry."

"Get real, Mike. I need to eat. Besides, I begged for a reservation in a great place."

"It can't wait 'til later?"

"What you have in mind will have to wait. Hell, I missed lunch today, am famished. You don't feed me, you won't get me in the mood."

"Then by all means, let's eat, but light. Don't want you stuffed, sluggish, and burping in my ear. Which of the four restaurants in this place you have in mind?"

"Not here. I'm thinking special and romantic."

"Not too time consuming. Want you ready before you fall asleep."

"Don't worry, lover, your matches light my fire."

"Yeah, yeah. Let's go. Where is this place you want to eat?"

"Not far. We can walk." She emptied her glass and slid off the stool.

#

They strolled along Royal Street, hand in hand, winding among bar-hopping revelers and window-shopping tourists. At Bienville they headed toward the river for two blocks to turn east again on Chartres. Cars, taxis, and horse-drawn buggies filled up the roadway, as did people spilling off the sidewalks. Strains of music as well as arresting aromas wafted from the myriad restaurants to intermix with the peal of revelry. Kaylee pointed ahead to the canopy with the legend: BACCO.

Mike shrugged acquiescence. "I'm okay for Italian."

"The best," she said as she led him indoors. "It's operated by the Brennan family, which is what makes it unique."

"There's one for the books," Mike said, "the Irish operating an Italian restaurant." But he groaned at sight of the capacity crowd, with many waiting to be seated. However, he sighed relief when the maitre'd recognized Kaylee and directed them to a small table for two by the window in the main dining room, set and waiting for them.

"Looks like you enjoy a little juice here," Mike kidded her.

"Some cops know how to appreciate perks."

Chuckling as he sat, Mike glanced around at the glut of diners occupying tables and chairs in the center of the dining room as well as the banquettes with bench tables lining the walls. He tried to read the poetic stanzas written on the leather upholstered banquettes but couldn't translate the Italian . . . Or was it Latin?

The ambiance of Bacchanalian delight influenced him to order a bottle of Barbera, a full-bodied red with a satiny taste—worthy of being expensive. He pushed his menu to Kaylee. "You make the selections since you're familiar with the place."

She beamed as she anticipated sharing mussels steamed in sweet vermouth, accompanied by red onions and spicy pancetta. Foregoing salad, both enjoyed a veal T-bone with ziti in the best marinara sauce

204

Mike could remember.

#

Stuffed and giggling, they left the restaurant with arms linked to traipse back to the Monteleone Hotel to get their cars. Barhopping revelers crowded the streets in even greater numbers than before.

Kaylee tensed at the flash and jerked to a stop. "A camera," she exclaimed as she scanned her surroundings. "They're taking pictures."

Mike searched around, his face wrinkled in bewilderment at why photography upset Kaylee. Before he had a chance to comment, Kaylee growled: "That bastard Symmonds must have called Shayde."

"So what? Who cares?"

"You should. They're targeting you—gathering substantiation. Don't you understand how desperate the bastards are to discredit you?"

When he scoffed, she warned: "They're not above scandalizing me to get at you." She pointed to the flash of a camera from a car across the street. "There! Those guys are NOPD—snapping photos to make an example of me as well. They'll be used to claim you're an incorrigible womanizer, then passed around the squad room to make fun of me."

Mike's face hardened as he darted between vehicles backed up in traffic to cross the street. The two occupants in plain-clothes seated in the unmarked car pretended unawareness of him. But they gasped when he jerked open the passenger-side door and grabbed the camera off the guy's lap. Both yelped objection. But Mike slammed the door and stepped back while breaking it open and tearing out the disc.

The two guys wrenched open their doors and clambered out, demanding their camera. He tossed it to the closest one. The guy caught it and stared at it in disbelief. The other one kept moving toward Mike, brandishing handcuffs and yelling: "You're under arrest for vandalizing police equipment."

205

Mike caught him with a left in the gut and a right on his jaw. When the guy crumpled against the side of the car, bobbling the cuffs, Mike swung around to the other one, who advanced on him wielding the camera. He ducked the swinging object and drove a fist into the guy's side. When the man bent over from the force of that blow, Mike cold-cocked him with a back-of-the-neck chop. Then he spun around and laid a right on the jaw of the guy struggling to pull himself up from leaning against the car.

Kaylee reached Mike's side to see both detectives laid out on the street. "Get out of here! For Christ's sake, get out of here!"

"Why? They came at me."

She searched beyond the milling carousers and gawking spectators. Those people and the endless traffic helped to conceal them. "If there are others they'll likely shoot you. Get out of here!"

"Hey, I'm a cop too."

"But you're in enemy territory, Mike. There have to be others around and they'll be spitting mad. Get the hell out of here!"

He ground his jaws but overcame his obstinacy and joined Kaylee in dodging around and between revelers to hurry back to the Monteleone to command the valet to get their cars. "Meet you at your place," he told her.

"Don't be crazy. It's the first place they'll look."

"Hey, I'm not some dumb civilian. I'm with the AG's office. I'm also—"

"That won't stop you from taking a few bullets for resisting arrest. Face it, Mike, you pissed them off big-time. Give it time to cool off."

"You saying we're not going to enjoy tonight . . . and the weekend!"

206

"It's too risky. You need to be out of reach for two or three days."

"Hey, I'm not going to run and hide from local cops."

"You will if you have good sense. The department will whitewash those guys—believe me! Shayde might even put them up for commendation. Get out of sight for a couple of days, until it cools off."

"But what about us?"

"We're on hold until this blows over. Believe that Shayde will sanction any use of force by his men to avenge those two guys."

"Will any of it affect your career?"

"Sure they'll scuttle it without a second thought. But their main interest is you. Best thing you can do is hie your ass up to Baton Rouge until this thing blows over."

"I got real lucky and found you, Kaylee. No way I'm going to abandon you."

"Please, Mike! Use your damned head. You get hurt and it'll tear my heart out. I found you too. You're important to me."

"Okay, every problem has a solution. What say I book a room out of town . . . even out of state?"

"Yes! Go now!"

"Together."

"No, Mike. They're probably surveilling me—have my car bugged. You need to go to where they can't harm you."

"Not without you. Doubtful they bugged my car."

"Be reasonable, for God's sake. Get the hell out of here!"

"Only on the condition that we hook up tomorrow. We'll drive there separately and meet at noon."

Kaylee paced in a small circle, impatient for their cars, her face drawn with concern. She shook her head. "Where will we be safe?"

"Over the border—in Mississippi." He rolled his eyes back to search his memory for where they could meet. Biloxi was the first place that came to mind.

"Where in Biloxi?" she asked, excited by the prospect.

"The Beau Rivage." Then he wanted to bite his tongue for selecting a place that expensive. But it was the only one popped in mind.

Kaylee brightened. "Oh yeah! It's a short drive—but beyond the watchful eyes of big brothers. Go there tonight. You'll be safe."

"Super. Meet me there in an hour."

"They'll be watching me, Mike, hoping I'll lead them to you. Better I don't leave town tonight. But you have to split."

"Don't worry about me. I can take care of myself. But I'll be miserable as hell for missing out on spending the night with you."

"Let's concern ourselves with spending tomorrow night together, and surviving to enjoy many nights thereafter."

# #

Chapter Forty-Three

Mike leaned his elbow out the opened window to bask in the Saturday morning sunshine while tooling east in the light traffic of US 90. Sparse lowland vegetation offered little in the way of interesting scenery. At intervals swampy areas overgrown with sedges and spiky grasses interrupted the endless scatterings of stunted and straggly trees with an occasional sprawling live oak festooned with Spanish moss.

Despite swamp stenches invading his olfactory organ, he bubbled with anticipation, counting every mile that brought him closer to his rendezvous with Kaylee. However, the sporadic cumulus clouds cast intermittent shadows that diminished hope. God, she couldn't disappoint him by not being there . . . for whatever reason.

No, he denied himself considering the possibility of their hurting her, a fellow officer . . . or what he'd do if they did. That concern reminded him of the encounter with those two dicks last night. Yes, he wished it hadn't occurred, aware it amplified enmity with the NOPD. But chivalry incited his transformation to the knight in shining armor that defended her honor.

It also increased the likelihood of one of the psychotics of that department stepping over the line by shooting him and claiming he resisted arrest. Of course that cop will insist he never became aware the guy he attempted to take into custody was with the AG's office.

Cops exceeded their authority all too often, committed atrocities that civilians never expected. In the largest cities, with the most sophisticated police forces, civilians have been shot down by over-eager cops. Worse thing is the cops often get away with it, whitewashed by superiors who endorse the Blue Line rather than defend society at large.

That awareness had him checking the nearby vehicles while leaving New Orleans. But he felt more secure once he'd crossed the border into Mississippi. He doubted those yahoos were that crazy to chase out-of-state after him, lacking jurisdiction to shield them. Besides, they had to expect him to return to his office in New Orleans Monday morning, so needed only wait for him.

Okay, he'd enlist Jace to intervene, certain that one telephone call from the AG would let the air out of the emotional balloon of the NOPD executives. Believe that they'd pass the word down through the ranks, defusing the situation.

He'd stayed at his hotel last night, obstinate as well as disdainful of whether the local cops knew where to find him. No way he'd give them the satisfaction of thinking he ran scared. Better believe he'd tucked his Beretta semi-automatic pistol with its fifteen-round magazine of 9-millimeter bullets under his pillow to shoot the ass off any yahoo had the impudence to bust in on him.

Awakening in the morning after sleeping fitfully, he set out for Biloxi, smug for having survived a perilous night. But he kept a wary eye out for ambushing vehicles. Nothing untoward occurred. Nor did he now spot any vehicles that appeared to be tailing him, certainly no dusty pick-up truck, especially that one with its murderous battering ram.

Miriam's death shocked the hell out of him. Why had he and Arlene not seen any of the signs? Sure as hell Arlene had to have had heart-to-heart talks with her about relationships and sex. Young guys had begun to call on Miriam, provoking memory of his horny youth and raising suspicion that they wanted to bounce on his daughter's bones.

But he needed to relegate those thoughts and all that pain to a remote chamber of his temporal lobe and stop beating up on himself about things he had no control of. Arlene was dead because some inconsiderate som'bitch ran a light, augmented by another dumb-ass exceeding the speed limit in a high-traffic area. And he had no capability to undo that tragedy or bring her back.

Miriam had taken her own life, and he couldn't specifically say why. Sure she mourned the loss of her mother, but she might have accidentally overdosed, having nothing to do with her grief. Kids on dope are their own worst enemy.

Rehashing it didn't change anything. He had to move on, despite having foolishly let that grief blind him to the realization that Melody played him. He'd seen her as a sweet gal, the reincarnation of Miriam. Her year-old daughter filled his heart with joy, then sadness when he realized she was the closest he'd ever come to having a granddaughter. He sure thought about grand-adopting little Louellen. Damned if he wouldn't have.

That's what led to his feeling sorry for a teen-age single mom with no record—in Louisiana anyway. That was another dumb mistake. He sure ought to have checked with neighboring states and might've learned that she'd been indicted a number of times and convicted once in Arkansas and once in Texas. Believe that if he'd known she had a rap sheet he'd never have been that big a sucker.

But he'd deluded himself into believing he gave a decent kid a new start and a chance to go through life without a criminal record. He really believed he was saving her. Little did he know she'd already become entrenched in crime.

No way he'd considered any kind of sexual relationship. Hell, he treated her like his daughter. Man, was he dumb—stupid!—totally brain-dead!

That experience soured him on females in general, diluted

yearning to interact with them . . . until Kaylee came along.

They meshed from the git-go, culminating with one hell of a consummation. His grin sparkled anticipation of the two nights ahead.

Had he been a doofus by passing up sleeping with her last night? Had those lobos made the mistake of coming after him at her place, he'd have blown them out of the doorway—with legal justification.

But he didn't want to put her in jeopardy, so had caved to her reasoning. Dammit, he wished he'd gone there. And he didn't give a damn if Sebastian Shayde scandalized it. They had a right to be together. But he feared endangering Kaylee, and damn sure didn't want her caught up in a shootout against her own brothers and sisters in blue.

Glancing ahead he recognized the Beau Rivage silhouetted against the skyline, larger and more impressive since being rebuilt after Katrina's devastation. Holy shit!—he'd been driving for a little over an hour, unaware of the passing of time. Straightening up in the seat he viewed huge machinery busily restoring the expanse of beach. He smiled as he inhaled sea air. Yee-haw! Only a few more minutes.

Yeah, his heart sang with anticipation as he gazed out of the large openings in the garage wall to see the sun sparkling on the tranquil waters of the Gulf of Mexico. He hoped to hell Kaylee had arrived, uncertain how he'd react to disappointment. He searched for but failed to spot her Chevy among the countless cars parked in rows. Okay, if she hadn't as yet arrived she'd be here soon. He needed to believe that.

He scrutinized the few vehicles that had followed him into the garage, then watched those occupants pull luggage out of their trunks before trundling off toward the hotel concourse. Noting nothing threatening, he assumed they headed for a happy weekend.

Relax, son, you're on holiday. But impatience impelled his stride as he trekked the length of the long concourse from the garage,

212

towing a weekend bag on wheels and oblivious to the upscale stores lining the right side, as well as the open-walled cafeteria teeming with diners on his left.

He arrived at the desk to check in, and glowed when he learned his wife had already arrived. Damned if he didn't angst with impatience while the elevator took him to the fourth floor.

Opening the door to his room, he saw her near the bed unpacking her bag. She'd shed her blouse and skirt and shucked her shoes; wore only a lace-trimmed bra and panties. Both grinned; neither needing words of greeting.

Mike swung the door closed behind him, abandoning his luggage in the alcove as he strode to her and gathered her in his arms. She grasped his face and brought their mouths together.

Mike unsnapped her brassiere and Kaylee slithered out of it and let it fall to the floor. She groaned her delight when he ran his lips down her neck and bent to suckle her nipples. After wriggling her panties down to her ankles, she kicked them off. Anticipation glowed on her face as she sat on the bed and watched him peel down.

Mike left his clothes where they fell. And when her silky hands grasped his buttocks to pull him to her he obediently shuffled the short distance. Impatient to consummate the act of love, he pushed her down on the bed and lay atop her. She groaned ecstatically when their naked bodies fused.

#   #

Chapter Forty-Four

  "You've exhausted me," Kaylee moaned. ". . . Blown me away."

  Mike chuckled while snuggling her nakedness deeper into his embrace. "Just getting started, gal."

  "Like hell. It's time to take a break . . . To find us a different pastime . . . get us some damn lunch."

  "Why don't we just munch on each other some more?"

  "While it satisfies everything else, lover, it doesn't nourish me. You need to replenish my energy to keep getting me in the mood."

  "Same story as last night at that bar," Mike said, mirth twinkling in his eyes. "You are one hungry woman."

  "Glad you came to the realization that feeding me increases your level of familiarity with this booty."

  "Okay, we'll go down and feed our faces. Then we'll come back up here and repeat that incredible half hour."

  "You got that much energy in you?"

  "You'll infuse me, darlin'. Just press all that gorgeous nakedness against me and I'll sure as hell rise to the occasion."

                              #

  Mike held her hand as they strolled among those traversing the second floor corridor. They pushed the glass doors open to pass into the outside snack-area near the pool. Having covered bathing suits with cabana outfits, they resembled the myriad others relaxing under colorful umbrellas spread across the wide veranda alongside a huge pool. Hilarity reigned, with every chaise lounge occupied, as were the chairs surrounding metal tables.

They beamed their luck when three people vacated a table. Sitting, they ordered sandwiches and cold drinks.

"Coming to Biloxi was one smart idea, lover man. I needed this break. And necessary, with all of the hullabaloo going on back in town."

"Screw them. I'm only interested in you, even though your bosses assigned you to keep tabs on me—possibly to impede progress?"

"In the beginning. Then it occurred to Shayde that if you hit on me they'd claim you're an obsessive sex fiend, incapable of not approaching females—bolstering the claims of that young gal in Shreveport."

Mike started to object when the waiter interrupted to set their orders in front of them. So he relaxed as both took a few bites and sips. After sighing approval, Kaylee informed: "They plan to continually publicize charges against you of taking advantage of that juvenile."

"Hate to burst your bubble, but that kid induced in me a fatherly complex."

"You told me that the accusations were false. I believe you, Mike."

"Thanks. Too few people do. Those scandal rags continually running photographs of her in skimpy outfits and sexy poses make folks believe I took advantage of her. And they keep paying that mercenary a bundle to pillory me. She takes the money without compunction about enriching herself at my expense."

Kaylee nodded. "A bitch without conscience."

"Not one damn thing I tried to do for her instilled ounce one of gratitude. You're looking at a giant sap."

"Then open your eyes and understand why we have to avoid being seen together in Naw'lins for a little bit. They'll make something

215

out of whatever they can to take you down and eliminate you as morally qualified to head up the investigation."

"I know Shayde hates my guts and maybe Montrose wants a piece of my hide. Who else is in it with them?"

"That's obvious. You ran into Shayde when you visited Kenman and Boheemer. Don't ask me what all and how all they're connected because I honestly don't have all the answers. Truth: don't want to know."

"Sure blows my mind," Mike said, "knowing Shayde for a champion among cops, and deservedly so. But I can't, for the life of me, understand why he plays palsy with the two most obvious suspects of engineering that massacre."

"Blows mine too, Mike. But, honestly, I'd rather not learn the truth about that."

"Why not? It's your department."

"Right now, big guy, I'm more concerned with your situation."

Mike made a face to dismiss that. "The heat of passion is past. They aren't about to take on the AG's office."

"No, babe, only you. Believe that a few are crazy enough to bring you down."

"In the words of a past president: bring it on. I need to, I'll take on those dicks and their bosses, including that lieutenant."

"Don't confuse your thinking by including Montrose. He's as honest and sincere as they come. But some of the others will go to any lengths to prevent you exposing something that might be detrimental to them."

"You saying some of your boys in blue might be complicit in that assassination?"

"No I'm not. But there's all kinds of damn corruption in

216

Naw'lins. My take on it is everybody's fretting whether exposure of that killing opens one hell of a can of worms."

"Is it possible that there's official blanketing of that business?"

"I'm trying my best not to learn any of those answers."

"But you have to be concerned that justice prevails."

"More important to me, Mike, is not to end up with the reputation of the whistle-blower who brought them down. I've taken enough scorn serving on the rat squad."

When Mike stared obliquely at her, she explained: "It's important to me to remain a member in good standing in the cop universe. I like living and working in Naw'lins."

"Even at the cost of letting assassins go free?"

"Just don't want to finish my career despised as a rat and forced to leave the city."

"Glad I don't suffer your qualms about taking down dirty cops."

"Be careful, Mike. They'll resort to anything to prevent your clearing the case. Some of those guys are crazy enough to murder when they feel threatened. Cops gone rogue suffer from authority-induced insanity."

"Let them do their worst. I damn sure intend to find the killers of three prominent African-Americans."

"How close are you, incidentally, to something fundamental?"

Mike blinked, aware they were touching on a subject he didn't want to discuss. Unsure how loyal Kaylee was to her department deterred him divulging too much. "Do we have to talk shop all afternoon? Let's take a sabbatical from police work."

"Works for me. What would you like to do after lunch?"

"How 'bout we go back to the room for an encore."

"We haven't even taken a dip in the pool yet."

217

"That's not exactly the dip I have in mind, sweet thing."

"C'mon, we need to dunk our parts in that water."

"It's only March, for God's sake. That's too damned early to go swimming."

"Don't be a baby, Mike. It's a beautifully warm day. And the pool is heated."

"I've got a different heat needs attention."

"After we've dunked in the pool, big man. I see a pool like that and there's no way you can keep me out of it. I can even postpone sex until after I immerse myself in there. Well, that is, I can postpone the encore."

#   #

Chapter Forty-Five

"Fifteen minutes of splashing is enough for me"

Kaylee chuckled while accompanying Mike in climbing out of the pool and searching for two unoccupied chaise lounges. They considered it a miracle to find them side-by-side amongst those pool-siders, stretched out like seals roosting on shore rocks.

Kaylee turned over on her side and studied Mike. "I checked up on you and discovered a full-fledged enigma. What motivates a guy with an engineering degree to become a cop? And don't sluff me off with some high-minded claptrap about serving the public weal or occupying an envious position in the upper echelon of the AG's office as superior or something."

"You saying you want to hear a boring history?"

"Nothing about you will bore me. Well, some things do a really good job."

They laughed together. "Born and grew up in Lake Charles," Mike said. "Did a hitch in the Coast Guard after finishing high school—where policing harbors became my first cop work. After mustering out I took my daddy's advice to get educated."

"Another late-bloomer," Kaylee remarked.

"With no idea what I wanted to do with the rest of my life. My daddy, a drilling crew foreman, advised me to become an engineer and I'd never be broke. So I studied mechanical engineering at Louisiana Tech in Ruston. Meanwhile I worked part-time as a guard in a warehouse on the river. It wasn't as exciting as a number of incidents in the Coast Guard, but it allowed me to strut my stuff and brandish

219

authority. Upon graduation I landed a job with a farm machinery manufacturer in West Monroe."

"Sounds really mundane."

"Yep, it wasn't work I became enthusiastic about. Fact is, the prospect of performing repetitive tasks for a lifetime depressed me. Had a few buddies practicing law. Prosecuting or defending criminals sounded more exciting than shuffling diagrammed drawings all day and filling out check-sheets on the various machinery. So I quit and moved to Baton Rouge, where I became a state cop and enrolled in law school at LSU."

"How long it take you to finish?"

"Didn't. Realized after a year of it I wasn't enthralled by jurisprudence any more than I was by engineering. Since I liked cop work I switched to criminal justice."

"Which served to advance you in the state police."

"Believe that. Got real satisfaction contributing to society."

"Don't engineers contribute to society?"

"Of course, but not as immediately as cops. Engineers check on quality control and do R and D that makes a product more serviceable in the future."

"Isn't that important to society?"

"Of course it is. But cop's work is hands on, remedying a crisis on the spot, protecting people from predators. The daily challenges kept me wired."

"Like most of us," Kaylee said, "that make cop-work our career."

"Within three years they put me in the investigative bureau, and I knew I'd found my niche. Truly enjoyed examining shippers, warehousers, importers and exporters for fraud. There were no end of those slicksters trying to pull all kinds of swifties, and it gave me satisfaction to bring them down."

"Nothing like toppling the mighty," Kaylee said. "And, I imagine, you made yourself a hell of a reputation, which resulted in Jace Morreau appointing you to head up his investigative body."

"That's the way how it went. What attracted you to police work? Women are less likely than men to pick that profession."

"You're living in the past, like most small-minded men. Women today seek careers, with aspirations not limited to what used to be considered female-type pursuits."

"So what inspired a really good-looking lady to strap on a gun, when she could have pursued any number of more prestigious vocations?"

"Not all that eager to attend any of the big-time colleges, I settled for a two-year stint in Community College. During that time I worked part-time as a clerk in Municipal Court, which brought me in contact with cops, especially the female variety. When I turned twenty-one I applied for the job and got accepted."

"That's interesting as hell. But you know what? It's time to go back to the room and take care of business."

"God, you're a bull."

#   #

Chapter Forty-Six

They panted exhaustion and lay on their backs to recover from the exertion. Kaylee ran her hand across Mike's chest and murmured: "You're quite dark. I heard you're Mexican and part Indian. Or should I be politically correct and say Native American . . . Native Mexican, or one?"

"Say any damn thing you want. It amounts to the same thing. My daddy was Mexican and my mama was Cajun and Choctaw."

"That's interesting. How'd they happen to fuse?"

"The oil exploration company my daddy worked for in Texas sent him to ramrod a drilling crew in the Calcasieu River. He met my mother waitressing in a little café in Lake Charles."

"So you're a quarter redskin, which is as politically incorrect as I can get."

"Fact is, I'm more than a quarter. My daddy, whose parents came from the state of Coahuila in Mexico, were also part Indian. How 'bout you? For someone with an Irish name you sure don't resemble a freckle-faced colleen."

She chuckled. "My family on both sides descended from the French Creole settlers, with an intermix of German. Got stuck with that moniker by marrying an Irishman mixed with Creole."

"Every damn person I meet is mixed," Mike said. "The whole damn population is polyglot."

"And getting more so," Kaylee said, "with each succeeding generation."

"Imagine what our kids would be like," Mike said.

222

"Let's not have any. I'm forty-one, too old to raise kids. Didn't have any when I was married, mostly because the one time I was pregnant the child was stillborn."

"Sorry to hear that."

"It's a depressing experience. My ex and I never tried again—mostly because the marriage had begun to deteriorate."

"What did he do, to leave you so well off?"

"Had a couple of vintage clothing stores—one on Toulouse in The Quarter, and the other on Gentilly near Dillard. He did real well, selling costumes for Mardis Gras and other holidays. But he got wanderlust and sold out to move to California."

"Just like that?"

"Don't know what kind of bug bit his ass, but he was hell bent on going there."

"Maybe another woman?"

"Wouldn't have surprised me. Sonofabitch had more side stuff than the Brewhouse has choices of po'boys."

"Which apparently didn't bother you."

"We'd already agreed to disagree, had separated while not yet divorced."

"At least he split the take with you."

"Not voluntarily. But I had a good lawyer—a woman."

"And you never found someone else you wanted to marry."

"Nor did I find anyone wanted to marry me."

"No way I believe that." He leaned over and kissed her breast. "You 'bout as fine a specimen of woman as I've ever met. Doubt I'll ever get enough of you."

"Hope I don't see encore in your eyes."

"Sorry, darlin', I don't think there's enough energy left in this

223

ole' body. However, no harm in trying to stoke my boiler."

"I'd rather get a drink."

"I'll call room service."

"Hell no! I need to get out of this room and get me some damned respite."

"Done," he said as he jumped out of bed, grasped her hand, and pulled her into the shower with him. They laughed and giggled as they lathered each other.

#   #

Forty-Seven

Wanting to look and feel festive he donned a Hawaiian styled shirt, its tail worn outside of his chinos, and slipped his feet into loafers without bothering with socks. But since he dressed quicker than she, he groaned impatience until she did her hair, finished putting on a face, and wiggled into a form-fitting pastel sundress.

He beamed his approval as he took her hand and they descended in the elevator to the main lobby. There they joined the human eddy traversing the concourse in every direction. They knew they neared the casino because of the buzz emanating from it—a cacophony of hysteria and forced hilarity punctuated by bells reverberating in a concert of machines gobbling up money.

Spotting the bar on their right, their brows wrinkled at its legend of EIGHT75. But they shrugged off the enigma and sat at a small table in the back end, the furthest from the din of the casino.

Kaylee ordered a hurricane, a mixture of light and dark rum with passion-fruit juice and limejuice, shaken with ice, then strained. Mike opted for his usual, Knob Creek on the rocks.

"You're boring," she said, "with your choice of drinks anyway."

"First you call me stodgy, now you call me boring."

"But I'd never say you were disappointing."

He lifted his squat glass to clink against her tall one. "May it never end."

"But let's hope it slows down a peg. We keep this up another day and a half and I'll have trouble walking on Monday."

Mike chuckled—then gawked. He struggled to swallow while

225

gesticulating to the far end of the bar close to the casino.

Kaylee gasped when she saw pudgy Nicholas Boheemer, with his unmistakable hangdog look ease onto a stool. A tall, Italianesque-looking man in wire-rimmed glasses mounted the adjoining stool.

"Holy shit," Mike said, "I think we struck the mother lode."

"He's probably just down here for the weekend, same as us," Kaylee said.

"Sure he is, and shacking with a guy answers the description of the tall guy who shot all three of those people at Belmonde's."

"A lot of men are tall. You're tall."

"He's taller than I am—wears wire-rimmed glasses—and appears to be Italian."

"You have any idea how many Italian-type men there are in Naw'lins, much less Lu'ziana?"

"We're in Mississippi." Then Mike sniggered when Boheemer passed the guy a stuffed envelope. The man thrust it into the inside pocket of his tweedy sportcoat. The bartender served Boheemer a drink and appeared to ask his companion if he wanted one also. Tall-guy shook his head as he rose and loped down the concourse toward the main lobby. Boheemer remained there, sipping his drink and lazily scanning the gamblers, seemingly without concerns.

"I'm going to tail him," Mike said. "You keep track of Nicky boy."

"Aren't you jumping to conclusions? Besides, we're here on a break from the job. Or have you forgotten that we agreed to put police work on hold for the weekend?"

"Hey, come on, girl, we can't just sit here and ignore them."

"For God's sake, Mike, let it go."

"Let it go, my ass." Mike rose and sidled around the wide

226

opening, hoping to conceal himself in the swirl of humanity to prevent being spotted by Boheemer . . . didn't want the pudge alerting Tall-guy by cellphoning him. Arriving in the main lobby he grimaced disappointment when he failed to see Tall-guy's head protruding above the swirling crowd.

Spotting the glass entrance doors, he assumed the guy exited the hotel. Hell, Tall-guy hadn't taken a drink or gambled. Why stay? Mike accepted if he chose wrong he'd lose the guy. Hell, he'd come to a casino and so far this was his only gamble.

#   #

Chapter Forty-Eight

Mike pushed through the glass doors to peer around the outer vestibule. There! . . . folding his lank into a taxi. Mike flexed to jump into the next taxi in line.

But a number of people queued up for taxis, with a doorman assisting them. Shit! If he waited his turn he'd be fourth in line and likely lose sight of Tall-guy's cab. Not anxious to squabble with the doorman or those waiting, he ran up the line to the last taxi and jumped in. "I need you to follow that taxi already headed down the ramp."

The cabbie swiveled around to frown disbelief at the bossy guy in the raucous-colored shirt who'd audaciously bi-passed those waiting in line.

"It's imperative. I'm an investigator for the Attorney General's office." Mike omitted informing that he worked for Louisiana, not Mississippi.

"Mind showing me some kind of identification?" the cabbie drawled.

Mike patted his pocket and realized he hadn't taken his creds, not expecting to serve in any official capacity when he and Kaylee went down for a drink. It also occurred to him that he hadn't taken a weapon. Damn! He felt naked.

"Left it in my hotel room. Came here for the weekend to relax. Never expected to happen on that perp in the casino—a guy on the fugitive list."

When the driver stared dumbly at him, Mike said: "You need to accept that I'm a law enforcement agent—on a critical mission."

But the cabbie stared at him, without indicating doing as bid.

"I'm not planning anything dangerous," Mike said, "only tailing that other taxi to see where it takes its occupant. Then I'll call in the local police. That service, incidentally will earn you a twenty besides the fare."

The guy tilted his head in consideration, then turned forward and nosed into the driveway between incoming and outgoing vehicles. The next two taxis in the front of the line had taken on fares and pulled out, leaving no alternative but to follow them. Both Mike and the driver ignored the reproachful gesture of the doorman.

By the time they reached the bottom of the ramp, the target taxi had made a left onto Route Ninety. But the light changed, denying the taxi in front of Mike's from turning—consequently his as well. Mike flagged his head but refrained from instructing the guy to violate traffic laws.

Squirming on the edge of the seat, he glared at cars and trucks whizzing past while wishing to hell for a green arrow to permit them to continue the chase. He felt like he'd run out of breath before that occurred.

Shit! They no longer had the target taxi in sight. "Mind speeding up and maybe catching up to them?"

"That thing's a good bit up the pike by now, Hoss, and I'm not all that anxious to lose my hack license for speeding."

"Don't worry. I'll cover you."

The cabbie half-turned and snickered. But after a moment he grudgingly pulled into the left lane and passed a few cars. Meanwhile Mike peered up every side street they passed, in case the quarry turned off. With the beach on the left, he only needed to scan streets on the right. But realization daunted him that spotting the tail end of a taxi

229

wasn't going to mean he'd found his guy.

He clenched his teeth to contain impatience. Whoa! He did a double take when they whizzed past a lighthouse in the center medium of the highway. Why? But, concerned with the pursuit, he dismissed that incongruity.

A slow-up ahead detained a number of cabs, so Mike peered into them and brightened when he believed he identified the tall guy with wire-rimmed glasses in the lead cab. When the light changed he coaxed the driver to pass slower vehicles. He ignored the man's grumbling, anxious for them to move close enough to positively identify Tall-guy.

"Not too close!" Mike admonished. "Stay two or three cars behind." With vehicles turning off, it concerned him that the driver or occupant not make them. Gangsters are edgy, and this guy more than likely continually glanced over his shoulder.

"Speed up a little," Mike prodded when they fell too far behind.

But a little farther along Mike instructed: "Slow down. Give them space so we don't get made."

"Jesus sakes alive, sure hope I ain't unlucky enough to get any more of you pickity state cops."

Mike gritted his teeth to stifle retort, sure didn't want to provoke the man into having a tantrum and quitting. So he hunched forward and stared out of the windshield, suppressing edginess as the pursuit led them quite a distance. Finally, a little past Route Forty-Nine the target-taxi turned right onto Rodenberg Road and rumbled along for two and a half blocks before pulling into the parking lot of an economy motel.

"Pull up on the outer perimeter." Mike directed. When the man complied, Mike climbed out and sneaked into the closest rows of cars to watch Tall-guy stroll to one of the doors and knock on it. Mike couldn't see the person who opened the door to let him enter. So he hurried back and told the cabbie: "Need you to wait while I reconnoiter."

"No way, Hoss. You slip off without paying and I'm stuck for that money. Still ain't seen nothing to prove you any kind of official— city, state, or otherwise."

Mike peeled off two twenties and handed them over. "That take care of it?"

"Sure does, Hoss. Be waiting right here for you."

Mike stooped to reduce visibility while slinking between parked cars to where he had a clear view of the door the tall guy entered. No doubt in his mind that the fat envelope he'd observed had been stuffed with greenbacks as a payoff for the assassination he believed was engineered by Kenman and Boheemer. Now he needed to prove that.

Spotting a car pulling into the lot, he flattened himself behind a bulky pick-up truck and watched two men get out of it. Holy shit! One of them answered the description of the chubby guy that had fired high over Kenman's head. What the hell was his name? Yeah, Chucho Banzini. The chub looked like a donkey with his head bobbing as he led the way toward one of the motel units.

Remembering one of the salient features of the guy's description, Mike sniffed the air, but wasn't able to discern his aftershave lotion. Accepting that the distance prevented that unless a breeze wafted it his way, he remained concealed and watched those two go to the same door as Tall-guy had. One knocked and a minute later they were let in.

Did he really have the assassins in that room? . . . Been blessed with that stroke of luck to take them down? There were at least four of them, and probably five, maybe six considering a driver more than likely stayed with the blue van outside of Belmonde's.

Whatever, they outgunned him. Hell, he didn't have a gun. He patted himself again and cursed himself for not having taken his weapon. He didn't even have credentials, besides being out of his jurisdiction for chasing bad guys.

Nor had he brought his cellphone to call the locals to assist him —goddammit! If he had the cabbie call it in it'd probably take ten or twenty minutes before a patroling cruiser arrived . . . even a half hour if they considered other calls more urgent. No way one solitary trooper is going to undertake the arrest of five or six armed hoods. And Mike cursed himself for not having a gun—making himself feel useless.

Best thing was to take the taxi to police headquarters. Hopefully those mooks didn't book before he got back with the troops. He jotted down the license plate and a description of the two-year-old gray Mercury the pudgeball arrived in, then hurried back to his taxi.

# #

232

Chapter Forty-Nine

The cabbie scratched his head and gazed around as if groping in memory.

"Don't you know where the police station is?"

"Had to think on it for a minute. Yeah, I remember now—up Porter Street. It's not somewhere I go all that often, thank the good Lord."

Mike struggled not to squirm as they drove mile after mile back up Highway Ninety . . . with time ticking away. How long would those yahoos remain at the motel? They approached that lighthouse in the median, hitting Mike with the realization that they'd gone almost all the way back to the Beau Rivage.

Hell, it might serve him to have credentials to get the police moving off their tails, and save time waiting for them to authenticate his authority . . . giving those miscreants time to fade away.

Gritting his teeth as he made the decision, he instructed the cabbie: "Stop at the hotel first since we're that close, so I can pick up my credentials."

The cabbie grumbled compliance, but when he parked he again grouched: "How I know you don't cheat me out of the fare on the meter. Still haven't seen thing one verifying you're a cop or nothing, Hoss."

Mike gave him another twenty, then dashed up to his room. It didn't surprise him not to find Kaylee there, since she surveilled Boheemer.

After gathering up his wallet and credenials, he tucked his off-duty gun, a twenty-five Beretta semi-automatic, in the back of his belt, concealed by his sportshirt. He'd locked his nine-millimeter in the trunk of his car and didn't want to take the time to go to the garage and back, so accepted he'd make do with this and hurried back to the taxi.

The cabbie rolled out of the circular driveway and turned west on Route Ninety again, for a couple of blocks to turn north when they reached that lighthouse in the highway divide. Mike grunted, too much on edge to be amused by sight of that incongruity for the third time. It occurred to him that he hadn't noticed it when first arriving at the hotel.

He dismissed that as they pulled up to the modern two-story building with glass doors extending across its front, giving it the appearance of a library or museum. But the legend on its front of Public Safety Center convinced Mike that they had, indeed, arrived at the local cop house.

He paid the cabbie, no longer needing him, and hurried up the four steps to enter and gaze around, at the courtroom on one hand and doors to somewhere on the other. Spotting the directory he found the office of Director of Police listed as room 2059. So he jogged up the angled stairway in the center of the entrance hall. Finding that suite, he entered to encounter two mature women in civilian dress, one white and one black, at desks constructed as high counters.

The white one glanced up, then returned to her paper work, ignoring him. The black one stared at him as her way of inquiring about his visit . . . typical municipal clerks. He flashed his credentials. "Like to have a word with the officer in charge."

The black woman gave him a critical once-over, then a twice-over of his colorful shirt. "And your reason, sir?"

"It's an important matter that I'm hoping not to have to repeat while going up the hierarchy of command." He gestured to his creds. "Time is of the essence, so please let me discuss the matter with the officer in charge."

The woman sighed as she slid her bulk off her stool and ushered Mike into an inner office where a stout and balding guy in uniform gazed at them from behind a desk. "This is Assistant Chief Arlen Bouwill. You have you a visitor, sir."

That chubby man eyed the visitor quizzically. After perusing Mike's credentials the assistant chief half rose to shake his hand and gesture to a chair near the desk. He looked askance at Mike's attire.

Mike sat, ignoring the appraisal and leaned toward him. "A group of men suspected of murdering three people in Louisiana have gathered in a motel room on Rodenberg Road. I need them taken into custody."

"I'm going to assume you positively identified said suspects," the assistant chief said, slouched in his swivel chair, his demeanor bereft of enthusiasm.

"You must have received the APB sent out from Baton Rouge a few days ago of an Italian-looking chubby male by name of Banzini."

"Got so many bolos from every which place, ain't no way I can keep them all in mind. Now you real sure you positively identified those so-called fugitives?"

"I'm not a neophyte, Assistant Chief, having twenty-four years in police work. Those skels answer the description of the perpetrators of a mass murder in New Orleans."

"Mind explaining how you happened upon them here in Biloxi?"

"Spotted one meeting at the bar in the Beau Rivage with someone we suspect of being complicit."

"But you didn't bother taking anybody into custody."

"It's out of my jurisdiction. That's why I followed the guy to that motel, where he met up with a few other fugitives."

"And the names of those others?"

235

"I don't know their names, only—"

"Maybe y'all arrest folks in Loo'ziana on something that flimsy, but we don't here in Mississippi—not in Harrison County anyway."

"I need this done. And there's no time to waste. I'll take the heat for it if I'm wrong. You came to Louisiana we'd do it for you."

"But I'd make sure to have me a whole bunch more to go on."

"Good God, assistant chief, you can't just sit there and let a bunch committed a triple homicide slip through our hands."

"Let's not make this *our* hands. Those is *your* hands, Hoss. And I'm not about to go out on a thin plank and arrest some Eye-talians because you think they may have killed somebody in Naw'lins."

"Call your superior then, to get authorization."

"Don't think it'd be a good idea to disturb the Director of Police while he's on a long weekend with his wife and kiddies visiting relatives in Pensacola, over in Florida."

"Then you have to make the decision on your own, assistant chief, and without further delay. This is imperative."

"To *you*, Hoss. I don't see where that applies to me."

"It damn sure will if they're not apprehended and the media broadcasts your lack of cooperation across every state on the Gulf."

"Tell you what," Assistant Chief Bouwill said, running a chubby hand through his thinning hair as he sat erect, "I'll see if I can reach someone in our attorney general's office who can make that decision. But I'm not all that optimistic that'll happen this late on Saturday afternoon."

Mike anguished as the minutes ticked away, watching the assistant chief make half a dozen phone calls in lackadaisical fashion. He chatted for a minute or two with whoever answered, then shrugged to Mike to indicate he'd come up empty.

236

As a last resort, the assistant chief contacted someone in the Harrison County DA's office with enough clout to sanction detaining out-of-town suspects. Groaning as he hung up, he pressed a button on his intercom and growled into the device: "Put out a call to some of the boys to come in and help take down some out-of-state bad boys."

#   #

Chapter Fifty

Mike gritted his teeth to conceal angst for the nearly two hours it took to assemble a group of six patrolmen and one detective to comprise the Emergency Service Team, Biloxi's version of SWAT. He and the assistant chief accompanied them in three police cruisers to the motel.

Mike granted them their due as a law enforcement team since they looked the part in Kevlar helmets and flak jackets while carrying heavy armaments. Two had bolt action Winchester 70s, rifles capable of knocking over a full-grown bull. Another two had Remington 870 shotguns with seven-round magazines. The detective toted a CAR 15 carbine with a folding stock.

Considering that kind of firepower, Mike had to concede that they weren't as Toonerville as he first perceived them to be. But they didn't exhibit the verve he'd have liked to see. Fact is, a couple of them didn't impress him as all that anxious to get involved in a shoot-out. Two griped about being called in on Saturday, which this week happened to be one of their days off.

Arriving at the motel, they ascertained that the target room had no rear exit or other means of egress. They then took up positions, two cops on one side of the door, with Mike, the assistant chief and the detective on the other. Four cops spread out behind nearby cars in the parking lot.

The detective snickered when Mike brandished his Beretta. "Best you stay out of the way if all you brought is that toy."

"Besides," the assistant chief added, "we need to avoid any kind of problem, such as a cop outside his jurisdiction shooting someone that turned out not to be the fugitive they sought."

Mike nodded and stepped back. Hell, they all holstered big-ass semi-automatics to back up their assault weapons. The Assistant Chief had his fist wrapped around the handle of a long-barreled forty-four Magnum, capable of knocking over a Sumo wrestler.

The detective rapped on the door and yelled: "We the damn police. Open this damn door!"

Receiving no response, he growled; "Open up 'fore we break this damn door down!"

No response, so the detective put his ear to the door. "Don't hear sound one."

One of the cops positioned near the parked cars trotted to the motel office and returned a few moments later with the manager. That man used his master key to open the door . . . to a vacant room.

Still, the detective and one of the cops ventured in with guns at the ready. "All clear," one of them yelled out. The assistant chief went in to survey, and after a few minutes waved Mike to join in examining the interior. It had a tiny closet and a bathroom barely large enough to accommodate the necessary fixtures. But they didn't find even a scrap of paper to indicate anyone had been there.

Not a single thing appeared to have been used, including the two glasses with paper covers near the ice bucket; not that lifting fingerprints would be helpful. Hell, they'd like as not lift countless fingerprints from a motel room. Mike hurried into the parking lot in search of the fat guy's car, though he didn't expect it to still be there.

"They must have spotted you casing the place," the assistant chief said.

"Or got tipped," Mike growled.

"We'll check the lugs," the detective said. "They made or

239

received a phone call, we'll trace it to the source."

"Not if they used one of them prepaid rent-a-phones," one of the uniforms said.

Mike shook his head in frustration. Then he turned to the manager. "What's the name of the person who rented this room?"

"Most who pay in cash use Smith. Don't require no identification when they hand over greenbacks."

"How 'bout you describe him," Assistant Chief Bouwill said.

The manager scratched his head. "Must be nigh two dozen folks rented rooms today—more'n a few with a gal waiting in the car. Most look alike after a while. 'Sides, danged few hang around all that long."

"Perhaps you'll accommodate me," Mike said to Bouwill, "by putting out an APB on the car. I have its description and license number. Catch Chucho Banzini in it and we have one of them—maybe two, with the possibility he'll lead us to the others."

"One or two of how many?" the Assistant Chief asked.

"Many as six. Don't rightly know. But bagging at least one beats the hell out of ending up with none."

The assistant chief shrugged. "If that assistant district attorney approves it."

"Appreciate everything you've done," Mike said to placate the guy, knowing he'd rankled him earlier. Hell, he had no right to criticize the way they operated despite their exhibiting too little enthusiasm.

"One of the boys'll drop you off at yo' hotel," the Assistant Chief said. "I'll call you if the bolo turns up anything."

"Really appreciate it. Here's my cellphone number as well as my room number." Sighing concession, he hoped he'd get that call and resume the chase. Damn it to hell! So close, yet so far.

#   #

240

Chapter Fifty-One

Mike plodded through the teeming lobby of the Beau Rivage, aware of the reverberations of clanging machines and hyperventilating voices punctuated by shrill laughter. Hurrying back to the little bar in the corner of the casino he grimaced disappointment for not spotting Kaylee—or Boheemer.

Only two customers slumped over their drinks. The bartender chatted with a grinning waitress at the service end of the bar. Neither had a clue regarding the two people Mike inquired about.

He called his room on the house phone. Since no one answered he trod up and down aisles between clanking and blinking machines, narrowed by avid players. Goddammit, why can't he spot Kaylee? Damned if he enjoyed running around like a chicken with its head cut off. Nope, he didn't need to encounter Boheemer, having nothing to pin on him.

Even if he confronted the chub he didn't dare let himself get carried away since he had no legal right to shake the guy for information based merely on having observed him handing an envelope to someone fitting the description of the assassin. Wasn't a judge alive wouldn't reprove him for not having a scintilla of substantiation that money changed hands or that Boheemer was involved in a criminal conspiracy.

Grimacing resignation, he weaved through the swirling gamblers and spectators, groaning disgruntlement while rounding the banks of flashing machines, scouring every crowded, bell-ringing aisle. Where did all theses addicts come from?

More importantly: where in hell had Kaylee gone? No, he

doubted Boheemer harmed her, considering all the witnesses. Besides, Kaylee wasn't no pushover. He hoped to hell she hadn't followed that mook out of the hotel, put herself in jeopardy.

Passing the Hurricane Bar in the center of the action, he resisted the urge to stop for a drink, yearning for the palliative effect of Knob Creek on his tonsils. Then his head jerked when he caught a glimpse of her slumped at a slot machine—in a congestion of mesmerized players. He scanned the area but didn't spot Boheemer.

Approaching her, he asked: "What are you doing *here*?"

"Fighting another losing battle." She snickered as she plunged coins into it.

"You keep track of Boheemer?"

"Tried to, but he disappeared in that shuffle of humans. Figured I'd kill time until you got back, from wherever the hell you went . . . hours ago. What took so long?"

He grimaced as he wrestled with how to account for his time without sharing everything with her. Her attitude since spotting Boheemer with the lanky guy with glasses didn't fill him with confidence. Actually, she impressed him as being averse to pursuing Boheemer or even suspecting the guy as complicit. And it galled him to think that whatever he divulged might get back to Shayde. To sidestep her question, he said: "I'll check to see which room he's staying in."

"Did that. He's not registered in the hotel. Either he didn't intend to stay or he used a fictitious name."

"Great!" Mike punched the machine in frustration. Its lights flashed. Eight coins clunked out. They stared at it in awe.

"Looks like the right way to play this thing," she said, forcing a chuckle. "Most I've won. What'd that tall guy lead you to?"

"Evaporated." Mike averted his eyes as he deliberated how

242

much to disclose. His feelings for her nagged him to be candid, but his concern for too much getting back to Shayde repressed doing that.

"So what in hell kept you occupied for three, four hours?"

"Had them in sight for a while."

"Them?" Kaylee's narrowed eyes probed his face.

He winced. "The tall guy and the taxi driver."

"You blowing smoke, Mike?"

"Why in hell would I do that? Too bad you lost Boheemer. My take on it is that he came here to deliver that payment. Having accomplished that he split. Ain't proud to admit it, but I lost Tall Guy."

"Okay, don't beat up on yourself over something you weren't prepared for. Those events took us by surprise. But what in hell took you three, four hours?"

Mike threw his hands out while groping for an explanation that might wash. No way he dared share it all with her, not with his suspicion-bell ringing. Her reaction when they spotted Boheemer with the tall guy replayed in his head, as did her objection to his shadowing the suspected assassin. It robbed him of confidence to be open with her.

Her hard-eyed stare prompted him to explain. "The guy made a couple of stops, leaving me no alternative but wait for his next move. Next thing, he vanished."

"Why do I get the feeling you're blowing smoke?"

"No more than you are. How in hell can you lose a fat moose like Boheemer?"

"You saying you don't believe me?"

"No, nothing like that. But that tall guy got spooked. Was pretty sure Boheemer hadn't spotted me when I sneaked past him. Yet somebody tipped the tall guy."

"What in hell you insinuating?"

243

"Nothing. Just running things over in my mind. Okay, I'll corral Nicky boy Monday and shake some answers out of him."

"Not a good idea . . . not in Naw'lins. Not with Shayde all that friendly with them. Besides, you'll be taking on Kenman, which is to say one powerful political organization headed up by Big Willie Hoke."

"I intend to take them down."

"Without one damn thing to base your accusation on? Chill, Mike, or you'll likely end up knee-deep in some rank-smelling do-do."

"They don't worry me."

"They should, considering you're still on the hook for slugging two dicks and may end up being the one taken down."

# #

Chapter Fifty-Two

"You've been distant since striking out with those alleged bad guys," Kaylee said. Resentment edged her voice as she glanced across the small table in the cafeteria at the garage end of the hotel concourse. She glared at Mike, desultorily munching a buttered corn muffin with coffee for his breakfast. She'd opted for a croissant with butter and jelly with hers.

When he didn't respond, she asked: "You blaming me for that tall guy getting away?"

When he shook his head without raising his eyes to her, she added: "You ran out of passion after encountering Nicky Boheemer and that Italian guy."

He made a wry face but didn't contest her statement. Scowling, she asked: "Is it that you don't trust me to share with me? Or do you suspect me of aiding and abetting Boheemer?"

He flailed a hand about while searching for words to refute her allegations—without revealing anything that might get back to Shayde.

"You're sure as hell not being open with me," she said. "Fact is, rather than desire me last night, you all but recoiled when I rolled close to you. Are you only interested in pleasuring yourself when you're not chasing bad guys?"

"That's not it, dammit. That's not one bit of—"

"No, of course not. It's not me and it's not you. However, you won't even share what happened when you tailed that tall guy—for three, four hours."

"Oh, God! Back off, Kaylee, before a good thing goes to seed."

245

"Seems to me it went fallow yesterday after—"

The trill of Mike's cellphone interrupted her. As a result of not being prepared yesterday by not having it when he needed it, he took it with him this morning, and answered it. "Hello. Morning, Armand. Tried to raise you last night. Glad to hear it, good buddy. You deserve to enjoy a night out with Ysette."

He shifted about on the seat, considered turning away from Kaylee, but accepted that wouldn't prevent her from hearing every word . . . besides pissing her off. No, he didn't dare get up and stroll away. Hell, she heard to whom he spoke. He sure didn't want her to conclude that he was being secretive. So he shrugged and said: "Can I call you back in a bit? You're on your way out and won't be available until late afternoon?"

He clenched his teeth. "Okay, got a few things I need to share with you. Yep, got news. No, it's not all good. Ran across a tall guy fitting the description of the one alleged to have taken out Darby Williams and the others. He met with Nicky Boheemer yesterday afternoon here in Mississippi. Yep, I'm in Biloxi. I'll explain it later. Yep, had a run-in with a couple of the locals. You cooled them down? Good. And Jace called them too? Even better."

He winced at Armand's request to hear what happened. Glancing at Kaylee, he compressed his lips, then responded to Armand's question. "Yep, tall guy later joined up with Chucho Banzini at a seedy motel not far away."

He peeked over at Kaylee, hoping she hadn't been alert to that Italian name. But seeing the expression on her face he knew he'd let the cat out of the bag. Hunching acceptance of needing to explain a heap of things when he got off the phone, he continued with Armand. "Short story is that by the time I rounded up the locals to make an arrest, the

246

bad guys had booked. Nope, haven't the slightest. But authorities here have a statewide APB out on them, including the description and license plate of the car Banzini is traveling in. Do the same in Louisiana and get a bolo out in Alabama and Tennessee. I'll fax you the plate number and car description from the hotel desk to avoid any mistakes. Absolutely, good buddy, will keep you informed."

While clicking off he glanced at Kaylee. God, he hoped she didn't realize he'd said he'd fax the information to deny her hearing it. Nor did he need her going ballistic. Dammit, he wished he didn't have to be secretive. However, memory of her reactions yesterday, along with intuition, prevented him from sharing with her.

He shrunk into his shoulders when she leveled anger-darkened blue eyes on him. "You told me you never heard thing one about that fugitive with the Italian name."

"To prevent things getting back to Shayde and Kenman."

"Don't trust me?"

"Couldn't, with so much on the line, and uncertain where your loyalty lies."

"Slept with me—bounced on my bones—had your lips on my parts—but don't trust me. Fed me a lot of romantic tripe while deceiving me."

"Try to understand, Kaylee, I—"

"Understand what . . . that you have so little regard for me?"

Shit! How was he to explain that he didn't feel free to share it all with her?

"You going to trust me," she asked, "and fill me in, or go on leaving me out?"

"You going to respect that information as privileged, or pass it on to Shayde?"

247

"I report to Lieutenant Montrose, not Shayde. And you committed to share discoveries with him."

Oh shit! Feeling boxed, he turned to stare at the large windows as he wondered how much to divulge and how to justify not revealing the rest. The scraping sound of her chair brought his eyes back to see her rising from the table. God, no, he didn't want her to go . . . fretted that if she left she might not come back . . . considering her unforgiving nature.

"Since we have our own cars," she said, "I won't have to spend an hour of driving back to Naw'lins with you moping about some mooks giving you the slip—and blaming me for it. Maybe I'll see you back there." She snatched up her purse and spun away.

"Hold on a minute. We need to—"

But she strode out of the cafeteria to intersperse with those traversing the wide concourse of window shoppers along with those arriving and those departing. Slamming down his napkin he started to rise with intent to pursue her when his cellphone rang again. Answering it, he recognized the drawl of Assistant Chief Arlen Bouwill.

"Good damn news, director. Our state police picked up yo' Eye-talian by name of Banzini for speeding on Route Fifty-Five, up north near Hernando."

"Super!" Mike's memory fixed Hernando on the map of Mississippi, just south of Memphis. Obviously the mook headed for familiar precincts. Elation from receiving that news momentarily blanked the problems with Kaylee.

"Got me a chopper warming up at the airport," Bouwill said. "A cruiser is on its way to pick you up. It ought to be at your front door in a minute or two."

Mike thought of going to the room for his weapon and a jacket, then decided against encountering Kaylee and having to make her privy to things he'd prefer not getting back to Shayde and the NOPD. Yes, he hated himself for shutting her out, but had long ago accepted that duty overrode personal considerations.

He'd worn a blue business shirt, while not a necktie, nor a jacket. Thankfully he had his wallet and his creds. He could always borrow a weapon from the locals.

He headed for the entrance, clenching his jaws to suppress guilt for leaving Kaylee out of it, and winced from memory of her caustic words ringing in his ears. Somehow he'd make it up to her. But for now he attended to business, so trundled down the concourse to pass through the front entrance and peer around for the police cruiser.

#   #

Chapter Fifty-Three

Mike waved a greeting as he climbed into the helicopter, joining Assistant Chief Arlen Bouwill on the bench seat behind the pilot. No sense trying to talk with that thud-thud-thud from the spinning rotor. He noted that the detective from the motel raid sat up front. They immediately got airborne to skim across the flat countryside covered in pinewoods and crisscrossed by riverlets and streams, an expanse of forests and wetlands. Upon landing a state trooper chauffeured them from the airport to the police barracks.

There, a sergeant ushered Mike and Assistant Police Chief Bouwill into the stark interrogation room. Because of limited space the detective waited outside. A chubby guy on the far side of a metal-legged table glowered at the two uniformed cops prancing on the opposite side of the table, then at the new arrivals. Mike suppressed grinning and exposing elation when he sniffed the sweet smell of the skel's aftershave.

"Now we got us four guys, Chubby-guy scoffed, "for a friggin' traffic ticket."

"You don't mind," Bouwill said to Mike, "I'll just sit here and observe while you employ the finer points of interrogation. Might be I'll learn how y'all in the AG's office do things." He dropped into the metal chair across from the detainee, leveling on the man a toothy grin that reflected more menace than friendliness.

Banzini stared obliquely at him, then at Mike, while mouthing the words: *AG's office.* He jerked around to Bouwill when that man taunted him with: "You got you a warrant out for murder, which is why this gentleman here to take yo' ass back to Lu'ziana."

Banzini's eyes bulged—he looked about to choke. His head trembled as he watched the two state troopers trudge toward the door, to leave him with the two arrivals. "I want my lawyer!" he screeched. "We gonna' fight extradition."

Mike gritted his teeth as he dropped onto one of the hard metal chairs at the table. He choked back lambasting Bouwill for running his big mouth. By a US Supreme Court ruling the interview terminated the moment the perp asked for his lawyer. But, God a'mighty, Mike knew he couldn't wait the weeks, possibly months, it'd take going through the system to get the guy extradited before he'd have an opportunity to shake information from him.

Chances of convicting him deteriorated over time. Doubtful information obtained months from now will serve to collar the rest of the murderous crew. The moment that tall guy becomes aware he's hunted he'll disappear. Kenman and Boheemer will have been alerted to cover their tracks, resulting in the case being laid to rest in the cold-case file.

No, Mike knew he needed to pump this guy here and now to wrench information out of him that will lead to the arrest and conviction of those who engineered the thing. But that damned assistant chief had provoked Banzini into demanding a lawyer, denying Mike the legal right to question him.

Bouwill gazed at Mike with innocent-rounded eyes. "What we going to do now, Mister Chief Investigator?"

One of the state troopers clomped back to whisper in Mike's ear. "We didn't mirandize him."

Mike grimaced as he turned to level hard eyes on the detainee. "You have the right to have a lawyer, and we're going to see that you get one, either one of your own choosing or a legal aide lawyer provided to

251

you at no cost to yourself."

"I got my own," Banzini snapped—glaring defiantly at Mike, then at Bouwill and the troopers, and back to Mike.

"Your choice," Mike conceded, nodding and spreading his hands. "However, I'd like to introduce myself. Mike Molino of the Louisiana Attorney General's office. Now, you can stonewall us much as you want, but your best chance of avoiding a death sentence is to cooperate."

Banzini sniggered.

"Sure you can claim you fired high," Mike said, "and missed your target. True, you never shot anyone in that restaurant. But no lawyer in this land is going to convince a jury that you're not complicit in that cold-blooded murder of three politically important black men."

Assistant Chief Bouwill jerked around to stare wide-eyed at Mike. The two troopers paused at the open door, then shrugged and exited, pulling the door closed behind them.

Mike held his breath, hoping the assistant chief didn't object to pursuing the guy for shooting blacks, which just might encourage the skel to continue stonewalling him.

"There's going to be a big-ass hue and cry to fry yo' ass," Bouwill said, leveling that mocking grin to Banzini. ". . . Most especially from the black community."

Mike noted the sweat beads on the fat face of the sweet-smelling guy. So he added: "You need to help yourself. Y'all dug you a deep hole when you shot a renowned black banker and the former mayor of New Orleans, the first black man with a good chance of running for governor in the state of Louisiana. That leaves us no choice but go for the death penalty."

Banzini winced, then shook his head, as if in denial. He shrunk into his flabby shoulders.

"Lord knows," Bouwill said, "you not going to be happy facing that jury in Naw'lins, which likely will have more black faces than white ones."

"No doubt about that," Mike agreed. But he wished Bouwill would shut the hell up before he screwed up the interrogation worse than he already has.

"Betcha' one damned good mule," Bouwill said, flashing his ghoulish grin, "that any white ones serving on that jury will be the bleeding fucking heart kind, that sympathize with the black community."

Banzini stared vacantly from one to the other; his blinking a sign of concern.

"They going to want to skin yo' white ass, boy," Bouwill said, grinning. "You don't tell this investigator what he wants to hear, he going to see that yo' ass fries for killing those black folks."

"You gotta' prove I was there," Banzini said.

"We have fifteen witnesses," Mike said, "ready and willing to identify that sweet aftershave you wear. And, oh yes, they will describe your fat, sloppy body to a tee."

Banzini scowled at the uncomplimentary descriptions. His beady eyes glimmered with concern as he sputtered without getting a word out. And he winced when Mike said: "Plus we have one witness capable of identifying you by name."

Noting how Banzini's eyes widened, then fluttered, Mike forged ahead. "I'm not going to identify that person so your goombahs can silence him. But I will tell you he gave us your name, the kind of car you drive, and its license plate number."

Banzini's jaw fell. After a moment of sputtering, he got out: "Nobody told us them mullenyams was somebody important."

253

"You often get paid that kind of money," Mike asked, "for lighting up unimportant people?"

Banzini blinked, then averted his eyes. "Had a bad feeling about taking them out when I saw them—in suits and all. But I didn't set it up—and didn't shoot any of them."

"Who did?" Mike asked. Then he suppressed a smirk when the guy stared morosely at the tabletop. He interpreted the skel's reaction as inner conflict, a positive sign. Being Italian, consequently more than likely Catholic, Banzini probably had the compelling ritual of confession implanted at an early age.

"Now you know we put out a bulletin on you," Bouwill said, "after your car been spotted at that motel in Biloxi."

Mike clenched his teeth; wished that big mouth had the good sense to shut up. But, thankfully, Banzini slumped in his seat, defeat in his posture. "What I gotta' do to stay outta' the death chamber?"

"Give us the tall guy," Mike said. "Yep, we're onto him too."

"No way," Banzini said. "I'll be dead before you get me to court."

"Okay," Mike said as he rose and took a step toward the door.

Bouwill snickered as he rose also. "Guess we're no longer going to offer this ole' boy a chance to save his ass."

"Let him deal with a black jury in New Orleans," Mike said as he reached the door.

"How you gonna' protect me from Long Louie?" Banzini whined. "He hears I ratted him out he puts a hit out on me."

Mike paused with his hand on the doorknob. "We have ways of protecting you."

"What kinda' ways? They can reach me in stir as well as outside."

254

"We have dozens of ex-hoods in protective custody," Mike said, turning toward the detainee.

"Kept out of stir," Bouwill added, "so they can't be shanked."

"Many have survived more than a dozen years," Mike said, trying not to grit his teeth—not expose being irritated by Bouwill.

"By which time," Bouwill added, "they're forgotten by their old hood buddies. Fact is, by then most of their goombahs doing time or stuffed in a casket."

Skepticism twisted Banzini's face.

"Hey, you either trust us," Mike growled, "or risk conviction and being put to death."

"I hear that needle is something awful," Bouwill said. "That chemical makes you writhe in pain for long-ass minutes. Seen it done four, five times. Woo-ee! It's one awful sight—too painful to be described."

"When that stuff finally gets to the brain, Mike said, "it causes tremors, babbling, and saliva foaming from the mouth and nose."

Banzini shuddered. "I gotta' have a guarantee you'll protect me, that you'll never leave me alone with any other con."

"You have it," Mike said, "but only if you cooperate here and now and stop trying my damn patience. I walk out of here and all your chances go down the damn drain."

"Best you listen to what this man tells you," Bouwill said.

"Okay. Okay. But you gotta' understand I didn't shoot nobody. He told me my job was to shoot high, not to hurt a hair on that white guy's head. Louie blew away all three of them titsoons by himself. Capiche?"

"First things first," Mike said as he strode back and grasped the top of the chair. "I want Long Louie's full name."

But all he got was silence. *Please, God, don't let him quit talking now.* Okay, if he had to he'd go to the wall again. So he shrugged as he half-turned toward the door.

"Luigi Guglielmo."

Mike barely heard it. He suppressed grinning elation before turning back. "Where is Luigi Guglielmo now?"

Banzini shrugged. "When we got the phone call we split."

"Phone call from who?"

"Louie got the call on a cellphone he said he rented. All's he told us was heat was coming and we needed to haul ass out of there."

"Did he meet with Nicholas Boheemer at the Beau Rivage?"

"Don't know where he went or who he met with. He never told us nothing. Brought a envelope fulla' money and gave us our shares we been waiting for since the shooting."

"You weren't told that Kenman, the guy you were to pretend to kill, paid you for your services."

"Was kinda' obvious, even though nobody dealt with me or the others—only with Long Louie."

"If you had to guess," Assistant Chief Bouwill asked, "where do you think Long Louie headed?"

Banzini stared blankly at the round-faced man. Bouwill slapped a fat hand on the tabletop, startling Banzini. "Answer the damn question, boy!"

"He's a Memphis boy, like me. But I doubt he'll go there right off, with cops on him. More'n likely he'll hide out somewhere . . . which is what I shoulda' done instead of heading for home like some kinda' mama's boy."

"Okay," Mike said, "you be real smart and we'll take good care of you. First thing is, you tell the locals that you don't really want a

256

lawyer. Second thing is you sign a statement saying you've been mirandized, then a waver of extradition."

"No way I'm going back to Naw'lins—with them mullenyams head-hunting me."

"I'll have you taken to Baton Rouge," Mike said, "not New Orleans."

"Where you'll be a whole lot safer," Bouwill said, "than that Big Easy overpopulated with black folks."

"Police here," Mike said, "are going to put you up and keep you safe until we send Louisiana State Police to escort you to Baton Rouge."

"Long as it ain't Naw'lins. We hid out there after the shooting. All you saw was them kind strutting around and flashing their teeth and loud-talking. They ain't like us. No way I want to be taken back there and share a goddam cell with any of them."

Mike made a wry face as he considered the irony of the remark, but stifled the urge to tell him he would spend a lot of years hobnobbing with black inmates.

#   #

Chapter Fifty-Four

"Hope y'all learned a damn lesson—to stay alert because you just might stumble onto the bad guys anywhere and any time," Mike quipped after being applauded by his staff in the conference room .

"We hear you," Armand Dupuy assured.

"Why'd you need to drive all the way to Biloxi to roll dice," Chi Chi asked, "instead of crossing the street to that monster-sized casino."

"And did you go there alone?" Nelda asked in her acerbic way.

"Important thing is I got my man," Mike replied.

"Suspect you got you a woman too," Nelda said.

Mike ignored that by focusing on Armand, who said: "Let's hope we hold onto him. The DA here in Naw'lins is claiming jurisdiction because the felony occurred here. He's filed for extradition to bring Banzini to be tried here in town."

"They want to play games," Mike growled, "we'll—"

"Better let Jace Morreau handle that part," Armand said.

"Right on," Nelda said. "You got you enough grief in this town."

"Word on the street," Chi Chi said, "is you slugged out some local fuzz."

"A couple, three in the coffee shop downstairs," Julie Provenzano said, "mouthed off how they out to get you."

"But I convinced their brass," Armand said, "that any harm comes to you will bring major heat down on the entire department."

"Meanwhile," Gustave said, "Kenman and Shayde are notching up that Shreveport smear-campaign against you."

"Let them have their damn fun," Mike said. "We get hold of Long Louie and we'll likely send Kenman and party to the slammer for some hard years."

"Some of it," Armand remarked, "might splash onto Shayde for playing footsie with the wrong politicians."

"Damn shame," Nelda said. "Lord, I don't want to believe Sebastian Shayde has gotten into bed with the killers of Darby Williams and Jerome Sessy."

"Probably doesn't realize it," Julie said.

"How in hell can he not?" Nelda retorted.

"Self-delusion," Gustave said. "He's so fixated on opposing Mike he'd climb into bed with the devil."

"Meanwhile," Chi Chi said, "we got us a reason to celebrate."

Mike shook his head. "Premature. This case is a long damn way from wrapped up. True, Banzini can give us Long Louie, and we should be able to convict both of them. But how do we tie Kenman and Boheemer into it?"

"Hell," Armand said, "offer those skels a deal to testify against the two pols."

Mike shook his head. "Banzini didn't have any connection with anyone except Long Louie, consequently can't testify against those that devised the thing. And, if we're lucky enough to nab Long Louie, there's no way we can let that hump off the hook after viciously murdering three of the most prominent black men in Louisiana."

"Amen," Nelda said.

"Then let's get our noses back into it," Armand said, "and dig up the evidence necessary to indict those two political slicksters."

#   #

Chapter Fifty-Five

Mike leaned back in his office swivel chair and closed his eyes, wearied by a frustrating case. He and his staff hadn't accomplished a whole lot more after stumbling onto Long Louie at that casino bar, resulting in the arrest of Banzini, a would-be shooter hired to miss the mark . . . with no connections to the crime's instigators.

Nope, they weren't anywhere close to busting the suckers that devised that atrocity. And the populace isn't so dumb it'll settle for that donkey. He sure as hell expected the black community to clamor for a more definitive conclusion.

Fact is, he'd have to satisfy a whole passel of media gasbags as to why the case dead-ended with Banzini, or even with Luigi Guglielmo if they got lucky enough to root him out. The minute that skel learns Banzini is in custody he'll dive into a deep hole.

Mike slapped his forehead and sat up, jolted into realizing that since the local prosecutor demanded jurisdiction over Banzini, the media had knowledge of that arrest. That meant Luigi Guglielmo and the others of that mob would soon become aware that Banzini had been taken into custody . . . if they didn't already know.

The media won't stop blabbering about the case—along with endless loquacious guests. And believe there are those around the state who'll continue clamoring for a conclusion of that Shreveport debacle. He still had a bumpy road ahead. So he contacted Armand by intercom and instructed him to utilize everyone available to make calls to convince the media—in surrounding states as well as Louisiana—to sit on the arrest of Banzini for a couple of days so as not to spook the other perps. He sure hoped they complied to keep all those complicit from running for the hills.

Oh shit! Kaylee came to mind and he worried she might never speak to him again. Yes, he needs to call her and placate her for those confused antics in Biloxi. Accepting that the longer he waited the more difficult reconciliation he picked up the phone and dialed.

"Sergeant Boyle is out of the office," a clerk responded. "No, sir, I'm not authorized to give out information as to the whereabouts of the sergeant. If the caller wishes to—"

Mike left his name, then called her cellphone—to be aggravated by a digitized voice telling him that no one answered, so to leave a message. Clenching his teeth, he called a few other places, including her apartment; though he didn't expect to reach her there this time of day.

Dammit, he had a strong feeling for that gal and wished he'd been forthright. But he did what he considered wisest, considering her questionable reactions, as well as her having been planted in his office to spy for Shayde. His first and most important consideration had to be to fulfill his obligation to the State of Louisiana for allowing him to serve as Director of Investigations.

His phone rang and he grabbed it off the hook, hoping to hear Kaylee's voice. But it turned out to be State Police Headquarters in Baton Rouge informing that all extradition forms had been exercised and that two of their detectives had been dispatched to Jackson, Mississippi, to transport Banzini to Baton Rouge.

After hanging up, he decided to go there and accompany the detectives. Maybe, during the long ride back to Louisiana, he'd be lucky enough to extract vital information from Banzini. So he called the New Orleans Lakefront Airport and booked a flight departing at twelve thirty.

#   #

261

Chapter Fifty-Six

Kaylee affected a pretense of nonchalance as she approached Shayde's office. Sure, she'd be raked over the coals, certain that pudgy Nicky Boheemer had reported her being in Biloxi with Mike. Plus she prepared herself to take heat for that fiasco with those two dicks on Friday night.

Those cops Mike punched out sure as hell liked to pitch a bitch because of her pointing them out to him. But she damn sure intended to argue to get Mike off the hook, not withstanding the lack of prospects for prolongation of that relationship. His lack of faith in her precluded any chance of continuing the affair. Damn shame. She'd pretty much fallen for the guy . . . wished it ended differently . . . wished it didn't have to end.

Inhaling resolve, she passed into Shayde's office, then blinked, incensed to encounter Kenman and Boheemer lounging in chairs around the captain's desk.

"You have a lot to explain," Shayde called to her from behind his desk.

Kaylee stared innocent-eyed at him as she spread her hands, having decided to let him do the talking, knowing he'd over-talk her anyway.

Shayde gestured her to a chair. "Hopefully you were in Biloxi to suck Molino into an embarrassing situation."

"Suck may be the proper term," Kenman commented.

"I don't like that kind of talk," Kaylee snapped at Kenman as she stood alongside the chair her boss had indicated.

262

"Like, don't like." Kenman sneered, slumped in the chair with his legs extended. "You hauled his ashes, like you were assigned."

"Keep it up," Kaylee growled, balling her fists as she stepped toward him, "and you and me are going to waltz."

"Think you can stand up to me?" He rose to confront her, though he wasn't any taller than she. "You may have to suck me to keep your job."

"Put a muzzle on that kind of talk," Shayde barked.

"Just letting her know her place," Kenman said.

"We're not going to insult the sergeant or any other officer of this department," Shayde growled.

"Then gag her sassy mouth," Kenman said, backing down no more from Shayde than from Kaylee. "I can hurt her career, and most anyone else's without half trying."

"I can stick a forty-caliber Glock up your nose," Kaylee retorted. Her hand went to the handle of her weapon.

Shayde flapped both hands as he stumbled out of his swivel chair and rounded his desk. "Settle down, everybody."

"Then tell Slick Willie to stay off my case," Kaylee said.

"I got your damn slick," Kenman growled.

Shayde hurried between them. "Enough—both of you. Sit!"

But Brent Kenman remained standing for a moment, while Kaylee obeyed her boss. After a moment of grinning defiantly, he sat.

"Explain Friday night," Captain Shayde demanded of Kaylee. "And your story better not differ no whole lot from those detectives."

"With all due respect, sir, that's police business, not something to be discussed with these *civilians*."

Shayde shuffled a few steps backward and perched himself on the front edge of his desk. Leaning forward he addressed Kaylee in a sibilant whisper. "It'll be discussed when and where I demand it to be. So just explain it here and now."

"First," Kaylee retorted, "you explain to me why the hell two dicks clicked pictures of me. Who in hell authorized anyone to—"

"You know goddam well," Shayde said, "they were targeting Molino."

"The question," Boheemer interjected, "is why did you squeal them out?"

Kaylee clenched her teeth as she kept her attention riveted on her superior, denying Kenman's chubby henchman the satisfaction of knowing he irked her. "They were snapping pictures of me. Whose goddam—"

"It isn't about you," Shayde hissed at her.

"How'd you happen to end up in Biloxi with Molino?" Kenman interjected.

"Aiding and abetting his escape," Boheemer said, "from arrest for battering cops."

"What the hell were *you* doing there?" Kaylee snapped at a sniggering Boheemer. "Serving as a bagman?"

Boheemer's jaw fell. His eyes bulged with shock then alarm.

"How dare you make that accusation?" Kenman demanded.

"Only reporting what I witnessed," she replied. "Looked to me like a payoff to a guy answering the description of the tall shooter at Belmonde's."

Boheemer bounced to his feet, his fists balled. Kaylee did also. Kenman rose to stand alongside his companion. Kaylee's hand again went to the butt of her pistol.

Shayde popped up from his desk and stepped between them, waving his arms. "Everybody take their seats!"

264

Kaylee sneered as she sat. The other two continued to scowl at her for a few seconds before they also dropped into chairs.

Shayde backed up to again perch on the front of his desk and focus narrowed eyes on Boheemer. "Why in hell were you in Biloxi?"

Boheemer sputtered and twirled his hands.

"Nicholas made the mistake of running a big account with his bookie," Kenman spoke up for him, "and went there to pay the guy, having been threatened if he didn't."

"This the damn truth?" Shayde demanded.

"Nicky has avowed," Kenman spoke for him again, "that he's learned his lesson and will quit gambling."

"That's a crock," Kaylee said. "But if that's the story you want to put out—"

"Don't call me a liar!" Kenman snapped at her.

"Enough!" Shayde barked. "We're supposed to be working in concert, not opposing each other."

"Tell that to this female," Kenman said.

"I'll remind you again," Shayde growled at Kenman, "that we show respect to Naw'lin's finest." Then he turned to Kaylee. "Expect you to be a team-player."

"With cops," Kaylee retorted, sneering at the two *civilians*.

"With whatever damn team I assign you to," Shayde retorted. "So for now let's all chill out, while giving everybody the benefit of the doubt."

"Okay," Kaylee said, "suppose I deserve this treatment after sacrificing my body all weekend to Molino, who, I might add, is insatiable."

"Enough!" Shayde waved a hand to dispel that. He rose to stroll behind his desk and drop tiredly into his leather swivel chair.

265

"We're not asking for that much description. And I don't want to hear any more of whatever that's supposed to mean." Then he stared at the two civilians. "Can't for the life of me understand why I let myself get snarled in this confused mess."

"Common cause," Kenman said, "to knock those AG investigators back on their heels and off the NOPD."

"Hope to God that's it," Shayde said. "I'm beginning to wonder if I'm backing the wrong horse."

"Or beginning to see the light," Kaylee corrected.

"What exactly does that mean?" Kenman demanded.

"It means," Shayde said, "I hope I don't discover that you two are involved in that mess at Belmonde's."

"There's a thought worthy of consideration," Kaylee remarked.

Kenman scoffed. "You really think someone in our position would do anything that outrageous? We're the front-runners. Why in hell we need to kill off the also-rans?" Then he turned to Kaylee. "Let's accept that we're on the same team. Forget the remarks I made and I'll forget those you made."

"I don't forget all that easily when someone insults me," Kaylee retorted. "And I share the district commander's suspicions."

"Put it to bed," Shayde said to her, "get all of that behind us."

"Including that slugfest on Chartres?" Kaylee asked. "Is Molino forgiven too, and not being hunted by any of those dicks?"

"Why are you so concerned for him?" Kenman asked.

"We're putting all of that behind us," Shayde grumbled. "All of it. I've already called the hounds off Molino."

"Why?" Boheemer asked. "This is the time to keep pressure on him."

"It's more important," Shayde said, "to save the department

266

from being stained by any sort of incident that might result. Besides, I'm not about to butt heads with the AG's office, who demand we put a blanket on it."

"Where do we go from here?" Kenman asked.

"Word came down," Shayde said, "that two dicks from the state barracks have set out for Jackson, Mississippi, to transport that Banzini fellow to Baton Rouge."

"Thought the Naw'lins DA applied to extradite him," Kenman said.

Shayde shrugged. "Morreau got to the muckamucks in Mississippi," "so they ignored our request . . . said to duke it out in Lu'ziana."

"Y'all need to take charge of this Banzini," Kenman said, "to control the investigation and the trial. The AG's office clears this damned thing before the NOPD does the media motor-mouths will never stop accusing the locals of incompetence, if not complicity. Bite the bullet and stop Molino."

"What in hell you suggesting?" Kaylee demanded.

"Simply to prevent those folks from stealing the credit from New Orleans," Kenman replied. "They violated the agreement and assurances they made with Lieutenant Montrose by not sharing that information. So let's turn those angered cops loose on him. He punched them out. Let them punch back, and if he foolishly resists arrest—"

"It won't happen," Shayde growled.

"Those cops and their buddies," Kenman argued, "are champing at the bit to put a real hurting on that wise-ass."

"As well as a bunch of cops seething from that exposé last year," Boheemer added.

"Let the boys deal with Molino as they will." Kenman said. "If that results in something excessive, Molino will no longer be a thorn in New Orleans' side."

Kaylee's face hardened. But she exhaled when Shayde said: "Revenge on Molino has been called off. I don't want anybody going hog wild with this thing."

"Then what *do* we do?" Kenman demanded.

"Been tipped that Molino booked a flight out of Lakefront to join up with those state dicks in Jackson," Shayde said. "We've managed to delay that flight."

When Kaylee glanced questioningly at Shayde, he explained: "Don't want him gaining the advantage by grilling that perp during the trip to Baton Rouge . . . wearing the guy down and getting a heads-up he doesn't intend to share with us."

"Wise." Kenman mock-clapped his hands, so they didn't issue any sound. "He doesn't get to Jackson and maybe we have a chance of rerouting Banzini to New Orleans."

Kaylee grimaced, unhappy to hear all the antagonism toward Mike. Dammit, why did everything have to happen the way it did and confuse what could have been a hell of a relationship? Yes, she came real close to falling in love with the guy. And she still yearned for him. Her breath caught at memory of his throbbing in her loins.

"Keep us informed," Kenman said as he rose to leave. Boheemer hauled his girth out of his chair and tailed Kenman to the door. Shayde rose and saw them out.

Kaylee wondered to what depths Sebastian had been drawn into their conspiracy? She knew him as a stubborn man, but a basically honest one. Had he let his zeal build a wall around the department lead him into a dark passage with implications in things he might have been wiser to avoid?

268

When the door closed behind Kenman and Boheemer, Kaylee asked: "What the hell ever possessed you to get into bed with those two schemers?"

"A common enemy."

"For the love of Jesus, Sebastian, don't get led astray by those silk-tongued lizards. Surely you have as much reason as I do to suspect they're possibly implicated in that triple murder. How in hell can you stick your neck out to defend them."

"The only damned thing I'm defending is this police department."

"Stop kidding yourself, Sebastian. You're a highly respected executive with a long record as a dedicated cop. Don't destroy that reputation because of hatred for Molino, by throwing in with those most likely involved in that massacre at Belmonde's."

"That's ludicrous! Think about it, girl: Big Willie wins that primary hands down—as well as the coming election. So why in hell they need to off Darby ? Our concentration needs only to be eliminating outside interference, like Molino."

"He's as anxious as you, Sebastian, to bag those murderers."

"My detestation for that smug bastard is because of his mucking around in our department and setting our officers up as corrupt."

"He couldn't have if they weren't."

"You defending that bastard?"

"I'm concerned for you, Sebastian, and what you mean to this department. Take a step back and consider this thing soberly. You're stubborn as hell but you're basically honest. Don't get on the wrong side and end up disgraced because of excessive zeal."

"Let me worry about my ass. You worry about yours."

They glowered at each other. Then Shayde ambled over to place a hand on her shoulder. "It pleases me to see that you're concerned about me. Maybe you have it in your heart to become Sebastian's woman again."

She shrugged off his hand and stood up. "Can't you register empathy and friendship for Christ's sake—without being motivated by that snake in your pants?"

"Hey, lady, we know each other well enough for me to say that."

Kaylee sneered at him as she left his office and clunked the door closed.

# #

Chapter Fifty-Seven

Mike paced the airport concourse, his lips compressed to stifle cursing every time they delayed the flight. Dammit, if he didn't depart soon he'd arrive in Jackson too late to accompany those two detectives and Banzini back to Baton Rouge. Remembering how quickly that hood captulated he hoped to wheedle some tasty tidbits out of him during the long and boring trip.

Yes, and he anticipated the publicity resulting from being with them when they arrived in Baton Rouge. Hell, it might reduce some of the disgrace resulting from that Shreveport goof, even gift him with an official sanction. Yeah, he could invite Kaylee to fly up and participate in his being restored in his old office.

Hell, she'd be proud to meet the attorney general. And seeing him officially cleared sure ought to diminish the enmity because of his less than candid handling of things heretofore and make things right between them. He sure hoped so.

Thinking about her, encouraged him to take out his cellphone and dial hers. It rang a number of times before transferring to voice mail. Shit! She probably had caller ID block his calls. He clicked off. Okay, he'd rely on time to heal that damn wound.

#

He felt like he seethed for an eternity before finally disembarking from the commuter jet in Jackson. Then it took a while for the taxi to wind through traffic. The bane of growing cities is that infrastructure rarely keeps pace with population expansion, resulting in crowded streets which increased his anxiety all the way to State Police

271

Headquarters.

"Those two detectives left a good while ago," a sergeant responded to his inquiry. "Yes, sir, they headed south on Fifty-Five in one of them long-ass black Chevy Tahoes."

"Where can I rent a car to try to catch up to them?"

"Ask me, that's not all that wise. Those ole' boys don't look like they dawdle on the road, and you don't want the embarrassment of being pulled over for speeding. Why don't I have a trooper take you in a cruiser and see if he can't catch up. Leastways, he won't have to worry about being involved in an interstate incident."

#

Mike forced himself not to fidget as they sped along the flat highway flanked by scrub interspersed with stands of pine. It frustrated him that despite high-speed-driving for the past hour they failed to overtake the two detectives. As they approached Magnolia, near the Mississippi-Louisiana border, the cruiser's radio crackled.

"Lord have mercy!" the black trooper exclaimed. "You hear that? A group of vehicles ambushed yo' dicks across the border in Hammond."

"Oh, my God! How fast can we get there?"

"I'm not supposed to cross that border, sir."

"Cross it anyway. Emergency. Come on! Step on it!"

Mike anguished the almost half-hour it took to pull off the highway just short of Hammond. He spotted the eatery designated in the communiqué, one of those chain establishments with architectural similarity to all of its locations. They tooled up a curving ramp that cut through a scrubby field to brake in a parking lot. Arriving among three Louisiana State Police cruisers and two local police cars surrounding a black SUV, Mike jumped out and flashed his credentials.

272

"Who're the two detectives that drove the Tahoe," he called out as he hurried toward them.

"Me and Kelly, sir. I'm Riegarten." They stood side-by-side with heads bowed and eyes downcast, remorse etched on tired faces. Of average height and weight, both wore jeans, long-sleeved plaid shirts, and sneakers. Their baseball-type caps with commercial logos lent them the appearance of two guys at leisure rather than police escorts, even though both wore empty holsters.

"What in hell happened?" Mike demanded.

"We were tuckered and dying for a break," Kelly said, "after driving up to Jackson, then all the way down here."

"Pulled in," Riegarten added, "to stretch our legs and get us some coffee when—"

"Were you aware of anyone tailing you on the highway?" Mike cut in.

"We wasn't expecting no trouble," Riegarten replied.

"Hell," Kelly piped in, "it was supposed to be routine. Nobody alerted us to be on the lookout for anything like what happened."

"Spell it out for me," Mike commanded.

"Almost the minute we nosed up to the building where we're presently parked," Riegarten explained, "two Ford SUVs flanked us . . . a black Flex on our left and a blue Escape on our right."

"And a dark Chevy Equinox pulled up so close behind us," Kelly added, "it tapped our rear bumper."

Both shuffled in place while Riegarten explained: "Before we had half a chance to react in any which way we realized guys wearing ski masks brandished shotguns through the windows of those flanking vehicles."

"The bulkiness of their black sweaters," Kelly said, "suggested

273

they had Kevlar vests under them, making us wonder if they were official issue."

"Those shotguns were more'n likely Remington Eight-Seventies," Riegarten said, "—twelve-gauge suckers with seven-round magazines, making them lethal enough to scare the rattles off'n the biggest som'bitchen snake out there."

"No way," Kelly claimed, "there was anything else for me and my partner to do when those ninjas yelled to hand our weapons out the windows."

"And those suckers had the smarts to demand our secondary weapons," Riegarten added. "If they weren't in the job, they were pretty danged knowledgeable about cops."

"A couple huskies with hand guns," Kelly said, "got out of the far side of the two flanking Ford SUVs and collected them."

"While their buddies in the vehicles kept their shotguns aimed at our heads," Riegarten added. "Two of them took Banzini out of the back seat and shoved him into the Chevy behind us."

Kelly tilted his head slightly to the side and rolled his eyes back to peer into memory, then murmured: "Something about the driver of that Equinox behind us made me think she was female. Never saw her face or nothing since she—or he—wore a ski mask that concealed the hair and all, but I just got that feeling . . . maybe the way how she moved or something."

"Anyway," Riegarten said, "it backed up and drove off. The other guys continued to cover us until the Chevy was long gone. Then they sped off."

"You didn't pursue them?" Mike demanded.

"They had our damn guns," Kelly said. ". . . All of them."

"Only thing we'd of gained," Riegarten said, "is getting our dumb asses shot off."

"Both of us got wives and kids," Kelly said.

"Did you manage to get some kind of description of the marauders?" Mike asked.

Kelly hunched his shoulders. "Besides they being white men— except maybe that white woman—no, sir, those ole' boys didn't intend to be identified."

"The one ordered us around pretty obviously disguised his voice," Riegarten said, "precluding voice recognition. Most mooks are too dumb to think of that."

"And they didn't waste a damned second," Kelly said. "They had that prisoner and were out of here 'fore we got our senses back."

"Few lowlife hoods have that kind of paramilitary precision," Riegarten said.

"Ask me," Kelly said, "I'd say they were SWAT cops."

"One thing though," Riegarten said, "the black Flex on our left had a small dent on its front right fender with a speck of red paint on it, like from a fender-bender."

"Did you get their license plates?" Mike asked.

"Sure," Kelly said, "they had to know we peeked them, but weren't too concerned."

"Because," Riegarten said, "they attached those plates with quick-clips."

"More'n likely changed them by now," Kelly said. "And they like as not split up, rather than stay in a convoy of recognizable SUVs."

"You people have an APB out on those vehicles?" Mike asked the State Troopers.

"Of course," one of them replied grumpily. "We got us enough sense to follow standard operating procedures."

275

"With that press of traffic on Interstate Fifty-Five and on Twelve," another of them opined, "it defies expectations that we'll bag any of them."

"Hell, there are more big-assed SUVs on the road nowadays," a third said, "than economy-sized sedans—in spite of their gasoline consumption."

"We have cruisers on both sides of Twelve entering Baton Rouge," the first trooper volunteered, "attentive to all Ford and Chevy SUVs."

Mike shook his head. "More than likely they'll head east on Twelve, to then take Ten into New Orleans, considering the likelihood is that they're out of there."

#   #

276

Chapter Fifty-Eight

A staticky announcement from the radio of one of the state troopers' cruisers captured their attention. They gathered around it to hear: "Local PD found a body some few hundred feet off County Road Twenty-Two near Springfield."

"Oh shit!" Mike hoped it wasn't who came to mind. "Let's go!" he yelled to Kelly and Riegarten. He thanked the black Mississippi State Trooper and sent him back to Jackson. Then he climbed into the black Chevy Tahoe with the two detectives to speed behind the two state cruisers down Fifty-Five, then west on Twenty-two.

Not more than a few miles shy of Springfield, they spotted a state police cruiser and two local police vehicles a couple of hundred feet down a dirt road. They carefully traversed that area of lazily winding bayous and stagnant swamps overgrown with spiky grasses and a maze of scrubby brush . . . gator habitats.

Mike blinked back the pain of recognizing Banzini the minute he saw the sprawled body. He flagged his head back and forth in commiseration of the loss of an important witness. The New Orleans crowd had outwitted him. It took doing to accept that it isn't unusual for people who wield authority to go that far off the deep end to defend their turf—probably convinced that their desperate act was justified. The radio of one of the state-trooper-cruisers crackled. The trooper near it relayed the information to the others. "Couple of our boys bagged a black Ford Flex with a red dent in the front fender."

"Where?" Mike called to him.

"Parking lot of one of those taverns along Lake Maurepas," the

277

trooper replied.

"Y'all remain to protect the crime scene from contamination while waiting for the ME and CSU," Mike instructed the local cops and the state trooper he'd encountered on arrival there. Then he directed the other state police with their vehicles to accompany the Chevy Tahoe with him, Kelly and Riegarten. They sped back up Twenty-Two with lights blinking and sirens screaming.

Branching onto Fifty-Five south, they careened along a highway elevated above the swamps, to swish past the upper portions of cypress and pine trees. Occasionally below them they saw crude dwellings along the bayous, most built on stilts, many afloat while moored to land. All had skiffs alongside, the only mode of transportation on the shallow and isolated ponds and lazily twisting waterways.

Racing down an exit ramp, they swerved around a couple of turns of a narrow road hard by the swamps. The pungent odor of mud and rotting vegetation hung like a mist over them. Only God knew what-all died in there and contributed to those combined stenches.

Rounding a blind turn, they pulled up to a weathered lakeside saloon with a sign that identified it as Pierre's Tickfaw Inn. At each side of the building narrow parking lots bordered the swamp, with a few cars and light trucks in each. In one they encountered two state police cruisers and the Ford Flex, with two civilians lounging next to it. Mike jumped out and yelled to the troopers as he approached. "Y'all searched that vehicle?"

"Didn't find anything will make your heart sing," an older trooper replied.

"They got identification?" Mike asked, scowling.

"Naw'lins police officers," one trooper said, handing Mike their creds.

278

"Any shotguns found?" Mike asked. "Kevlar vests?"

"Sure," the trooper replied. "Course, it's not unreasonable to expect big city police officers to be so equipped."

"How 'bout extra cop-issue Glock pistols?" Riegarten asked.

"And twenty-five Berettas?" Kelly added.

"Nope," the trooper replied. "Just their own."

Mike scanned their credentials and sorted out which of the detainees was Verbracht and which was Gatreau. They rolled their shoulders while sneering at him.

"Got a reason for being here?" Mike demanded.

"Some good catfish fillets along with cold beer," the one called Verbracht drawled, his lip curling in a surly manner.

"Which is all the information you're getting," Gatreau added, "without a PBA lawyer present."

"You'd better cooperate," Mike growled, "or face prosecution."

They sneered at him, then grinned smugly when one of the state troopers commented: "They're right not to talk without their PBA rep."

Mike scowled, pissed by that trooper siding with the mooks. But he conceded to the psyche of that cop to support the Blue Line. It always amazed and mystified him how cops embraced the police universe as their culture of brotherhood—a misguided loyalty that they stick together and shield each other, even if those they defend are dirty.

Mike understood the indoctrination that consolidated those attitudes—having shared dependence that developed trust and intimacy. As a consequence, many grow closer to partners with whom they rely upon to survive scary escapades than with family members, and even spouses. And because of that bond cops eventually become empathetic of other cops, unconcerned how that attitude negatively affects the community at large . . . even taking it to extremes at times that disgraces themselves and their departments.

Nevertheless, the wanton murder of Banzini couldn't be justified to Mike by the buddy system. That ruthless act violated the basic laws of man, as well as destroyed his maturing case. He glowered at the two detainees—his irritation amplified by the way they smirked at him.

"Book them anyway," he snapped.

"On what?" one of the troopers asked.

"On the order of the Director of the Investigations Division of the Attorney General's Office," Mike barked.

"You got it," the other trooper said. He cuffed the two men and handed them into the back of one of the cruisers. They grinned, offering no resistance.

"Take their SUV into the Baton Rouge garage for a fine combing," Mike said. He scowled as he watched them drive away, knowing damn well he didn't have anything substantial to pin on them. And they damn sure weren't going to volunteer any information. Not one clue would be uncovered in their vehicle . . . no fingerprints of Banzini nor his hairs or particulates since Banzini had been taken away in the Chevy Equinox. The whole goddam thing frustrated him, especially since it scuttled all his efforts and set his case back to square one.

# #

Chapter Fifty-Nine

Armand leaned into Mike's office. "Sorry to ruin your morning, Mike, but word just came down that Judge Beery dismissed all charges against those two cops."

"Didn't expect anything different, but had me a nettle in my craw that made me book them out of meanness."

"I hear you," Armand said. "Where do we go from here?"

"I've run out my skein, Armand. Did everything I could and came out a loser. Do me a favor and call a meeting in the conference room."

Mike gave Armand time to execute the request before he pushed himself up from his swivel chair to trod in there and confront his staff. "I want to thank y'all for trying your damnedest to build a case. Since we failed, I'm going to pack up and give you good folks back your office."

"You real, man?" Nelda asked. "We needs to be working this case . . . not let seven rogue cops walk free. Those rotten-asses murdered a witness in cold damn blood."

"They obstructed justice," Gustave added, "when they interfered with two police officers transporting a prisoner."

"And violated their damn oath to defend society," Julie said. "Let's get out there and take their rotten asses off the street." When the others emphatically nodded he reminded: "We got us two names to start with, so need to lean hard enough on their buddies and family members to tumble some dominoes."

"Don't depend on getting anything out of those two," Armand

said. "They've beat the system so far, so won't cave too easily."

"Then we need to find us new ones," Nelda said, "and work those suckers 'til they points us to others."

"I'm with you sister cop," Chi Chi said. "Let's partner up."

Gustave gestured to Julie. "Ready to hit the streets?"

"Without wasting any more time," Armand said, as he hooked his arm in Mike's and led him through the door.

#

Nelda drove, cruising the trash-littered streets of Tremé and Faubourg Marigny, two rundown districts where neglect marred most buildings. A few had been abandoned because of damage from Katrina and subsequent storms. Two had holes where windows used to be. Walls on some threatened to collapse. However, a few had been refurbished and looked spanking new, incongruous in that spread of dereliction.

On North Johnson Street she pulled alongside a dusty sedan parked in front of an aging three-story wooden structure that obviously had been converted to a rooming house. Two sleepy-looking black men in over-alls slumped in the front seat with hats brims pulled down.

"Hey, Roushon," Nelda called through her opened window to the robust driver. "You playing that sleepy game to trap some skells didn't show up in court?"

He brightened the moment he recognized her. The other guy peeked around the driver's bulk and waved. "What a big shot state investigator doing getting her shoes dirty in the ghetto?" he chided her.

"Same as y'all—hunting bad guys. Chi Chi, these are Rouchon and Baker with Warrants. Guys, say hello to my partner: Chi Chi O'Brien."

"Say what!" Baker exclaimed. "Chi Chi what?"

Roushon chuckled, then asked: "What brings you fancy cops down this way, sister?"

"Renegade white cops that murdered a witness up on Twenty-Two."

Both men shrunk into their collars and averted their eyes. "Nobody told us thing one about that mess," Roushon grumbled.

Nelda sucked her teeth. "Man, y'all going to tell me y'all don't have you no pride and going to cover up for some fey-ass motherfuckers don't have scruple one."

Neither responded, which impelled her demand: "Why y'all protecting bad cops?"

"You put some years in this department," Baker said, "and wise to why we can't turn those boys." A thin guy, he could barely be seen on the far side of jumbo-sized Roushon.

"You don't," Nelda said, "and I'm going to put yo' names on the street as lacking the kind of pride black cops need to have."

"We say one damned thing," Roushon said, "and we put our asses *under* the damn street. I'm talking about some badasses, mama."

"But that's not news to you, woman," Baker said. "You hip to the way those cats covers each other's rotten asses."

"You condone that shit?" Nelda asked.

"Now you don't believe that, woman," Roushon said. "Besides, ain't no black cops had nothing to do with that shit."

"Believe that," Baker said. "That bunch of *good-old boys* left over from the old days. But you know well as we do that that shit ain't dead."

"Point me in a direction," Nelda said, "that I can accidentally run into one or more of those rotten-ass motherfuckers."

Roushon rubbed his face with a big hand. "Damn, woman, you

asking a lot."

"I ain't covering their misdirected asses," Baker said. "That hard-ass Sergeant Lopinski organized that shit. 'Course, I never told you that."

"Scope out a cocky young motherfucker name of Tracy," Roushon said. "That smart-ass white boy strutting around the courthouse on Tchoupitoulas this morning bragging about squirrel hunting. That's the kind of shit my daddy said those motherfuckers spouted when they went out and did in a nigger."

"Where I can find this Lopinski?" Nelda asked.

"Tactical Unit," Roushon said. "All those guys with SWAT. Only kind of cowboys would think to pull that shit."

"Best you get you some white help," Baker said. "None of those boys going to sit around a table and gab with *you*, girl."

"And connection with the AG's office won't protect your black ass all that much," Roushon warned. "They'll do you as quick as they did that ginny-boy."

"They been talking about doing yo' boss," Baker said, "'til the word came down to back off."

Nelda thanked them while Chi Chi got on the cellphone to Mike.

#   #

284

Chapter Sixty

"Can you believe these som'bitches are stonewalling us?" Armand complained to Mike. He'd used his cellphone to call the NOPD Operations Bureau for information on Sergeant Lopinski of the Tactical Unit. Both agreed that they'd be more receptive to Armand, and more cooperative, than if Mike called.

Still, they jerked Armand around by handing him off to different divisions, with every person wasting his time by questioning why he sought that information, then claiming they weren't authorized to give it out, insisting they needed to transfer him to someone else.

"This is official business of the attorney general's office," Armand grouched to one after the other in an endless line of equivocators. "Lack of cooperation will result in official reprimands."

But they still passed him around, until finally connecting him to Sergeant Lopinski's commander. "Need to know the reason for the inquiry," that man responded.

"To learn," Armand said, "whether Sergeant Lopinski or any of his people were involved in that kidnapping and murder of the state's witness up in Springfield."

"Christ no! Our boys'd never take part in anything like that. My advice to you is to take a long look at state cops . . . or some from that parish. 'Course, it just might be the work of those hoods. That ole' boy's goombahs prevented him singing."

"We're looking at everyone. However, at the moment, I need to speak to Sergeant Lopinski."

"Ridiculous! Sergeant Lopinski wouldn't have any knowledge

of that since he's on a week's leave after a scary takedown of bank robbers in the Fauborg."

"I remind you, sir, my instructions came down from Baton Rouge."

"Who in hell they think they are to sully the reputations of our officers."

"Seeking information is not sullying."

"Whatever. You need to make your inquiries with the state police."

"I remind you, lieutenant, that local police forces are required to concede to the requests of the AG's office. So I'm reaching out to y'all to comply . . . saving me from bringing charges against y'all."

A moment of silence before the lieutenant groaned concern for putting his ass in a hard place. "I'll have my secretary give you his home address and phone number."

Armand smiled while waiting the few minutes for the secretary to satisfy his needs. Then he called the number she gave him. The phone rang a dozen times without being answered, each ring increasing Armand' exasperation. He called that secretary back and growled: "No one answered the number you gave me. That officer have a cellphone?"

"Sir, you received the information I've been instructed to give out."

"I'm not eager to indict you for obstruction of justice, ma'am, which just might result in termination of your employment—besides quite likely cancel any pension you hoped to get. And kiss your hospitalization goodbye."

She gasped. After a pause, she said in lowered voice: "Don't tell anyone I told you this, but Sergeant Lopinski has taken retreat at his cabin in Crown Point, on the northeast corner of Lake Salvador."

"With or without his wife?" Armand asked.

"The sergeant been divorced two years now."

Armand nodded while placing the location she gave as across the river and a good few miles south of the city. "Need the exact location plus his phone there."

"Far as I know, he'd never had a phone installed there. But here's his cellphone number."

Armand thanked her and dialed the cellphone, but it rang until answered by voice-mail. "Now what?" he asked, frustrated.

"Might serve us to take a trip down to Crown Point," Mike said.

"Assuming," Armand said, "he's there and not somewhere in Montana by now."

#

Mike slumped in the passenger seat, with his legs extended as far as the space allowed while Armand drove south on US 90 to Westwego, then took county roads to the lake. Both anguished while searching for the cabin; those things not having specific addresses. They exhaled exasperation until finding it set back off a dirt road in a wooded area where low bushes and weeds had all but overgrown the unpaved driveway, with a dusty pick-up truck parked on it.

"Shit!" Armand complained after receiving no response to their knocking on the front door; it had no bell. "Made this time-consuming trip for nothing."

"That truck's parked there," Mike said, "Just maybe he's hunting or fishing out in the backwater."

"So how long you suggest we wait around for him to return?"

Mike shrugged. "Don't rightly know—considering he'll probably stonewall us. But long as we're here we might's well have a look around."

287

Armand shrugged his lack of objection and accompanied Mike in ambling around to the back—carefully since less than a hundred feet from the house a grass-fringed swamp exuded the pungency of mud and decay. They remained alert while skirting what could be gator holes. A lonesome vulture glided with wide-spread wings above the treetops.

They trod carefully through weeds, concerned about stepping on a moccasin, a rattlesnake, or stumbling into a hungry gator. Spotting a small porch, they climbed the rickety steps to peek through the kitchen window. And both gasped, horrified by the sight of the man flopped over the table. One hand almost touched a Glock semi-automatic pistol.

"Likely got tipped," Armand said, "and took this way out to avoid disgrace."

#   #

Chapter Sixty-One

Gustave stroked his neatly trimmed beard and sighed, wearied by the inactivity of the stakeout. He and Julie sat in the car parked on the south side of the grassy median of Poydras Street, both bored by the endless parade of vehicles.

They tired of staring at the same buildings, including City Hall and the Courthouse, as well as the Superdome, a humongous concrete structure that dominated the area.

A number of people hurried along the sidewalks, their lightweight coats pulled tightly around them for protection against the unseasonable chill. Overcast skies not only denied them solar warmth but threatened to inundate their world.

Julie jerked to alertness, startled by the jangle and vibration of his cellphone. "Hey, boss. Yeah, we got him in sight. That Billy Tracy is some cowboy, strutting around like a damn rock star. He's rapped with half a dozen uniforms on the street. They been patting the yahoo on the back and treating him like a damn hero. A minute ago he and another guy went into an eatery half a block away."

Julie's facial expression changed to puzzlement. "Pick him up for questioning? Yeah, that hot dog is crazy enough to resist. Okay, boss, we'll do it quick as we can."

Julie signed off and wagged his head dolefully as he turned to Gustave. "That SWAT sergeant, Lopinski, ate his gun."

Gustave's jaw dropped. His mouth moved but no words emerged—reacting like most cops to hearing about the demise of a brother in blue. It affected them equally whether killed in the line of duty or by natural causes—and especially by suicide.

"They're sending three, four state cops to back us up," Julie said, "in taking Billy Boy to the office for a talk with Mike and Armand."

Gustave frowned, unhappy with instructions to take another cop into custody, as if that act indicted the police universe. But denied options they squirmed and groaned until two unmarked black SUVs parked behind them. Climbing out, they exchanged greetings with four grim-faced state cops in plainclothes; none of them eager to arrest a cop of any organization. Gustave led the procession into the drone of voices in the luncheonette, where the aromas of coffee and toast intermingled with the acerbity of fried foods.

Billy Tracy, a strapping blonde towhead in his middle twenties, blanched when he saw them. Quickly recovering, he rolled his shoulders and sniggered, affecting bravado as they strode toward him. The guy sitting at the small table with him, also in jeans and lightweight jacket, got up and wove his way among the approaching group, his hands held out in clear view to show he wasn't holding any weapons and didn't want trouble. He exited the restaurant.

"What you state hotshots want?" Tracy asked.

"We'd like you to accompany us to the AG's office for a talk with the director," Gustave said.

"Why not? I'll get my car and meet you there."

"Don't play us for saps," Julie said. "You're riding in one of ours."

Tracy shrugged, as if unconcerned. "What is it we have to go over to your office to gab about that we can't rap about right here?"

"You'll be told when we get there," Gustave said.

"Hey, how 'bout I call a PBA rep and have him meet me there?"

290

"You can call when you get there," Gustave said.

"Hey, I'm entitled to have my rep along if you guys intend to question me. Hear what I'm saying? I can even have an attorney present. Don't you state guys know that?"

"Your rights won't be abrogated," Gustave said.

"But if you don't get your butt into that car," Julie said, "I'm going to cuff you. You want that?"

"Okay. Okay. Don't muscle me around. I'm not some kind of hoodlum."

"Could've fooled me," Julie said.

#   #

Chapter Sixty-Two

"Thanks for coming in for an informal talk," Mike said, as he waved Tracy to sit across the conference table between the two state police detectives who drove him there and escorted him inside.

"What the hell you saying? Yo' bullyboys hustled me in here. Sure wasn't nothing voluntary about it."

Mike ignored the young man's cocky posturing and pretense of indifference. "A simple chat, between boys in blue," Armand said, seated on Mike's right. Julie and Gustave sat on Mike's left.

"Blue, my ass. You state guys wear civies. And this meeting is about as informal as a disciplinary hearing. Anyway, I'm not saying one damned thing without my rep here holding my damn hand. Hear what I'm saying?"

"Suit yourself," Mike said. "We've called your rep. When he comes we're going to charge you with murder."

Tracy swallowed—but a moment later pretended to swagger. "Try making it stick."

"Lopinski ate his gun," Armand said in quiet voice while pushing his black-rimmed glasses up on his nose.

Tracy's mouth fell open as he swiveled eyes widened with shock and disbelief to Armand, then to the others, beseeching someone to refute that announcement.

"Your mentor took the easy way out instead of facing the music," Gustave said.

Tracy shook his head. "Y'all bullshitting me."

Mike dropped a photo in front of the young cop, who gaped at the irrefutable evidence. Mike and Armand had planted a hand-written letter near the hand opposite that with the gun—the print too small to be read in the photograph.

"That note," Armand said, tapping it with his pen, "puts you in a world of hurt."

"Besides," Julie said, his eyes squinted as he stared intently at the young man, "you bragged to too many people out there on Poydras."

"We pressured a couple of those uniforms," Gustave said, "to testify to that."

Tracy blinked, revealing concern.

"It didn't require a great deal of persuasion," Gustave said. "They wisely considered continued employment and loss of pension and other benefits more important than covering your rogue ass."

"And Lopinski's note," Armand said, "seals your fate."

"Chet is dead? For real?" He looked dazed, blinked repeatedly while shaking his head in inability to accept reality. Turning to Armand, he again asked: "For real?"

Armand again tapped the photograph with his pen.

"We also know about Verbracht and Gatreau," Mike said.

"Sure, you collared them. But a judge kicked them loose."

"Because I didn't have substantive evidence at the time," Mike said. "We've got them now same as we've got you, thanks to Lopinski."

"No way I believe Chet would hurt us."

"Conscience," Gustave said. "Had a problem overcoming his grief and remorse for crossing that line, consequently couldn't live with what he'd done."

"After years spent as a model cop," Julie said, "he caved to doing the right thing. Probably had no other way of condoning stepping over that line."

"But you saying he spelled it out in that damn letter he left?"

"It's called confession," Julie said. "A cleansing of the soul . . . catharsis. Try it, you'll feel a whole lot better."

"We can get you a priest, you want," Mike offered.

Tracy shook his head, his eyes downcast, his cockiness dissolved.

"We're giving you a chance you don't deserve," Armand said. "Substantiate Lopinksi's dying statement and we'll make sure the worst you get is life."

"No way. No fucking way! I ain't flipping on my guys. Hear what I'm saying?"

Mike sniggered. "You don't think Verbracht and Gatreau will fink on you? Think again. Soon's we pick them up we're offering this one time only to one lucky winner to escape getting that needle. Don't be stupid enough to think that one of them won't roll."

"Or one of the others we haven't picked up yet," Julie interjected.

"During the years you're going to spend on death row," Mike said, "waiting for them to put a needle in your arm, you can mull over blowing the opportunity to survive."

Tracy hung his head and averted his eyes. "No way I'm flipping on my buddies—death row or no. Hear what—"

"You're running out of time." Mike growled. He knew *he* was, considering it wouldn't take long for Tracy to learn that Lopinski hadn't left a letter, or that no PBA rep had been summoned.

"I'll take my chances," Tracy said. He puffed himself up to project resoluteness. "Y'all hear what I'm saying?"

Mike rose from the table. "Your choice, sucker. You had one helluva opportunity to bail out." He turned toward the door.

294

"Need to think about it," Tracy said in subdued voice. Receiving no response, he turned pleading eyes to one after the other. "Can't you understand what you're asking? No way I can make a decision like that on the spur of the moment. Give me time to consider it and figure out which way is up for me. Hear what—"

"One hour," Mike said. "You get sixty minutes, not one second more."

"For God's sake, Director Molino, give me some reasonable time. This is a big thing you're asking. Hell, I need to think real hard on this. Hear what I'm saying? Give me 'til tomorrow morning to make that kind of decision. Please!"

"One hour," Mike repeated.

"Then forget it. No way I'm doing anything impetuous."

Mike's breath caught as it hit him that the young man was resolute. And he didn't know how to back-off being a hard-ass.

"He deserves more time," Armand said, realizing Mike's dilemma. "See if you have it in your heart to extend adequate time to consider everything."

"Let me have until tomorrow morning," Tracy implored, "to think on everything real hard."

Mike accepted he hadn't shaken the guy enough to induce him to talk. Hell, as a cop, with a few years experience observing suspects brought to the bar because of their impetuosity to strike a deal, he had more sense than do anything incautiously.

"Okay," Mike agreed as he leaned on the table and leveled hard eyes on Tracy, "we're going to keep you isolated until morning. But you don't cooperate then your ass will end up injected with one big-ass needle."

Tracy bobbed his head repeatedly, his eyes glazed.

295

"Put him under wraps until morning," Mike directed the two state cops. They stood him up and handcuffed him.

"But you have to spell the whole thing out," Julie Provenzano said. "We want the names of your superiors that put you up to it."

"Superiors?" Tracy scoffed. "Nobody had to tell us what needed to be done."

"Give it up," Julie said. "You guys aren't smart enough to do something like that on your own. It took strategizing—an area in which you muscle-heads are deficient."

"For your information, state cop, we decided to do what we did while talking about it in a bar."

"Just like that," Mike said, "you came up with the wild-ass idea to assassinate a state's witness."

"Y'all been leaning on our department . . . even blocking our bringing that witness to our jurisdiction. So Chet said we ought to go on up to the Mississippi border and take that witness away from y'all."

"And you were agreeable to something that daring?" Julie asked.

"Hell, man, I was gung-ho right from the git-go. Hear what I'm saying? A few of the other guys liked the idea too."

"Was it your idea," Mike asked, "to cold-bloodedly light up that witness?"

"No! I was in the Escape with Chet. And he cursed them dumb bastards when we heard about it. Simple-asses said they didn't dare drive into Naw'lins with him in the car . . . didn't know what else to do."

"Which of you geniuses thought it all up?" Julie asked.

"Chet laid it out, using SUVs confiscated in drug raids and quick-clips to change the license plates. No way we figured to get traced."

"So much for his brilliance," Gustave said. "He ended up

sucking on his own gun."

"Hey, it wasn't for those two yahoos stopping to celebrate with beer and shit at that tavern, you guys never pick-up on us."

"Your brag-assing sure helped," Julie said.

Tracy rolled his shoulders to shrug that off.

"You're telling me," Mike said, "that you guys hatched this without any of the brass involved. Horseshit!"

"The brass doesn't have the balls to do what we did . . . not without three weeks of deliberations. Hear what I'm saying? Those turkeys—"

"Besides Lopinski, Verbracht, and Gatreau," Mike cut in, "who were the others?"

Tracy snickered. "I ain't admitting nobody was involved until I think good on this thing. Hear what I'm saying?"

"Okay," Mike said, "but name the occupants in the Chevy . . . the murderers."

"Maybe in the morning. Maybe. Nothing now."

"Give us the female," Armand said.

Tracy's eyes widened. "How'd you find out about her?"

"We've learned about the whole operation," Mike said.

"But we didn't get her name yet," Armand said. "Give us that as a good faith gesture until the morning."

Tracy shook his head. Inner turmoil etched his face. "If I decide to talk, I'll give you everything in the morning. Nothing now, until I think it all out."

Armand held out a yellow pad and pen to him. "Okay, write out what you told us so far, even to excluding the brass as being involved."

"Hey, I write it out, it's evidence against all of us."

"You've already confessed," Mike said. "You want to save your

297

dumb ass from the needle, you write it out."

"Nothing I said is going to stand up in court. Y'all didn't mirandize me before I said those things. Fruit of the poison tree and all that jazz. Hear what I'm saying?"

"Then giving us the names," Armand said, "goes with the pre-Miranda ruling."

"I'm going to think real hard on everything," Tracy said. "If I decide to cooperate, we'll talk in the morning. Hear what I'm saying? Not uttering another word until then."

Mike motioned to the state cops to take him away.

After they left, Armand said, "There's no way in hell, Mike, you can let that idiot off the hook, being complicit in the cold-blooded murder of a state's witness."

"Don't intend to," Mike said. "But let's not enlighten the dummy until he writes out that confession, naming the others as well."

"Wait'll he learns," Armand said, "he's been conned."

"Yahoos like that don't deserve any better," Mike said. "The sad part is that it clears up the ruthless murder of Banzini, but doesn't nail us the guys who hired those hoods to blow away decent people at Belmonde's."

"Doesn't even move it off square one," Gustave said.

# #

Chapter Sixty-Three

Mike shuffled into his office, tired and grouchy after a night of fretting over a case that resisted resolution. His handling of Kaylee also nagged him, had him rehashing everything they said to each other and wishing he'd reacted differently.

. . . Especially last evening when he'd finally gotten her on the phone . . . but now wished he hadn't. That irritable exchange resulted in pushing them further apart.

Glancing up, he saw Armand stick his head in the office, wearing a morose expression. "What?"

"That kid Tracy hanged himself last night."

Mike gasped. "How?"

"With his belt."

Mike's eyes blazed as he came out of his seat. "Didn't they follow procedure, take everything away from him to prevent him doing anything like that?"

"They never anticipated anything like that."

Mike dropped back onto his swivel chair. "Need I remind you that suicide has a higher incidence among cops than among most professions? Need I further remind you that Lopinski ate his gun, which probably inspired that decision . . . being the young guy's mentor? How in hell'd they allow that to happen?"

Armand swirled his hands and sputtered, then stepped aside when a secretary appeared in the doorway. "Captain Sebastian Shayde of the NOPD is in the reception area—insists on speaking to you."

Mike hunched submission to show him in. "How'd he learn

about it so quickly?"

"Discovered the guy real early this morning," Armand said. "We weren't in yet and the state boys needed a ME to pronounce him dead, so reached out to the locals."

Mike wagged his head, burdened with that now. He winced upon seeing the tall visitor in the doorway, distinguished by his uniform laden with decorations. He rose, but Shayde scowled as he disdained Mike's proffered handshake. Stone-faced with the hint of a sneer, he stepped behind one of the visitor's chairs and clutched its top rail.

Mike dropped tiredly into his swivel chair to await the tirade. He frowned disbelief when Shayde spoke in calm and modulated tones. "You certainly put a quick end to a promising career for that young man in the Tactical Unit. For your sake, I hope you have substantive proof to back up whatever you alleged to detain him, thus becoming the instrument of his demise."

"Your young genius implicated himself with his braggadocios mouth," Mike quietly retorted.

"We've recorded everything," Armand said.

"You refer, of course," Shayde said, "to his exaggerated claims of participation in something he knew too little about. Other officers have assured me that Tracy didn't have enough facts to have been there. But his yearning for glory impelled the young braggart to claim to have been a participant in that incident."

"We'll play you the tape," Armand said.

Shayde ignored him as he addressed Mike. "You had no more on that young man than you did on the two detained and taken to Baton Rouge."

Mike and Armand grimaced but didn't contest him.

"He sought to increase his self-worth," Shayde continued, "to enhance his standing among macho cops. You should have sent him to a psychiatrist."

"Along with Sergeant Lopinski," Mike said.

"Very likely another psychiatric problem," Shayde admitted. "Not uncommon in police forces."

"Who should have been culled out by superiors," Mike said.

"Hereafter," Shayde growled, "I advise you gentlemen to go through channels. The Public Investigation Division was instituted for affairs of that kind."

"Wondered if you're aware of that," Mike said. "Y'all sure as hell were informed about the kidnapping and murder of Banzini."

"I remind you, Director Molino, that it happened outside our jurisdiction. However, had you shared with us that you had a witness able to shed light on the case, instead of concealing him from us, we may have been instrumental in safely transporting that person to Louisiana."

"Had your people done the police work we did," Mike growled, "you would have known about him as well."

"Who's to say we didn't? But we are not so impetuous as you, Director Molino, to grasp at straws, even to basing our case on the testimony of a very sick young braggart."

When neither Mike nor Armand responded, Shayde pushed the chair aside and turned toward the door. "Be assured that this badly managed debacle will receive full media coverage. So have a good retirement, Director Molino. You're retiring also, aren't you Special Agent Dupuy. Both of you enjoy life after police work."

Armand watched Shayde exit, then murmured: "A good man gone wrong."

"Self-appointed champion of the department," Mike said, "who's convinced himself that it's his obligation to defend the NOPD against all assaults, justified or not. Doesn't even weed out cops with mental problems."

"Psychopathic cops aren't born," Armand said, "but shaped by years in the job. How can you kick somebody out after the system transformed them into what they are?"

"Can't contest that," Mike said. "But I find it hard to believe a man that bright doesn't suspect Kenman and Boheemer as complicit in the Belmonde's massacre. How can he not realize his involvement with them amounts to conspiracy."

# #

Chapter Sixty-Four

Mike trundled into the conference room and glanced around at the expectant faces of his staff. "I suppose y'all are aware that a number of rogue-cop-cum-assassins will go unpunished. It scars my record and sure as hell puts an end to my career. So I'm bidding y'all good luck. You're a real good bunch of investigators and deserve the best."

"Where will you go?" Nelda asked.

"Retire. Have to face reality and accept that there's nothing left for me in this department, what with that Shreveport scandal hanging over my head, then failure here."

"We'll miss you," Gustave said. "I mean that sincerely."

"Yeah, homie," Chi Chi said. "I learned a lot from you, besides getting a whole lot of inspiration."

"You have a knack for handling hoods," Julie Provenzano said, "and shouldn't leave the business. The war against organized crime never ends."

"While those city cops get away with murder," Chi Chi said.

"That's the pity of it," Gustave said. "The system has never been perfect, and that incident is proof positive of that travesty."

"Whatever," Mike said. "It spells walking papers for me."

Nelda sucked her teeth. "Yeah, we fell on our damn faces. Now we need to get back up, brush our damn selves off and get back to work clearing this case."

"Meanwhile," Mike said, "Jace is pulling me to save the department further embarrassment, which is what I'd do if our roles were reversed."

"I'll damn sure pray for you," Nelda said, "to land on your feet."

The others murmured concurrence. Then all eyes turned to the jangling of the phone in the center of the conference table. Armand pulled it to him and answered it.

"Hello. Who? Sure, he's here. Hold on." Pushing his glasses up, he held the instrument out to Mike. "Somebody from the AG's office in Tennessee."

Mike's brow arched as he accepted it. "Molino here. You have? Fantastic! Believe, sir, that I'll be on the next flight there." Hanging up, he yahooed.

All eyes focused on him as his staff waited breathlessly to learn what elated him.

"That bolo on Luigi Guglielmo bore fruit. He's been apprehended in Memphis. I'm on my way there."

"I'll get ready," Armand said.

"Best you stay and man the fort," Mike replied. "Keep your damned ear to the ground to pick up whatever tricks the locals will pull this time."

"I'm your resident expert on mobsters," Julie said as he rose from his chair. "You need to take me along."

"Pack real quick," Mike said. "in case we need to stay overnight."

#   #

Chapter Sixty-Five

     Mike and Julie strode into the small interview room, rendered
dreary by plain oyster-colored walls devoid of decoration. They
acknowledged the two detectives seated across the small table from the
tall guy with wire-rimmed glasses slumped in the chair with an air of
unconcern. He glanced up and scowled at the new arrivals.
     Mike stifled snickering, noting that he wore the same tweed
jacket when Nicky Boheemer handed him a stuffed envelope at the Beau
Rivage. One of the detectives advised the detainee: "You're going to be
interviewed by Chief Investigator Molino of the Louisiana Attorney
General's office and his deputy, Agent Julius Provenzano."
     Tall-guy's head jerked back and concern lined his long face as
he stared at them while lip-syncing their names. Mike deduced he was
intrigued by their Italianesque names—though Molino would be Mulino
in Italian. But that might not be discernible in pronunciation.
Nevertheless, he wasn't about to inform Long Louie that he wasn't
Italian, and relinquish that possible edge.
     Both detectives rose to surrender their seats at the table to the
visitors. "Get anything out of him?" Mike asked.
     "Didn't try," the younger of the two said.
     "He been mirandized?" Mike asked, in barely more than a
whisper. And he winced when the older detective shook his head and
reminded that he'd been apprehended for questioning as per the bolo out
on him, and not yet charged with a felony. The two detectives leaned
against a sidewall to observe the proceedings.
     Mike sat and leveled hard eyes on the tall man with wire-rimmed

glasses. "You prefer Long Louie or Luigi Guglielmo?" When the man's brow arched with surprise, Mike said: "The fact that I have your nickname should clue you that I have enough on you to send you to the death chamber."

"Says who? Anybody can get them names. They even been in the news."

"I got it from Chucho Banzini," Mike said.

The guy's long face went sallow.

"He fingered you and has agreed to testify against you," Julie added.

Mike breathed relief when Guglielmo's gaunt face didn't indicate awareness of Banzini's death. Thankfully the various police agencies kept a lid on it and the media complied by quashing publication for a few days.

"Banzini gave us the particulars of the shooting at Belmonde's," Mike said. "Unfortunately he couldn't name the people who hired you. We know you can, since I saw you taking a packet of money from Nicholas Boheemer at the Beau Rivage in Biloxi. So I'll make an offer just this one time to take the death penalty off the table."

Mike knew damn well there was no way Jace or the governor was about to permit this hood to escape getting that needle after lighting up all three of the victims. Man, the black community would have a major blowout with Reverend Sharpton leading the protest if the state didn't do him in.

"Better take advantage of this one-time-only offer," Julie said. "Nothing else is going to keep you from writhing with those chemicals in your body."

"We can't finger Kenman, the guy we want most," Mike said. "Won't bore you with political matters. The long and short of it is that

306

I'm ready and willing to trade life in prison—no death sentence—if you testify against Kenman."

"Don't know him."

Mike gnashed his teeth. "Suit yourself. You just lost your chance to escape that awesome needle." Rising, he instructed the Memphis detectives: "Bundle him up for his trip to Baton Rouge, and his execution."

Julie pushed himself to his feet while shaking his head in criticism at Guglielmo. "You're going to regret that dumb decision."

"Hey, I never had no truck with nobody named Kenman."

"Stop bullshitting me," Mike growled. "I saw you with my own eyes with Nicky Boheemer at the Beau Rivage."

"Didn't say I don't know Boheemer . . . the only one I dealt with."

"Why," Mike asked, "did Banzini loudly mention Kenman's name at that shooting?"

"Instructions we got paid for. Figured he was in it somehow. Why else we were warned not to part a hair on his head?"

"You ready to testify to that?" Mike asked.

"If it keeps me out of the death chamber. But I want that in writing."

Oh shit. Mike knew that wasn't something he could do. So he said: "That needs to be done by the prosecutor in Louisiana, not here in Tennessee."

"So what's the story?" Guglielmo asked. "What do we do to get that done?"

"Wave extradition and come on back to Baton Rouge with me," Mike said, trying to sound matter-of-fact. He turned and again addressed the Memphis detectives. "Get this guy ready to travel." Then he walked out of the room with one of the detectives.

Julie stayed behind and spoke confidentially to Guglielmo. "Work with these guys to get all the paper work expedited. This has to be done without delay to assure you avoid that damned needle. Boy, that is one ugly way to go. Never seen anything worse than guys writhing for a long damn time foaming from their nose and mouth and their eyes bulging."

"So whatta' I gotta' do?"

Julie pushed the yellow pad and pen toward him. "Write it down. Nothing I can do to save your ass unless I have it all in writing. And sign this Miranda statement."

The detective accompanying Mike out of the interrogation room commented: "Don't sound like you're going to get the guy you want most."

Mike scoffed. "Boheemer is a weasel, won't go down alone. I'll work his flabby ass until he flips and testifies against Kenman."

"Think your boss going to accept a deal keeps the needle out of this scuzz-ball?"

"Not a chance. But it's not illegal to lie to a mook to turn him."

#   #

Chapter Sixty-Six

Mike waved to Jace while descending to the tarmac from the Beech Jet 400A. Yes it heartened him that even Jace's bushy mustache couldn't conceal his wide grin as he strode forward and vigorously shook Mike's hand while patting his shoulder.

Mike accepted that the flash of cameras were intended to publicize the attorney general being there when they brought in that perpetrator of the atrocity at Belmonde's. It was sure to bolster his reelection prospects, which were already strong.

Mike basked in the publicity with Jace, as they watched two detectives of the state police assist Julie in escorting a shackled Guglielmo off the plane and into a black Ford Expedition guarded by two uniformed state cops, with another half dozen, heavily armed state troopers on the perimeter.

Mike searched around. "The governor's not here to share the spotlight?"

Jace shrugged. "Doesn't appreciate the political value. But it helps you, Mike, in burying that Shreveport goof."

"You saying I'm off the hook now?"

"Soon's you have an indictment that'll stand up in court against someone higher up than Nicky Boheemer."

"You are one hard-ass boss, Jace."

"Hey, I've been doing you a bunch of favors by pulling your damn chestnuts out of a whole bunch of damn fires—ever' damn day."

"So why do I feel like I'm being burned at the stake?"

"Believe there weren't that many all that supportive of you, good buddy. Took a heap of talking to dissuade the governor from trashing you just last night at a fund-raiser."

"Good ole' Birch Murdock," Mike said. "Yessiree, the people's friend and the champion of state employees."

Jace chuckled. "Took doing to convince him to give you some damn time to do your thing and clear your name. You'll likely receive a lengthy message of gratitude from him, or should, considering Willis Hoke will likely pull out of the damn race when this barrel of shit hits the media fan."

Mike flagged his head side-to-side at the irony. "Despite four years of muddling, Murdoch will win reelection by default, while an efficient legislator with long service is forced to relinquish a well-deserved reward . . . for no fault of his own."

"Yep, that's the way how it goes . . . thanks to your stubborn investigating." Then Jace displayed a sneaky smile. "Damn truth be told, I'm one isn't complaining, being as term limits deny ole' Birch running for a third term."

"You saying you're in favor of that bumbler serving another term?"

"In four years I'll have a wide open door to run for the governorship, without having to contend with an incumbent like Hoke, if he runs and wins this time."

Mike rocked back on his heels. "So what you're saying is that you've been scheming and playing all sides against the damn middle."

Jace chuckled. "Been doing what politicians do best, Lu'ziana-style. Thank Huey Long for some damn good tutoring."

"Long as I receive the pass I've earned," Mike said, "to get my ass out of that roaring bonfire."

"Not until you hand us an airtight indictment against Brent

Kenman."

Mike grimaced while shrugging concession. "I'll go down to New Orleans in the morning and put this mess to bed."

"You'll go this afternoon. Got you a Learjet chartered over there. Armand Dupuy will be waiting at the airport."

"Thanks for not giving me one damn hour to rest. Want to tag along?"

"Wish the hell I could. I really do, Mike. But I have more damn things on my plate than any one man can process."

Mike nodded understanding, also having more than he needed.

"When you get back, Mike, after indicting Kenman, we'll have a press conference that'll clean up that damn Shreveport mess."

Mike's eyes narrowed with skepticism.

"Convinced that gal," Jace said, "to publicly proclaim that you never approached her for any kind of sex."

"Good looking out! What in hell did you offer that stubborn som'bitch to come clean?"

"Being as she's milked the damn tabloids for all they're willing to part with, she has no reason to keep claiming y'all was chummy, so accepted our offer of time served."

"I wasn't never *chummy* with her."

"Don't much matter. The thing is political until she admits you never touched her."

"Believe that I didn't."

"Yes, I do . . . reason I've stood behind you. We're demanding a comprehensive confession from her that absolves you and clears the air for me and Birch Murdock for standing by you."

"Since when was Murdock all that loyal?"

"What's done is done. Savor the damn victory."

"You ought to have offered her that right from the git-go," Mike grouched, "and saved me all that anguish."

"Threats of being sent to prison, which she knew all too well would result in taking away her baby girl, failed to deter that hard-assed mercenary from milking those damn scandal rags for more and more damn money."

"Tell me about it."

"Besides, she obviously reveled in the publicity, fancying herself a damn rock star. Thankfully the damn cow ran dry when this thing grew stale and other revelations captured the readers' attentions. Once the scandal sheets stopped paying she was ready to deal for time served, which allows her to keep her baby."

"My good luck, finally," Mike said. "Still, I don't feel good about a conniver like that getting off without punishment."

"Don't sweat it, good buddy. We've kept her under surveillance while out on bail. The bitch is dealing. Soon as she publicly clears you, we'll book her on new charges that aren't covered in the immunity agreement. Believe that she'll get a long stay in the slammer for those."

"I feel like the world's biggest asshole," Mike said, "thinking of her as a nice girl who needed a break."

"Think this damned case, Mike. Rise to the occasion one more once and tie up all those damn loose ends so I can get your ass back here to ramrod state-wide investigations. "

# #

312

Chapter Sixty-Seven

Armand drove the black SUV along Saint Charles Avenue, past fashionable residences in the Garden District. Mike perked to alertness when they turned west onto Octavia Street, lined by posh homes enhanced by manicured lawns and gardens.

"Always wanted to live here," Armand said.

"Which is to say you didn't grow up in these digs."

"Not that damn lucky. Nope, I'm from up near Burnside."

Mike rolled his eyes back while placing that town along the Big Muddy, a little more than halfway between New Orleans and Baton Rouge.

"My daddy was the foreman on a sugar plantation," Armand said.

"Live there all your youth?"

"Sure did. Was a homeboy who never saw the other side of the hill 'till I went to Tulane . . . down here in the razzle and dazzle of the Big Easy."

"How'd a Tulane graduate end up in the state police?"

"Got drafted, a few days after graduating college. Damn war was raging in Nam back then. Survived that morass over there and after two years got lucky to get discharged without leaving any parts behind. Needed a job when I got out of the army and the state cops were recruiting."

"Best thing you could get with a degree from Tulane?"

"Did intelligence work the last few months I spent in the army. Wanted to get into it in civilian life. Some folks advised me to get a few

313

years of police work on my résumé before applying to the FBI or CIA, to accelerate advancement."

"But you never went with the feds."

"Never wanted to once I got into the Criminal Investigation Bureau, seeing as how I did the kind of work I yearned to, without stepping foot outside Lu'ziana. Married Ysette and didn't hanker to spend time away from her. Then I really found a home when Jace Morreau recruited me."

"Well, you've had you one long-ass career, good buddy."

"Yep, it's time for me to smell me some damn roses while I can." Armand chuckled as he pulled up to a large two-storied house behind a tall wrought iron gate. White painted columns supported the roof of its wide porch. A lamp suspended from the center of the porch ceiling matched the sconces on each side of the decorative glass doors.

Mike took in the impressive home as he accompanied Armand up the walk flanked by a manicured lawn and flowering garden. Birds in the leaves above them stopped chirping when the men invaded their sanctum, then scattered when Armand clacked the brass knocker a few times.

Nicholas Boheemer, with his hangdog look, opened the door and stared quizzically at Armand then Mike. Barefoot, he wore faded dungarees and a gray sweatshirt stretched across his paunch. "What brings y'all calling?"

"You want to discuss everything out here and put your business in the street?" Armand asked.

Boheemer shuffled backwards, permitting them to enter a wide vestibule. His eyes glistened concern though he pretended nonchalance while brushing back his thinning blonde hair, all the while searching their faces for an explanation.

314

Mike waited until Boheemer closed the front door. "We've taken Luigi Guglielmo into custody."

Boheemer blanched. His head quivered and he looked like he might cry. Shaking his head, as if refusing to believe what he heard, he gestured them to follow him into a small den off the vestibule.

"Who's at the door?" an unseen female called out.

"People for me," he replied in cracking voice.

After waving them into the rustically furnished den, he closed the door and leaned on it. "Can I get y'all a iced tea—a beer—maybe something with a kick?"

"Nothing," Mike said. "This isn't a social visit. Best you take a seat. We wouldn't want your heart palpitating while you standing up."

"What has the person you mentioned to do with me?" Boheemer asked as he shuffled to the swivel chair behind a cherrywood desk. He waved his visitors to round-backed wooden chairs with decorative spokes supporting their curved rails.

"You forgetting," Mike asked, "I saw you passing him money at the Beau Rivage?"

"You never saw no money."

"Didn't need to," Armand said, "with Long Louie's spitting his guts out."

Boheemer gasped.

"In hopes," Mike added, "of saving his ass from the death house."

"Doubtful he'll escape the needle," Armand said, "any more than you will."

Boheemer looked even more hang-dog.

"Guglielmo is testifying to that envelope you gave him," Mike said, "as being full of greenbacks. And, as you're damn well aware,

315

Sergeant Boyle also witnessed you giving him that stuffed envelope."

"She's testifying against me?"

Mike's eyes darkened with anger. "Why shouldn't she?"

Boheemer twirled his hands. "Thought Shayde had her under his thumb."

"Maybe he did," Mike said. "But nobody, and I mean nobody, is taking a fall for you, buster."

"Wise up," Armand said. "Accept that we have enough to indict you."

"And circumstances being what they are," Mike said, "the black community is going to demand you get a death sentence."

Boheemer pulled a tissue from a plastic holder on the bookcase behind him and dabbed beads of sweat from his forehead. Worry lines creased his chubby face. His eyes filled with pleading as he glanced from one to the other. His lips trembled but words failed to emerge.

"Rather than send state troopers to pick you up and embarrass you and your family in front of your neighbors," Mike said, "we came here personally."

"Appreciate that," Boheemer mumbled, his head bowed.

"Plus," Mike said, "we're offering you the one chance you'll ever have of staying out of the death chamber."

"But you either ready to cooperate," Armand said, "or we're finished spending valuable time on you."

"Incidentally," Mike said, "consider yourself mirandized, or you prefer I recite the entire speech?"

Boheemer waved his hand to dismiss that necessity.

"Helping us convict Kenman," Mike said, "is the only way you avoid the death sentence."

"What will happen to me?"

316

"You sure as hell are not about to go free," Armand said, "after conspiring with Brent Kenman to have three upstanding citizens killed."

"Told Brent it was an extreme solution. Told him! But he insisted it was the only way to guarantee Big Willie's election."

"You really expected to get away with something like that?" Armand asked.

"Brent said the police wouldn't pursue all that hard because they was coloreds. He insisted we had to do it."

"Because of what Williams and Sessy had on Loren Hoke?" Mike asked.

"How'd you learn about that?"

"There are only a few loose ends we need tied up," Mike said, "like connecting Kenman to the conspiracy. So far he's kept himself detached from everything."

"But left you vulnerable," Armand said.

"You ready and willing to testify against him?" Mike asked.

"What will happen to me?"

"I'm reserving that decision," Mike said, "until we're satisfied you've cooperated fully. You do good and we'll be generous."

"More generous than you deserve," Armand said.

"I never wanted to do anything like that. He convinced me by reminding me the way Lance Pollard died of a sudden back in oh-six when he backed me for a run for the city assembly. No way Orly Drummond beats me out if Lance had been there to coach me through it . . . hadn't fallen off that eighth floor balcony."

"He wasn't visiting that pretty little quadroon," Armand said, "he'd never been there for that to happen."

"Point is, he did," Boheemer whined. "They destroyed my political career by killing the man who had the juice to get me elected.

317

It's what they do. No telling the success I'd've had if I could've broken through to the city council."

"So you had no compunctions about killing Darby Williams and the other two?" Mike asked, trying to conceal contempt.

Boheemer bent forward argumentatively. "You remember when Judge Boylan got killed in a hit and run accident while backing Brent against Eddie Grauer? And it wasn't no damned coincidence neither that Louis Villemer mysteriously died back in oh-seven when Brent lost to Jimbo Roark."

"Still no excuse," Armand said, "for you two committing murder."

"Those folks did," Boheemer all but screeched. "This is a hard-ass business and only audacious methods succeed."

Mike waved that off but Boheemer continued ranting. "Brent said we had no options. That shit about Loren was about to blow Big Willie's shot at that nomination, resulting in putting a big damn halt to our aspirations to be state-wide political bigwigs."

"That your only concern?" Armand asked.

"Was all we had left, having been defeated when we ran for office. Was our shot at political importance."

"Who's idea was it," Mike asked, "to have the assassins claim they were head-hunting Kenman?"

Boheemer averted his eyes, looked contrite. "Just kind of came to me when I was recruiting those hoods. Thought it was smart. Regret it now. It really pissed Brent."

"Who else conspired with you?" Mike asked.

Boheemer shrugged and shook his head, blinking his confusion.

"Now don't deny Sebastian Shayde wasn't part and parcel of that conspiracy," Mike growled. ". . . Or the cover-up at least."

318

Boheemer smirked. "Shayde got caught up in it because he's so damn anxious to strew roadblocks in your investigation, never willing to accept we orchestrated that assassination. The guy hates your damn guts and would do most anything to frustrate you, which became a blessing for us."

"You saying a guy as smart as Shayde didn't know he protected murderers?" Armand asked.

"Don't know why," Boheemer said. "It kept becoming as obvious as hackles on a barnacle, especially with y'all casting all those aspersions. But by then I guess he found himself in too deep to about-face."

"Hard to believe," Mike said, "that he covered up the ruthless murder of three prominent black men. What about Montrose?"

Boheemer made a wry face. "Jesse is straight as a saint. That's why we kept him in the dark, along with O'Shea, who's too blockheaded to be bought."

"How about Sergeant Boyle?" Mike asked, and held his breath.

"Shayde put her on you," Boheemer said, "to keep us informed. But Brent and I didn't have no whole lot of faith in her because she was sweet on you. Even so, took me by surprise to see you two together in Biloxi."

Mike scowled, annoyed at himself for having been spotted. At least it explained the telephone warning Long Louie received, and absolved Kaylee of suspicion of conspiring with them. But it didn't relieve his concern that she failed to shadow Boheemer in the hotel . . . or did, and lost him, like she said.

"You going to have to testify against Shayde also," Armand said, "and detail everything the guy did that contributed to covering up those killings."

Boheemer looked forlorn while nodding acquiescence.

"Hard to believe," Mike said, "that a guy with the success Shayde enjoyed would do something that stupid."

Armand nodded agreement. "Damn shame, considering how that old' boy overcame a ton of adversity to make it to that lofty level—only to compromise all of that because he hated you to a psychotic degree."

"Part of the bait to hook him in," Boheemer said, "was Brent promising him immediate promotion to deputy superintendent upon Big Willie winning the election."

"That's a big-ass carrot," Mike remarked.

"But not the whole one," Boheemer said. "Brent assured Shayde that within another year or two he'd be promoted to the top cop job in Naw'lins. No doubt existed in anyone's minds that Hoke beats Murdock hands down. Shayde bought the ticket, being too ambitious for his own good."

"It pricks my curiosity," Mike said, "that you didn't have your hired killers take out Josh Bigelow."

"He was supposed to attend that meeting so we could take out the three of them that had knowledge of that business with Hoke's son. But he didn't show. Darby said something about a meeting came up."

"So you took out Antwan Croix," Armand said.

"In spite of his having no knowledge of the Loren Hoke business," Mike added.

Boheemer waved his hands in a helpless gesture. "Wasn't any way we could communicate with those killers to instruct them not to hit the third guy as planned."

"Poor Antwan Croix," Armand said, "killed by error."

"Had all I could do," Boheemer said, "to stand there, knowing

320

those killers were on the other side of that little window. Any kind of dumb mistake could erase my ass."

"Ever occur to you," Armand asked, "that Kenman planned to erase you also and eliminate the only connection to him?"

"Worried about that. But figured I'd survive since I was the contact—the one to pay them off—to keep him unconnected."

"And you never considered sending your assassins after Josh Bigelow?" Mike asked.

"Those ole' boys were laying low and refused to do anything about Josh until they got paid for those they hit. Long Louie claimed he took out three guys just like he'd been contracted to do—didn't give a rat's ass if one of them wasn't one we wanted done. Wanted his damn money—plus extra up front to take Josh out."

"Why'd y'all meet in Biloxi?" Armand asked.

"They'd slipped out of town a few days after that assassination, and went into hiding in Mobile. No way he'd return, requiring I meet with him in Biloxi."

"You might want to slip into shoes and take a jacket," Armand said. When he and Mike stood, Boheemer blanched, realizing they intended to arrest him there and then.

# #

321

Chapter Sixty-Eight

Mike rubbed morning sleepiness out of his eyes as he joined his staff in the conference room. "Armand and I took Boheemer into custody last night. Had him incarcerated in the holding cells at the Supreme Court building with state cops keeping him under wraps. Yes, they took away his belt."

He waited for the snickering to end. "Then we spent half the night futilely searching for Kenman, concerned that he'd fled after somehow learning we'd busted Boheemer. His wife claimed he'd gone to the capital to spend the evening with Senator Hoke, with intentions to stay over."

"And she believed that jive?" Nelda commented.

Mike ignored that. "Called Big Willie's office in Baton Rouge to learn the senator was at his home in Shreveport. No, sir, his secretary assured, he had no appointment this weekend with Mister Kenman."

"A check of hotels in New Orleans, Baton Rouge and Shreveport," Armand said, "failed to locate the guy."

Nelda chuckled. "Bet a damn c-note he shacked up with a sharp little high-yalla' mama in The Quarter."

"Whatever," Mike said. "It delays going after Sebastian Shayde, fearful of tipping Kenman. So we had plainclothes state cops stake out Kenman's house and office."

"I want to be the one cuffs Shayde," Nelda said.

"There's a person I don't understand," Gustave said. "In spite of every obstacle a black man needs to overcome, Sebastian Shayde achieved incredibly, then threw it away in the most ridiculous cover-up."

322

"Damn fool!" Nelda spit out angrily.

"He took it upon himself to defend the NOPD against detractors," Armand said.

"Another of the human foibles resulting from attaining power," Gustave said. "We take ourselves too seriously, even to believing that we alone are capable of guarding the honor of the institution."

"Even by obstructing justice to accomplish it," Mike said.

"Because," Armand said, "we deceive ourselves into believing that whatever we do in the interest of the institution is righteous."

"But Shayde had more responsibility to the community at large than most," Nelda said. "When a black man or woman attains a position that high they automatically represent the black community. And they serve as encouragement to black kids, inspiring them that a good future can be attained."

Armand answered the ringing phone. He smiled as he hung up. "The state dick staking out Kenman's office reports that the man just arrived. No, the trooper said he didn't look the least worried; apparently hadn't been apprised of Boheemer being taken into custody, or the APB out for him."

Mike led his staff, along with four-uniformed state policeman in hurrying there in four vehicles. The sexy receptionist batted her eyes at Mike, then gasped when she and the secretary were brushed aside. Mike barged into the office, then paused in mid-step. He gasped upon encountering Kaylee Boyle, along with Shayde and Montrose. But he quickly composed himself and directed his attention away from Kaylee.

"What the hell is going on?" Kenman demanded.

"Who authorized this?" burst out of Shayde.

"We're taking you into custody," Armand informed Kenman, "on a charge of conspiracy in the triple murder at Belmonde's." He

323

gestured Chi Chi and Julie to cuff the guy.

"Get your damn hands off me," Kenman bellowed as he twisted to resist.

Chi Chi bent his arm behind him, roughly hoisting him half out of his chair to lean him over his desk, simplifying it for Julie to apply the cuffs.

"What in hell is going on here?" Shayde yelped, bounding to his feet. But Mike and a uniformed state cop blocked him from interfering.

"You have no basis for charging me with anything," Kenman yelled, "and won't get away with this."

"You may think you insulated yourself from that business," Mike said, "but your lapdog, Nicky Boheemer, has capitulated to helping us build one damned strong case against you." Kenman's face registered shock. Mike smirked as he directed: "Read him his rights."

Chi Chi recited: "You are under arrest for conspiracy in a triple murder. Anything you say can—"

"I'm better informed of my damn rights than you are," Kenman cut him off.

Nelda glared at him. "Your smart ass going to fry. No way you can have three black men killed and walk away scot-free."

"Bullshit!" burst out of Kenman. "I'll be out before lunchtime." He turned to his secretary gaping in the doorway. "Call Rick Bevins, and tell him to get me the hell out."

Mike and his people gawked at Kenman's gall to retain a black lawyer to defend him against conspiring to murder three prominent African-Americans.

Shayde swung his widened eyes from Mike to Armand to Kenman, his face scored with rage. "This is the epitome of asinine arrests, on top of all—"

324

"Not really," Mike said. " We have evidence that'll convict him of murder, as well as implicate you in a cover-up." He gestured to Gustave and Nelda to cuff the district commander.

"Are you insane?" Shayde tried to pull away.

"Don't make me hurt you," Nelda warned.

Armand spoke to him in a calming voice. "We're indicting you for obstruction of justice, Sebastian. You have the right to—"

"I know my damn rights!"

Lieutenant Montrose stood staring slack-jawed at everything occurring—uncertain what to do and reluctant to oppose the AG's office and the state police. "Are you certain of what you're doing?" he asked Mike.

"We have more than enough evidence to book Shayde," Mike said, "with the certainty that he'll be convicted."

"This true, man?" Montrose asked his district commander. "You betrayed the integrity of your office? You used your position in the department, a black man who achieved your position, to conceal a capital crime, obstructing the arrest of those responsible for the wanton murder of three prominent brothers?"

Shayde averted his eyes, looked defeated and ashamed as the detectives escorted him out.

Mike turned to Kaylee. "Were you in cahoots with that bunch?"

"No I wasn't! Have never violated this department."

"Failing to comply with surveillance of Boheemer in Biloxi sure as hell stretches ethical."

"Outside of my jurisdiction," she retorted. "You're the one violated ethics, having agreed to work in concert with this office, but concealed findings and information from us. You call that principled?"

Mike stared at her for long seconds, then wagged his head and

325

lumbered out of the office, leaving it to Armand to supervise the putting of Kenman and Shayde in separate state police vehicles. Having achieved that, Armand ambled to where Mike leaned despondently against the SUV.

"Had a real feeling for that gal, Armand."

"Put your mind on something else, good buddy."

"Makes me wonder if I'm derelict of duty for not having asked her or Boheemer if she warned him at the Beau Rivage."

"Boheemer said he spotted you two together. Leave it at that."

"Whether I do or not, I still have this pain from walking away from her."

"You're not supposed to serve your heart up on a silver platter until you know the score. And I mean thoroughly."

Mike spread his hands palms up. "How does a man not fall in love?"

"Count your blessings, Mike. She helped you throw off inhibitions allowing you to emerge from your cocoon of mourning so you can now live life fully. Celebrate that rebirth and look ahead, to new associations you can freely accept."

"With my heart torn out?"

"Time heals most wounds, Mike. Just maybe y'all will get past this. And just maybe you'll have a fuller life."

The End